MW00699665

Peter Atwater

PORTFOLIO
PENGUIN

PRAISE FOR *THE CONFIDENCE MAP*

"A rare, and beautiful, look at what happens in our heads when we try to make sense of the world."
—Morgan Housel, author of *The Psychology of Money*

"Over the years, Peter has proven to us that he has an uncanny ability to predict the future. And now he's revealed the secret source of his powers: *The Confidence Map*. It's a fascinating read that leaves you with a sixth sense of what's to come. Truly a powerful competitive advantage!"
—Ken Muench, chief marketing officer, YUM! Brands

"There are economic numbers, and then there is how people really feel about what's going on in the economy. Peter Atwater connects both, helping us to find the signal in all the market noise in ways that give us insights not only about business but about politics and society too. Atwater is one of my most important 'finger to the wind' sources for understanding the global economy today."
—Rana Foroohar, bestselling author of *Homecoming*; global business columnist and associate editor, *Financial Times*

"A thoughtful exploration of decision-making and the role of stress, focus, emotion, innovation, and lots more, all through the lens of confidence—not self-esteem or the appearance of confidence, but the feeling of being able to handle successfully what comes next. A fascinating read."
—Eldar Shafir, Class of 1987 Professor in Behavioral Science, Princeton University; public policy director, Kahneman-Treisman Center for Behavioral Science & Public Policy; coauthor of *Scarcity: Why Having So Little Means So Much*

"Soldiers and explorers are counseled to 'navigate from where you are, not from where you wish you were,' and it remains valid to leaders in every endeavor. *The Confidence Map* provides an exceptionally clear view of where we are, and how to move forward with real confidence. An approachable, entertaining guide to the daunting challenge of leadership."
—Gen. Stanley A. McChrystal, U.S. Army (retired), author of *Team of Teams* and *Risk*

"This is an important book. Peter Atwater's *The Confidence Map* is an instructive tool for analyzing the decision-making that drives outcomes in financial markets, business, politics, culture, and society. Those of us having personal or professional interests in these outcomes will eagerly and helpfully compare and contrast what we do to analyze, understand, and predict against what we learn from Atwater. Adding his valuable and comprehensive framework to our toolkit is reason enough to read this book. However, *The Confidence Map* also provides extremely beneficial, even startling, insights into our own decision-making process: why, for example, we all yearn for certainty and control and how we respond in their absence; and why we are drawn to overly confident or excessively pessimistic decisions at precisely the wrong times. Read this book; you will be better for having done so."

—Larry Pulley, dean emeritus, Raymond A. Mason School of Business, William & Mary

"Valuable insight into one of the most important, but least well understood, phenomena—the role of confidence in influencing behavior. Atwater provides tools for investors, company executives, board members, policymakers—and even just individuals looking to manage their career—to maximize returns while controlling risk."

—Craig Broderick, former chief risk officer, Goldman Sachs Group, Inc.

"Atwater shows us how confidence depends on two key factors—control and certainty—illustrating these ideas with personal stories, professional tales, and intriguing data. These ideas can help any reader to be more structured and thoughtful in addressing some of the most critical decisions that impact our lives."

—Wendy K. Smith, Dana J. Johnson Professor of Business, Alfred Lerner College of Business & Economics, University of Delaware; coauthor, *Both/And Thinking*

"I began *The Confidence Map* with an enormous dollop of skepticism. How, I wondered, could a single variable—confidence—possibly unlock the future movement of stocks, bonds, commodities, and currencies? How could Peter Atwater succeed where so many before have failed? I ended the book with the greatest Aha! moment of my long career in finance. Atwater promises (and delivers) a new way of thinking for investors, corporations, NGOs, governments, and societies."

—William Bollinger, cofounder, Egerton Capital

"Insightful and original, *The Confidence Map* explores how our feelings of certainty and control—and their connection to evidence or emotion—affect every choice we make and every risk we take. Atwater has made an important contribution to understanding the underappreciated influences that affect our decisions. Readers will use this fresh perspective to become more resilient in the face of uncertainty."

—Michele Wucker, bestselling author of *The Gray Rhino* and *You Are What You Risk*

"Everyone knows that human psychology affects economics, but previous explanations have been anecdotal. Peter Atwater now provides that explanation. His book is highly original and brilliant."

—Nassir Ghaemi, professor of psychiatry, Tufts University School of Medicine; author of *A First-Rate Madness: Uncovering the Links Between Leadership and Mental Illness*

"Confidence is a concept that we often discuss, but with little clear idea of how to define or measure it. *The Confidence Map* offers a simple way to do both. Without over-simplification, Peter Atwater breaks down confidence into its basic elements, and then reaches a series of fascinating conclusions as he applies his measure to investing and many other spheres of life."

—John Authers, senior editor and columnist, *Bloomberg*

"Peter Atwater's precise descriptions of what confidence is, how to gauge it, and how to leverage it are mind-blowing. It's hard to believe such profound insights have been hiding in plain sight for so long. Now that he's switched on the light, it's impossible to unsee the vital role that confidence plays in, well, everything."

—Lydia Saad, director of U.S. social research, Gallup

"Peter's ability to break down the nuances of confidence into an insightful, intuitive, and powerful framework can help any organization better serve its customers, employees, and other stakeholders in an uncertain world."

—Greg Dzurik, vice president, strategy, Collider Lab/Yum! Brands

"Based on the simple idea that confidence is a combination of certainty and control, Atwater is able to map his own finely honed business intuitions, which took him to the heights of finance, and brings them to his second career in the academy. His combination of business experience and social science research will guide you to better understand how confidence matters in your life, and better recognize how it drives the people you rely on. *The Confidence Map* offers practical, actionable advice on topics that range far beyond finance, from managing in a crisis to interpreting narratives."

—Benjamin Ho, professor of economics, Vassar College; author of *Why Trust Matters: An Economist's Guide to the Ties That Bind Us*

"In healthcare, patient confidence is vital to the healing process. What *The Confidence Map* provides is a new framework that aligns with that—shifting the focus from customer satisfaction to customer confidence and helping others feel more certainty and control in their lives. For leaders, and those aspiring to be leaders, this book provides tools to achieve better outcomes, no matter your business or industry."

—Terry Shaw, president and CEO, AdventHealth

"Atwater's guidance on how to understand human confidence—and the lack of it—is essential reading for any CEO or strategic leader. Clear, thoughtful, humane, and actionable: this is a framework for all who need to make decisions during periods of high uncertainty. In other words, for all of us, for the foreseeable future."

—Katherine Rowe, president, College of William & Mary

"I've known Peter Atwater for many years and have followed his career and its many twists and turns. Looking back, it all makes sense once I read his take on confidence and his explanation of the Confidence Quadrant. It's simple and complex at the same time. I encourage anyone struggling with decision-making to read it and use it."

—Rod Wood, president and CEO, Detroit Lions

"Since Daniel Kahneman won the Nobel Prize for behavioral economics, there has been a revolution in how we view the role of human emotions in decision-making. Peter Atwater has added to our understanding with his superb insights on the role that confidence plays in predicting outcomes. I am confident after reading his book that people will see the future much more clearly."

—Michael Powell, former FCC chairman, CEO of NCTA—The Internet & Television Association

"*The Confidence Map* is a compelling book on decision-making that focuses on what we do every day without appreciating why and lays out and provokes thinking about specific actions to take to improve your decision making—as a person, as a businessperson, and in life. Thanks to Atwater's framework and his life work in these areas, you will see your own choices, and the choices of others, in a whole new light."

—Rob Majteles, founder and managing partner, Treehouse Capital

THE CONFIDENCE MAP

THE CONFIDENCE MAP

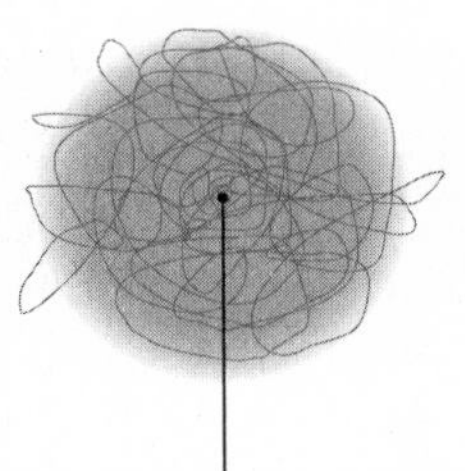

CHARTING A PATH FROM CHAOS TO CLARITY

PETER ATWATER

PORTFOLIO • PENGUIN

PORTFOLIO/PENGUIN
An imprint of Penguin Random House LLC
penguinrandomhouse.com

Most Portfolio books are available at a discount when purchased in quantity for sales promotions or corporate use. Special editions, which include personalized covers, excerpts, and corporate imprints, can be created when purchased in large quantities. For more information, please call (212) 572-2232 or e-mail specialmarkets@penguinrandomhouse.com. Your local bookstore can also assist with discounted bulk purchases using the Penguin Random House corporate Business-to-Business program. For assistance in locating a participating retailer, email B2B@penguinrandomhouse.com.

All graphics by the author unless otherwise noted.

LIBRARY OF CONGRESS CATALOGING-IN-PUBLICATION DATA
Names: Atwater, Peter, 1961– author.
Title: The Confidence Map : Charting a Path from Chaos to Clarity / Peter Atwater.
Description: New York : Portfolio/Penguin, [2023] | Includes bibliographical references and index.
Identifiers: LCCN 2023015023 (print) | LCCN 2023015024 (ebook) |
ISBN 9780593539552 (hardcover) | ISBN 9780593539569 (ebook)
Subjects: LCSH: Self-confidence. | Confidence. | Decision making—Psychological aspects.
Classification: LCC BF575.S39 A89 2023 (print) | LCC BF575.S39 (ebook) |
DDC 158.1—dc23/eng/20230501
LC record available at https://lccn.loc.gov/2023015023
LC ebook record available at https://lccn.loc.gov/2023015024

Printed in the United States of America
1st Printing

BOOK DESIGN BY TANYA MAIBORODA

To my wife, Janet,
and my children, Molly and Bennett

Look, I made a hat . . .
Where there never was a hat . . .

—STEPHEN SONDHEIM, "Finishing the Hat"

CONTENTS

Introduction *xiii*

SECTION I

The Confidence Quadrant

Chapter 1 VISUALIZING CONFIDENCE *3*

Chapter 2 THE CONFIDENCE QUADRANT AT WORK *30*

Chapter 3 THE CONFIDENCE SPECTRUM: INVINCIBLE TO DEFEATED *48*

SECTION II

The Stress Center

Chapter 4 THE STRESS CENTER AND ENVIRONMENTS OF LOW CONFIDENCE *69*

Chapter 5 INTRODUCING HORIZON PREFERENCE *86*

Chapter 6 BETTER PRACTICES IN THE STRESS CENTER *106*

SECTION III

The Comfort Zone

Chapter 7 THE COMFORT ZONE AND ENVIRONMENTS OF HIGH CONFIDENCE *125*

Chapter 8 CONFIDENCE AND COGNITIVE EASE *140*

Chapter 9 BETTER PRACTICES IN THE COMFORT ZONE *156*

SECTION IV

The Passenger Seat

Chapter 10 THE PASSENGER SEAT AND ENVIRONMENTS OF HIGH CERTAINTY AND LOW CONTROL *173*

Chapter 11 CONFIDENCE ELASTICITY *187*

Chapter 12 BETTER PRACTICES IN THE PASSENGER SEAT *206*

SECTION V

The Launch Pad

Chapter 13 THE LAUNCH PAD AND ENVIRONMENTS OF HIGH CONTROL AND LOW CERTAINTY *221*

Chapter 14 CONFIDENCE AND THE STORIES WE TELL *235*

Chapter 15 BETTER PRACTICES IN THE LAUNCH PAD *262*

Conclusion *280*

Acknowledgments *285*

Notes *289*

Index *303*

INTRODUCTION

EVERY WEEKDAY AFTERNOON, right after the stock market closes, reporters in the financial media go to work. They scour the major news stories from the day and interview professional investors with one objective in mind: come up with a clear and compelling story that explains why the market moved up, down, or simply sideways.

On election night, just after the polls close, political reporters do much the same, swapping in voters, turnout percentages, and hot-button issues to explain the victories and defeats of the night.

When big things happen, we like to know why. News reports and the stories we share help us do that. They organize what may be random, potentially unsettling events into logical timelines. They identify the deciding factors that brought about a specific outcome.

We have remarkably little difficulty identifying deciding factors when we work backward by following chains of actions and events upstream. With respect to the past and what has happened, cause and effect flow easily.

Things become far more challenging when we are asked to consider the future. Not only do we struggle to make accurate forecasts, we seem all but blind to those very same deciding factors that we can so easily identify later with hindsight.

But what if we had a framework in hand to better anticipate what will happen next—without waiting for 20/20 hindsight? What if we could see with crystal clarity the deciding factors that exist right now that will drive our future preferences, decisions, and actions?

Well, that framework is what this book is about. You see, I believe there is a single deciding factor that underpins the important choices we make and will make ahead:

Confidence.

Redefining Confidence

When most people think of confidence, what they're really talking about is *self-esteem*—how we feel about ourselves. The focus is inward, with self-help books on the topic hoping to help us gain a greater respect for our own abilities. That is not what this book is about.

Nor is this book about "confidence theater"—the *appearance* of confidence that seems to dominate corporate businesses and our culture more broadly. Mention "confidence," and listeners quickly conjure up figures like LeBron James, Elon Musk, Beyoncé, and countless other celebrities whose public behavior mirrors the attributes our culture associates with confidence. We believe that being confident—and being successful—means acting as they do.

Confidence theater generates a lot of attention, but as we see time and again in the world of sports, politics, business—and perhaps in our own lived experiences—confidence and success don't always align. Sometimes, confidence is a mask we feel compelled to wear along with high achievement, while internally we struggle with "impostor syndrome." Others, too, believe they must "fake it till they make it." They sport a full costume of confidence in the belief that, one day, they will wear it more comfortably. Ironically, between the relentlessness of social media and the pressure for ever greater success, many people who aspire to be or already are atop the ladder feel exposed and vulnerable. "Confident" is the last adjective they would use to describe themselves.

No, this book is about confidence itself—*real* confidence. It's a deep dive into an essential aspect of our lives whose specific definition we often can't quite put into words. Moreover, it is about why having or not having confidence matters so much—to how we feel, to what and how we think, and to what we do. This is a book about the role confidence plays in our decision-making.

Far different from high self-esteem and extraordinary accomplishment, and separate from how we make ourselves appear successful, real confidence is our natural internal barometer of how we *feel* about what is to come—and how successfully we believe we will handle it. Confidence is the combination of our feelings about the future and our feelings of preparedness for the future we imagine. As the pandemic and recent geopolitical events have shown us, we can have the self-esteem of a rock star and still have our confidence rocked.

For as much as we use the present tense when we consider confidence ("I feel confident"), we are always talking about the future. We are projecting an outcome and then determining the odds of our success in achieving it. ("I feel confident now because I believe that I will make the baseball team tomorrow.") Confidence is inherently forward-looking; it's our summary assessment of our expectations. We may try to live in the present, but how we feel right now, in this moment, has everything to do with what we imagine will happen next. Put simply, we feel confident when we think we know what is coming and we feel prepared for it—when we see success ahead of us.

This may seem simple and self-evident, but there are several important subtleties.

First, confidence is a feeling. It may have nothing to do with any of our five senses, but we instinctually put confidence in the same "perception" box. Changes in our confidence level foster a near-sensory response: we feel it in the pit of our stomach; we taste it at the back of our throat.

Second, our assessment process for determining our confidence level is hardly courtroom ready. While we may take in evidence as a jury does, we also decide which facts get presented for serious consideration—often unconsciously. There is neither a prosecutor nor a defense attorney forcing us to consider opposing viewpoints. We may have hit every single pitch at yesterday's practice, but does it even matter when all we're replaying in our head is our disastrous strikeout at last week's game? Our process for presenting and evaluating facts is highly subjective and personal. Others may try to encourage us to be confident, but ultimately, we alone make the call.

Our assessment process is also reflexive and self-reinforcing—in other words, how we assess our confidence depends heavily on our confidence level. The more confident we feel, the more rose-tinted our glasses, and the less apt we are to go looking for or put stock in counterarguments. We limit our view to belief-affirming evidence.

Conversely, when our confidence is low, we overthink things. If one thing has gone wrong, then so might something else. So, we go looking for problems, conjuring long lists of the many other ways things could go wrong. Our scrutiny level and our confidence level are inversely related.

Our confidence levels are also, well, squishy. There is no objective scale on which we measure confidence; when we say we feel confident about something, we can't transform that feeling into degrees Fahrenheit or measure it precisely on a Richter scale. We have only our personal scale to use, and, like stock-market bulls and bears, we do not all see the world in the same way. Confidence is highly subjective.

Certainty and Control: The Components of Confidence

If what I just shared about the nature of confidence seems too abstract to be useful, I have some encouraging news. Underlying our personal and subjective feelings of confidence are two very consistent factors that we can learn to diagnose and put to practical, everyday use in our analysis: our feelings of certainty and control.

We tend to lump our feelings of certainty and control together, believing that we can't have one without the other. That isn't true. When we are on an airplane, for example, unless we are the pilot, control rests with someone else. We have only a feeling of certainty—the presumption that the plane will land safely.

Typically, our lack of control while riding on a plane is of little concern. We believe pilots are rigorously trained, planes are well maintained, and air travel is highly regulated. There is ample evidence we can draw from to affirm our conclusion that flying is extremely safe. But when we experience unexpected turbulence, suddenly our lack of control can feel like a big deal.

To be confident, we need our "C & C." We need to feel things are predictable—that we have certainty in what is to come—and we need to feel we have the right preparation, skills, and resources to successfully steer our way through it—that we have control. When we are confident, we believe we will land safely and successfully on the other side of what's next. Feelings of certainty and control lie at the root of the decisions we make in business, investing, politics, and our personal lives. These two variables drive how we feel and, in turn, how we act. The more we understand their precise roles, the more accurately we can predict what we and others are likely to do next and calibrate our own decisions accordingly. Whether we're investing in technology stocks, designing the next ad campaign for a clothing retailer, or running an emergency room, by understanding how feelings of certainty and control drive what we do, we can predict trends, generate better outcomes, know when to trust or second-guess our natural instincts, and, generally speaking, make better sense of a world that too often feels chaotic.

This book is an all-weather guide to our feelings of certainty and control—useful no matter what your natural confidence level—and, as you will see, it comes complete with a handy map to help you better anticipate, and navigate, whatever the future may have in store.

Vulnerability: The Opposite of Confidence

When we think of confidence, we typically think of it as coming in three sizes: none, some, and too much. We lack it; we have enough of it; or we are overconfident.

As handy as this simplistic framework may be, when it comes to connecting decision-making to confidence, it isn't especially useful. Lacking confidence hardly seems like a powerful propellant for the kinds of dramatic decisions and actions that often accompany those low moments in our lives.

Though we don't typically think of it in these terms, the opposite of feeling confident isn't lacking confidence as much as it is feeling vulnerable. Vulnerability is what we experience when we feel that we lack certainty and control—when we feel somehow threatened, when what is ahead seems unclear and we feel powerless against some troubling force. Extreme vulnerability—the way we feel when we truly lack confidence—better explains the highly impulsive and emotional nature of the behavior we display at such moments, too. When we perceive an intense threat, we are urgently compelled to do something bold.

As you will see, feelings of vulnerability drive much of our decision-making. We are all but programmed to attempt to restore certainty and control in our lives when we've lost them.[1] Moreover, once we do restore them, we will do all we can to make sure we don't experience vulnerability again. As a result, and often without our knowing it, our choices reflect a relentless drive to achieve and sustain confidence in our lives. This is why confidence matters so much. Vulnerability inherently drives us to act—and, as you will see, it does so in very predictable ways.

A Little About Me

I make my living studying confidence and its impact on what we do. Every day, I use, and help others use, the concepts and framework I am about to share with you. It is a second career for me, and I came to it by working backward as I tried to better understand what drives investor decision-making.

I spent the first part of my career in financial services. Forty years ago, I was a pioneer in what is now called "securitization," among the very first to help banks and finance companies bundle up pools of credit-card and automobile loans and sell them to global bond investors. While the process has since become routine, there were no instruction manuals or roadmaps when I started. To succeed, I had to be persistent and I had to be innovative. From there, I went on to serve as the treasurer of a major regional bank, where I was ultimately responsible for a line of business that generated $900 million in annual revenue. On paper, at least, everything was going according to plan.

Then one day, as I was blowing out candles on my forty-fifth birthday, my eight-year-old son made a show of his newfound math skills and enthusiastically proclaimed that I was halfway to ninety.

Oof.

Halfway to ninety?!

Those three words stopped me in my tracks and made me reconsider my priorities. Right then and there, I decided it was time for a change. It wouldn't be long before my son and his older sister would be teenagers and then off to college. I knew I wanted to spend my "second half" differently. So, in 2006, unsure of what was next, I stepped down from my job.

"Next" turned out to be consulting for a small group of hedge funds and institutional money managers during the 2008 financial crisis. Given my expertise in securitization and my experience working with regulators and the rating agencies during my time as a bank treasurer, I not only saw the crisis coming but had a good feel for how it would likely play out. The consequences of the bursting housing bubble seemed straightforward to me.

What I didn't anticipate was that the crisis would send me down a deep rabbit hole. I had seen firsthand the collective euphoria ahead of the housing crisis and the hopelessness at the bottom. After witnessing the impact that changing confidence brings to bear on our decision-making, I decided I needed to gain a better understanding of its impact on the choices investors make. So, working backward, I started to study the role mood and sentiment play in the financial markets.

Which brings me to the present.

More than a decade later, I not only continue to work with professional investors but now also serve as a consultant to *Fortune* 500 companies. I help business leaders to better see the connection between consumer confidence and the choices their customers and employees make, enabling them to improve marketing, customer service, and their own decision-making.

I also teach classes on confidence and decision-making at William & Mary, my alma mater, and in the honors program at the University of Delaware. In both classrooms, we go well beyond the world of investing to explore the connections between confidence and our economic, financial, political, social, and even cultural choices. We look at everything from what we invest in to how we vote and what we eat and why—all based on our confidence levels. (As you'll see, there really is a reason we reach for the pint of Ben & Jerry's Chunky Monkey ice cream after a breakup.)[2] My class is an unconventional, interdisciplinary exploration of how confidence drives our actions, often in real time.

For example, as Election Day neared in the 2016 U.S. presidential contest, one of my classes began with a discussion of the pair of charts in Figure 1 and their potential implications for Hillary Clinton and Donald Trump. The first chart, from *HuffPost*, tracked the respective popularity of both candidates throughout the campaign, while the second tracked Gallup's U.S. Economic Confidence Index—a broad and widely used measure of consumer confidence—over the same time period.[3]

Setting aside questions of causation, correlation, or coincidence, it was clear that for almost eighteen months of the campaign, Hillary Clinton's popularity with voters had ebbed and flowed in near-lockstep with how voters *felt* about the economy, as measured by Gallup's index. Which was the cause or effect was irrelevant. The takeaway was clear: there was a connection between economic confidence levels and the choices voters were likely to make on Election Day.

After studying the two charts, my students concluded that if the trend held, the result of the election would come down not to party or platform but to how voters felt more broadly. The class's view flew in the face of the polls and punditry that led up to the election. But thanks to what they had learned, my students accurately forecast that if

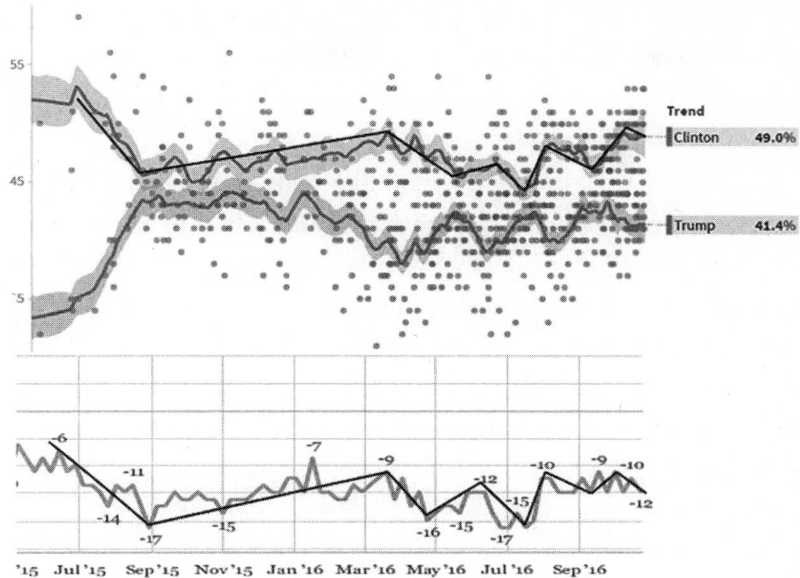

FIGURE 1: Top: Popularity of Trump and Clinton; Bottom: Gallup Economic Confidence Index.
Top: From HuffPost. ©2016 BuzzFeed. All rights reserved. Used under license. Bottom: Gallup, Inc.

economic confidence fell going into early November—which it did—Donald Trump would go on to victory. Voter confidence was the deciding factor.

In my day-to-day work in the classroom and as a consultant, I am part economist, part historian, part psychologist, part sociologist, and part anthropologist. I don't fit squarely into one box, nor does my research. That is what I like most about what I do—I bring a different lens to decision-making than other social scientists and experts. Where others tend to go deep within their specialized fields, I go wide, applying concepts from different disciplines and from the confidence framework I have developed to better understand and explain why we do what we do and what our behavior suggests lies ahead.

Because our mood transcends everything we do, simultaneously affecting us in multiple areas, its impact can be far-reaching, too. As a result, I often look for parallel behaviors across culture, politics, and society more broadly, comparing what is happening in music, for example, with what is happening in government, business, and the markets.

In late January 2020, Billie Eilish's surprise sweep of the Grammy Awards over highly favored Taylor Swift was as noteworthy to me as the decision made the same week by Italian policymakers to shut down their economy. While seemingly unrelated on the surface, both were important reflections of deteriorating confidence. Our music selections mirror our mood, and Taylor Swift, like other pop chart–topping artists such as Justin Timberlake, does best when confidence is high.[4] The sudden rise of Billie Eilish, like the rise of indie music more broadly, cautioned that behind the scenes, consumer mood was already deteriorating. Even before the pandemic hit, we were getting anxious.

Throughout my career, I have been told repeatedly that I think differently—that I see connections others miss and bring a different perspective to a discussion. That is the point of this book: to help you look at confidence and its impact on decision-making in a new way.

My Approach

The concept of confidence—and even the concepts of certainty and control—can too easily feel abstract. To counter that tendency, I have found that the best way to explain these concepts and their impact on our decision-making is to use familiar, real-life examples. In my classroom, that means we explore the choices my students made while on spring break in contrast to the ones they made as they awaited their college acceptance letters. In sessions with business leaders, we discuss how they felt when they made their best and worst acquisitions and how they felt and acted during a crisis.

In this book, I use familiar and real-life experiences, too. Some are major moments in history; others are far more mundane. My hope is that the contrasts in these examples will help you see the behavioral parallels, similarities, and patterns that arise at different levels of confidence. While I may sometimes mention well-known people, they aren't my real focus; I am less interested in who was in the room where it happened than I am in how those in the room felt and why they made the choices they made—i.e., how feelings drive history.

Just as seeds need the right soil to germinate, the same is true for our ideas and actions, and I believe popular culture and social movements all have their roots in confidence.

Too often, we focus on major events and their consequences, moving quickly past the conditions that existed prior to their inception. We focus on specific *actions* as deciding factors, rather than the *feelings* that led those actions to be taken. This book is about the backdrop of certainty and control in those preceding moments—the mood just before investors bought shares in GameStop or Vladimir Putin ordered the invasion of Ukraine.

Throughout this book, when I cite examples from recent history, I encourage you to take a second to recall how you felt in those moments. I believe that by doing so—by looking at our shared experiences through the lens of our feelings of certainty and control—you will come away with an appreciation for how not only is the "unprecedented" remarkably predictable but so is the nature of our response to it.

Relatedly, I won't bombard you in these pages with minute facts and lots of objective data. What interests me—and what I believe drives our decision-making—is how we *feel* about facts and data. In other words, it doesn't matter if it is 65 degrees outside; what matters is whether we think 65 degrees feels warm or cold. It is our personal, subjective assessment—the story we tell ourselves about how we feel—that determines whether we put on a T-shirt or a sweatshirt before we head out the door.

We routinely act based on stories—on the adjectives we ascribe to facts. As I observe regularly in the financial markets, the same objective data can generate far different outcomes depending on the feelings of the crowd: profits of two dollars per share one quarter can "beat earnings estimates" and "surprise analysts," while the exact same figure a year later can "disappoint" and "anger investors." What the crowd is certain of, just moments before earnings are released, determines the story about the data and, in turn, drives the response.

My approach may make some readers uncomfortable, particularly when I discuss major business, political, and social decisions. Some may want me to take a side on certain issues. I will leave it to others to argue over whether the choices that were made were good or bad, right or wrong, rational or irrational, or how the decision-making process itself could have been improved. My objective is to reframe how and why choices were made in the first place as a means to a deeper understanding of decision-making, *not* in order to assess their appropriateness or correctness.

At the end of the day, I want you to be able to apply the concepts and framework of what I call "confidence-driven decision-making" to your own life and work. I want this book to be a source to help you confront moments of uncertainty and powerlessness in your life—personally and professionally—and to be a tool to better understand and anticipate the decisions and actions that you and others make.

You see, I have no idea whether there will be another global pandemic, or a housing bubble, or what exactly our future will bring. But I do know that whatever happens, our decisions will be guided by our feelings of certainty and control.

The Journey Ahead

This book is divided into five sections. The first explores confidence in more detail and examines how changes in our feelings of certainty and control alter how we feel more broadly. From this overview, you will gain a better understanding of how and why confidence is such a deciding factor in our choices. The remaining four sections are deeper dives into the four distinct confidence environments we routinely experience. Along the way, I will introduce tools and practices that I hope will improve not only your decision-making but your resilience and your ability to navigate uncertainty and powerlessness.

With that, let's open up the Confidence Map.

SECTION I

The Confidence Quadrant

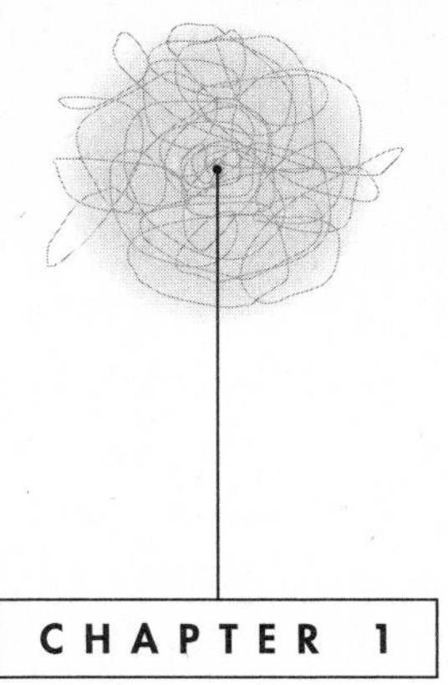

CHAPTER 1

Visualizing Confidence

When I was growing up, we had one of those supersized National Geographic atlases—a blue, hardcover treasure trove of detailed maps of the world, about the size of a front-door welcome mat. My dad traveled a lot, and when he returned from a business trip, he would pull the atlas from the shelf next to our kitchen table, open it up—all but covering the table—and leaf through it until he found the specific map detailing the city he had just visited. As he spoke about his experience and pointed his index finger to different locations on the page, the maps helped me visualize where he had been and how far he had traveled to get there.

With each new trip, more pages of the atlas were highlighted. I gained a better sense of the world around me: individual cities and countries didn't stand alone but instead fit into a broader patchwork of geography. When my dad flew to Dubai or Saudi Arabia, which he did often, I knew not only his exact location in the atlas but, more broadly, that he was in the Middle East. Specific cities and countries began to fit together.

When I grew older, the atlas became more than just a series of maps I could use to assess relative distances and understand the broader geographic configuration of the world. As my father shared different experiences from his trips, the atlas formed the framework for a rich, unwritten travel guide filled with interesting stories detailing what things looked like and how people behaved in different places on the map. I knew that on page 194, people ate sushi and drank sake. On page 179, they wore a *thawb*. On page 174, they spoke Russian and used the Cyrillic alphabet.[1] Cultural norms added depth to the geography on the page. Later in my life, when I was the one traveling, I carried these associations with me. When I landed in London or Tokyo, I had a general sense of what to expect. I felt prepared. There was a line of understanding stretching from my childhood travels with my dad across the pages of the atlas to my real-world adult journeys abroad.

When I became a parent, one of my first purchases was an atlas of my own—and a globe, too. Like my father, I wanted my children to see that dots on maps were more than just locations; they represented people with stories and cultures—places where distinct things happened.

Little did I know how helpful this perspective would be in my second career.

Introducing the Confidence Quadrant

A few years into teaching my class on confidence and decision-making, I realized my students were struggling. The concepts I was trying to share felt too abstract to them; students were having trouble "seeing" the connections between their own actions (as well as the behavior of others) and confidence. Trying to separate confidence into two distinct feelings, certainty and control, didn't help matters—I had simply created a jumbled-up word cloud. Not only did I need a way to show that specific feelings drive behavior, I also needed to show how and why that was the case. I needed to turn the word cloud into a simple, easy-to-use framework that made it clear that different mixes of our feelings of certainty and control lead to different outcomes in our preferences, decisions, and actions. Moreover, the framework needed to acknowledge and allow for the fact that our feelings routinely change, altering how we act. I realized that, like my father with the atlas, I needed a map that enabled my students to see specific feeling locations in relationship to others, on top of which I could then layer stories that revealed the norms and behaviors unique to each location. With that map in hand, my students would better understand why our feelings of certainty and control matter so much, and what happens as these feelings change when we move from location to location around the map.

With this in mind, I developed a tool I call the Confidence Quadrant (Figure 1.1). As you look at it for the first time, ignore all the labeling. Just think of it as a map made up of four distinct states—like a map of the Four Corners region of the American Southwest.

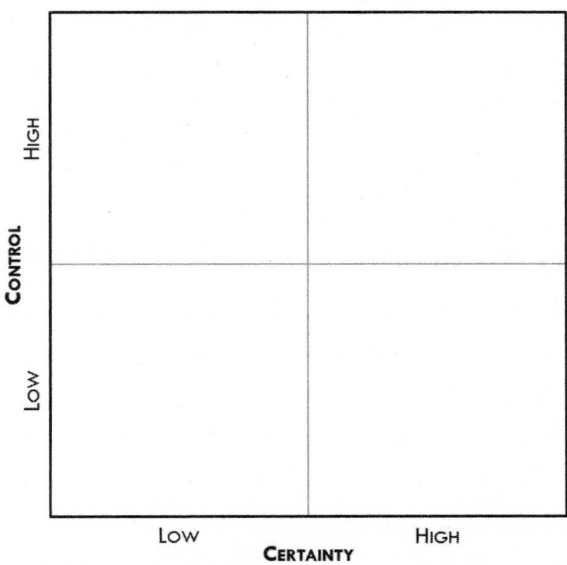

FIGURE 1.1: The Confidence Quadrant

If you've traveled to Four Corners, where the boundaries of Utah, Colorado, New Mexico, and Arizona all come together like the center of the image above, you will have seen that the differences from state to state are indistinguishable. Without the granite monument and the small bronze disc at its center showing where one state ends and the next begins, you'd never know where one state ends and the next begins.[2] But the farther away you drive from that marker, the more unique the culture, the norms, and the topography of each state become.

Rather than subdividing a physical region, like the Four Corners, into four unique states, the Confidence Quadrant divides our feelings of confidence into four unique environments that reflect the relative mix of certainty and control we feel in our lives. The horizontal axis of the Quadrant measures the relative intensity of our feeling of certainty—how sure we feel about what is ahead—while the vertical axis measures the relative intensity of our feeling of control—what level of influence we feel we have over the outcome.

Just as at Four Corners, our feelings of certainty and control are indistinguishable at the center of the Quadrant, no matter which of the four environments we are in. But as we move away from the center, each of the four confidence environments of the Quadrant becomes increasingly distinct. There are consistent patterns of behavior—cultural norms, as it were—that characterize our presence in each box. Different combinations of certainty and control change how we feel and, in turn, how we act. There is a clear relationship between our location on the Quadrant and our behavior.

Before I go any deeper into these connections, I think it's important we start with a quick tour of each of the four confidence environments of the Quadrant.

The upper right box, where we feel high levels of both certainty and control, is our "Comfort Zone." We are confident in this box, relaxed and optimistic about what we see ahead. Here, things feel familiar to us. We believe we will succeed at whatever it is we are undertaking.

When athletes are in the upper right box, they describe it as being

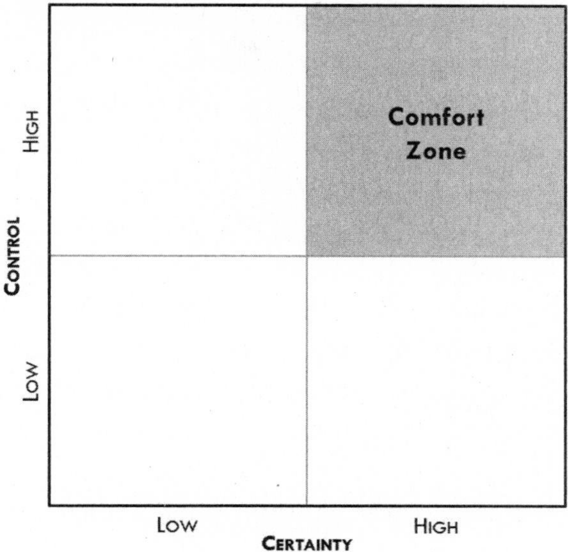

FIGURE 1.2: The Comfort Zone

"in the zone": time passes quickly; actions seem effortless. Likewise, business leaders routinely map their greatest successes to the Comfort Zone—positive outcomes like expectation-beating product launches, career promotions, and stock-option gains. The Comfort Zone is where leaders feel most valued, appreciated, and rewarded. It's also where we have fun. When prompted, my students always identify the Comfort Zone as the location of experiences like spring break and prom—unless, of course, their date was a dud.

Those dud experiences typically show up in the lower left box—the "Stress Center." This box is where we feel powerless—we lack control—and the future feels uncertain. We feel vulnerable here. We are anxious, pessimistic, and doubtful of our ability to handle things. In the Stress Center, even easy things feel hard.

A few years ago, a student rushed into my class late, making profuse apologies: "Professor," she said, "I'm so, *so* sorry I'm late, but I'm in the lower left box! Last night, I had a fight with my roommate. Then I

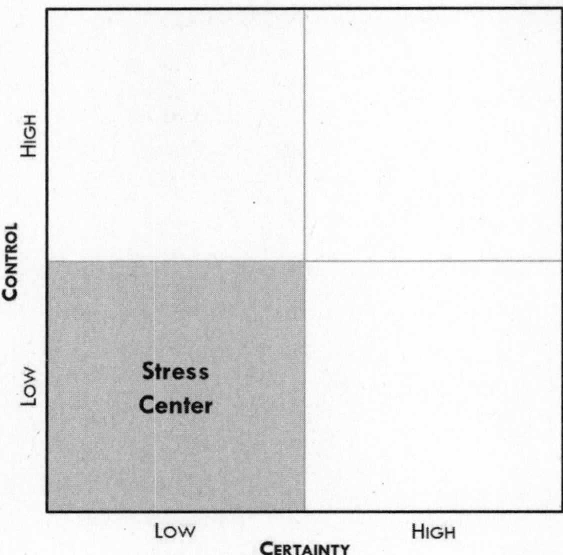

FIGURE 1.3: The Stress Center

overslept this morning. And to top it all off, I have an organic chemistry test this afternoon that I didn't have time to study for!" In her exasperation, she perfectly captured what it feels like when we are in the Stress Center—it seems as though *everything* is going wrong at once and there is little we can do to stop it.

Business leaders describe the Stress Center as the place where they work hardest and get recognized (and paid) the least. It is where they experience their greatest failures, too. Demotions, firings, and the fallout from flawed decisions all cluster here. So do feelings of shame and embarrassment.

The upper right and lower left boxes of the Quadrant are the mountaintops and valleys of our lives—our *Wide World of Sports*'s thrill of victory and agony of defeat, respectively. It is as if there is a spectrum of confidence that runs from the upper right corner to the lower left corner of the Quadrant. The farther into either box we go, the more extreme our feelings become. When we think about being or not being confident, the Comfort Zone and the Stress Center are what first come to mind.

The other two boxes of the Quadrant are a little fuzzier in our minds and more challenging to capture. These are environments of mixed feelings, where we have *either* certainty *or* control. We often overlook these states of being—if we acknowledge they exist at all. Typically, we lump together our feelings of certainty and control, believing that we can't have one without the other.

We can and we do—and far more often than we realize.

The lower right box, where we feel certainty but have low control, is the "Passenger Seat." This is an environment where we feel someone or something else has the steering wheel, but there is predictability and stability to our circumstances. Being on an elevator is a common Passenger Seat experience; so, too, is getting a haircut or an oil change. Passenger Seat environments involve a loss of agency, where control has been taken by or ceded to someone or something else.

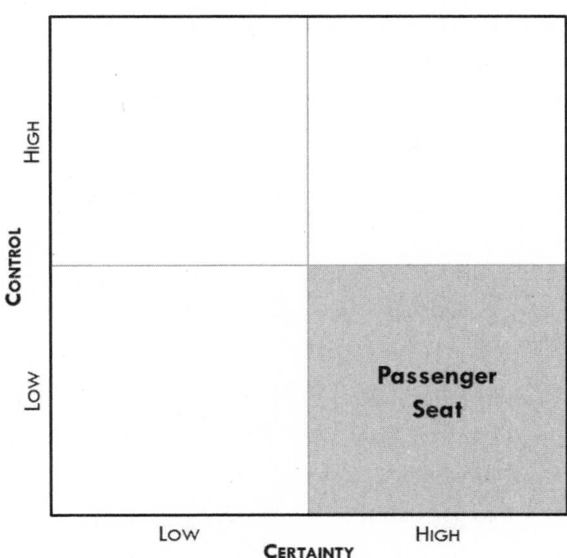

FIGURE 1.4: The Passenger Seat

In the workplace, the Passenger Seat tends to encompass those environments where employees are told what to do. It's full of assignments, training, and projects where workers are instructed to follow the clear direction of others. And here is where the lower right box gets interesting: the experience of certainty without control can feel pleasurable, or it can feel prisonlike.

We like it when a Passenger Seat experience is voluntary—when we have chosen to cede control. But even that may not be enough. To be comfortable in the Passenger Seat, we also typically need a very high level of certainty in the outcome we desire. We must feel like we are on the far right side of that lower right box. We wouldn't get on an airplane if we had only a 50 percent chance of arriving safely at our destination, nor would most of us get on a plane with even a 90 percent chance—we require 99.99999 percent certainty. When we are in the Passenger Seat, we are comfortable only when we are hugging the right edge of the box.

As a result, and especially when the consequences to us are dire, even a very small decrease in our feelings of predictability or stability can quickly move us from the Passenger Seat to the depths of the Stress Center. Because we have one but not both of our requirements for confidence, there is an inherent fragility to our feelings when we are in the lower right box. If you've ever tried to teach your children to drive, you have experienced that Passenger Seat fragility firsthand.

The final box is the opposite environment to the Passenger Seat. Here, in the upper left box of the Quadrant, we have high control but low certainty. This is the "Launch Pad." It is where we control a decision or action but the outcome of that choice is still unknown. The Launch Pad is where we are when we pull the lever on a slot machine, when we are rock climbing and begin our ascent up the side of a cliff, or when we've updated our résumé and hit "Send" to deliver it to a potential new employer. When experts talk about "decision-making amid uncertainty," they are almost always discussing a choice we make in the Launch Pad. In these moments we have control—agency—but the outcomes re-

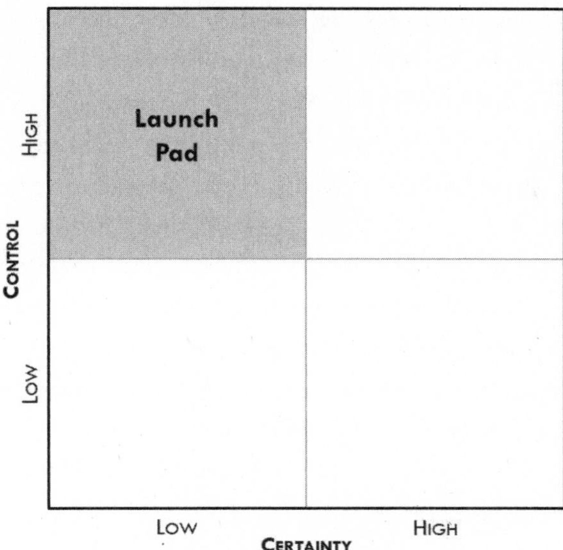

FIGURE 1.5: The Launch Pad

main uncertain. We don't know whether we will hit the jackpot, reach the mountaintop, or be called for an interview; if we'll come away successful or licking our wounds.

Some have suggested the upper left box is akin to the early moments of the hero's journey—that it is the moment when "Sully" Sullenberger took back control and decided to land US Airways Flight 1549 on the Hudson River; or when Tom Hanks set off on his raft in the film *Cast Away*. Others have suggested that I should simply call the upper left box "TBD."

No matter what we call it, we try to compensate for the uncertainty of the upper left box by doing something to make us feel like we have both our hands on the wheel. We want to be at the very, very top edge of the box. The more control we feel we have, the better we feel. Just as we require near-absolute certainty to feel secure amid the powerlessness of the Passenger Seat, we require near total control to feel secure amid the uncertainty of the Launch Pad.

To be fair, there are some people who love spending time in this box, particularly thrill seekers and entrepreneurs. But most people view the Launch Pad as a necessary means to an end, a temporary environment they must endure in order to reach or return to the Comfort Zone.

Not surprisingly, business leaders tend to map those experiences in which they deliberately took a risk in the Launch Pad and succeeded. They often draw a circular path from the Comfort Zone over to the Launch Pad and back, forming a visual victory lap that celebrates the outcome of their successful risk-taking. Few leaders volunteer to discuss experiences where they willingly left the Comfort Zone for the Launch Pad, failed, and ended up in the depths of the Stress Center.

While opposite environments, the Launch Pad and the Passenger Seat often generate similar feelings of anxiety. Both involve elements of risk-taking, since either certainty or control is missing. In the Launch Pad, we hike up a steep, winding trail to reach the summit of a mountain on our own. In the Passenger Seat, we ride a chairlift that dangles from a thin cable above our head. Both get us to the top, but they do so via different paths on the Quadrant. Moreover, in both cases, we look forward to the experience being over and successfully returning us to the Comfort Zone, where we once again have certainty *and* control in our lives.

Taken together, the full Confidence Quadrant looks like Figure 1.6.

According to the different mixture of our feelings of certainty and control in each box on the Quadrant, we feel, and in turn act, differently.

Earlier, I shared that our choices fall into two broad categories: we act either to retain confidence once it has been achieved or to restore it once it has been lost. As Figure 1.6 shows, any time we are outside of the Comfort Zone, we feel vulnerable. There is something unknown and fragile about the environment, so in order to feel relaxed and secure, we must return to the Comfort Zone. Having once returned to its safety, we will do whatever it takes to preserve the certainty and control we feel there.

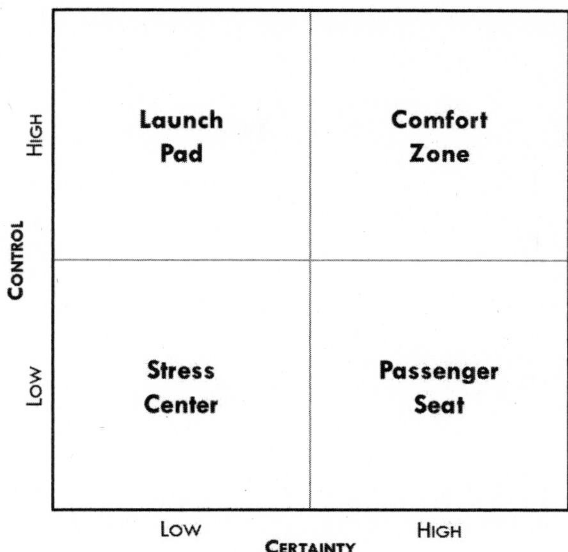

FIGURE 1.6: The four environments of the Confidence Quadrant

Mapping Experiences Using the Confidence Quadrant

Despite what many well-intended self-help experts suggest, confidence is not a steady state. When we have it, we don't keep it forever. As much as we might wish otherwise, especially when we are relaxed in the Comfort Zone, real life moves us around the Confidence Quadrant. To help illustrate this idea, I'd like you to join me on an airline flight.

Early in my career, I frequently flew cross-country, from New York to Los Angeles, for business. It was a trip I took so regularly that when I made my reservation, and then later arrived at the gate for my flight at Kennedy airport, I naturally felt a high degree of confidence. As I boarded the plane, my feelings of certainty and control put me in the upper right box (Figure 1.7).

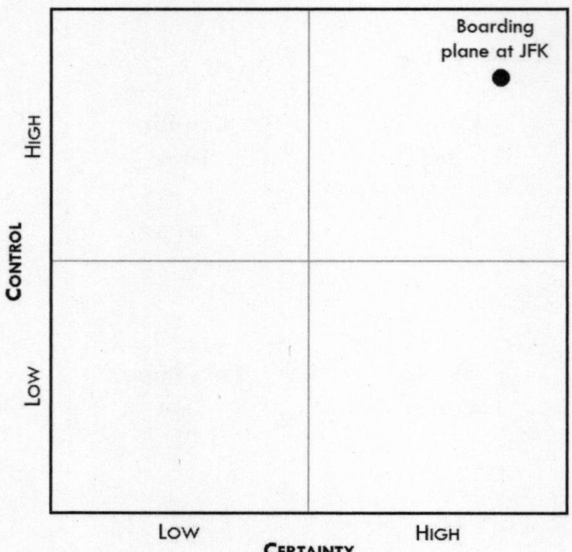

FIGURE 1.7: Mapping a plane ride, boarding

As the plane took off, though, I felt different. The sense of control that I had on the ground was gone. I didn't have control of the plane; the pilot did. I was both literally and figuratively in the Passenger Seat. All I had was certainty (Figure 1.8).

That evening, as we came in for our landing at LAX, there was heavy fog around us. At the very last minute, our pilot realized the plane was not correctly aligned with the runway. Immediately, he aborted the landing and gunned the engines, sending the plane rocketing skyward. As we made our ascent, the plane shook violently, and I suddenly experienced an unmistakable sense of uncertainty and powerlessness. Panic filled me. In that moment, I was squarely in the lower left corner of the Quadrant—the Stress Center (Figure 1.9).

After what felt like an eternity, the plane leveled off and the pilot spoke over the PA system to reassure us that everything was OK. Not twenty minutes later, we landed safely.

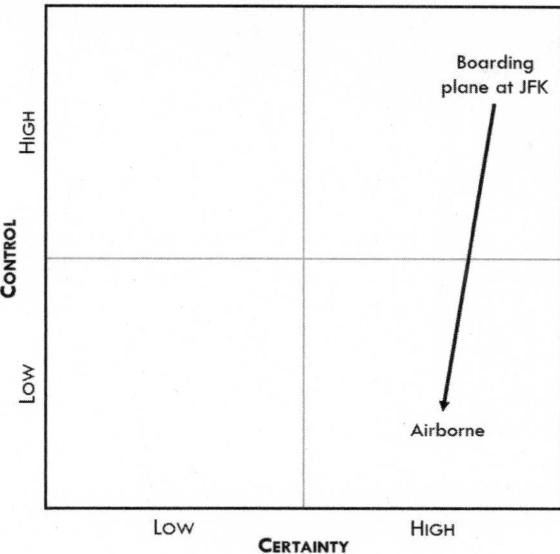

FIGURE 1.8: Mapping a plane ride, airborne.

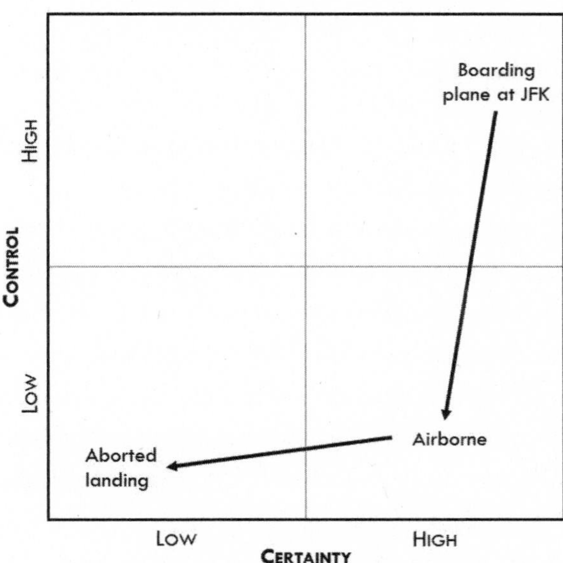

FIGURE 1.9: Mapping a plane ride, aborted landing

By the time the plane pulled up to the gate, my five-hour flight to Los Angeles not only had taken me cross-country but had sent me on a highly emotional tour around the Quadrant (Figure 1.10).

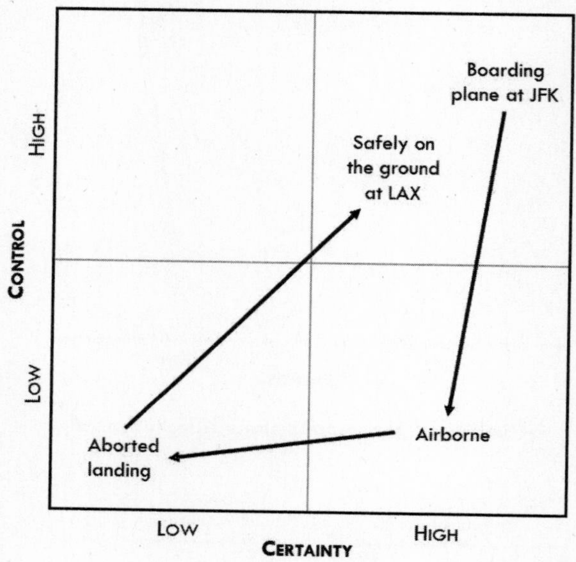

FIGURE 1.10: Mapping a plane ride, safely on the ground

Figure 1.11 imagines how a very nervous flyer on that same flight might have mapped this same experience.

You'll notice his map has a new first step. When our nervous flyer made his reservation, he was in the Launch Pad—in control of his actions but intensely aware that he was taking a risk by initiating his travel plans. Moreover, once he got to the airport, anxiety likely had already started setting in—even before he boarded the flight, his sense of control was declining. Once airborne, our nervous flyer likely felt none of the certainty I did, leaving him low on both components of confidence. When the plane aborted its landing, he may have found himself in the very deepest depths of the Stress Center, and after finally deplaning, perhaps his fear remained so intense that he decided to cancel his return flight and drive back to New York. All told, our nervous flyer would

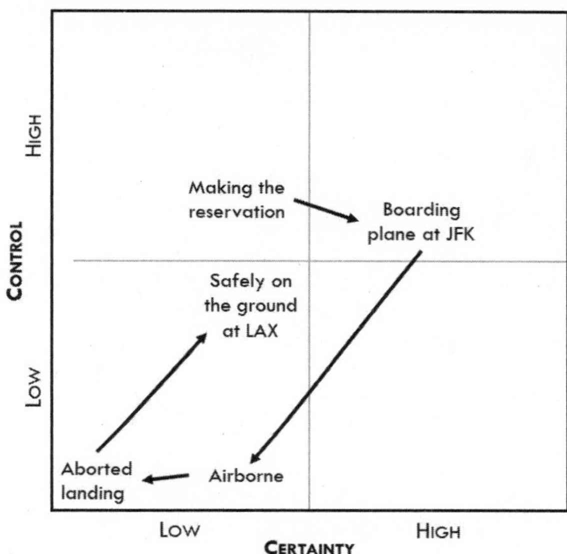

FIGURE 1.11: Mapping a plane ride, fearful flyer experience

have mapped a very different experience from the one I mapped, even though we were both on the same flight.

One of the things I see repeatedly when using the Quadrant in group mapping exercises is the varied nature of human experience. From plane flights and roller coasters to cocktail parties and first days of school, no two journeys are exactly alike when we measure them in terms of a person's feelings of certainty and control.

And there are other interesting things that mapping reveals.

We just looked at my map versus the map of the same flight for a nervous flyer. Figure 1.12 imagines the map an extremely confident passenger might draw for the same flight.

Our extremely confident flyer might not even have registered that when the plane took off, she had no control. Moreover, she might have been unaffected by the aborted landing; she may have traveled so frequently that she had come to see such events as merely routine. If she even entered the Stress Center, it may have been only for the briefest

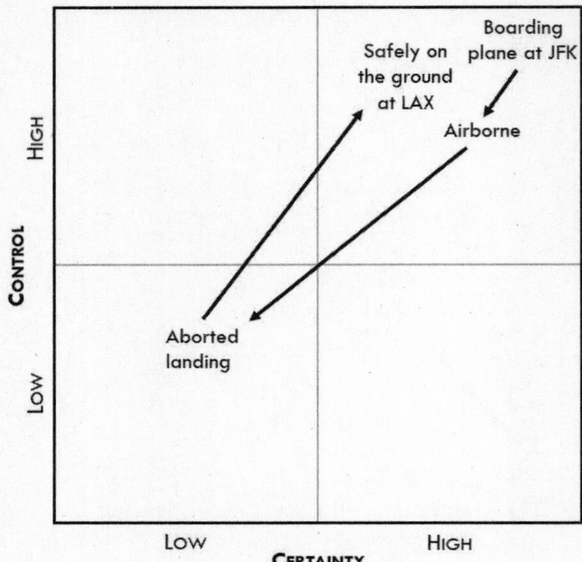

FIGURE 1.12: Mapping a plane ride, frequent flyer experience

moment. Maybe, as the woman next to her clutched her armrest in terror, our confident flyer stifled a yawn.

This one flight yielded three very different journeys as measured by the flyers' feelings of certainty and control. Here's why that matters: In this particular case, our extremely confident flyer's perception of the experience is *factually* incorrect. When the plane took off, she had no control. If only to reflect the reality of the situation, her second point, "Airborne," should have been placed somewhere in the lower right box. Other than the pilots, everyone on that plane was in the Passenger Seat. Air travel is an environment of high certainty and no control, no matter how good or bad we may feel about it.

In fairness to airlines and airplane manufacturers, I should also point out that the map our nervous flyer created was factually incorrect, too. Air travel is remarkably safe; statistically, there was far greater certainty midair than our nervous passenger acknowledged.

Finally, I should also add that there was far more certainty than any of us on the plane appreciated when the pilot aborted our landing and gunned the engines. The experience—a "go-around," as it is called—is something pilots regularly train for; moreover, commercial pilots actively prepare for its possibility. Specific go-around procedures are outlined and discussed as pilots go through their preflight and pre-landing checklists. While those of us in the back of the plane were unprepared for the go-around when it happened, the cockpit was at the ready.

When I asked a commercial pilot friend to map how he thought the captain on our flight would have captured the experience, he shared the image in Figure 1.13.

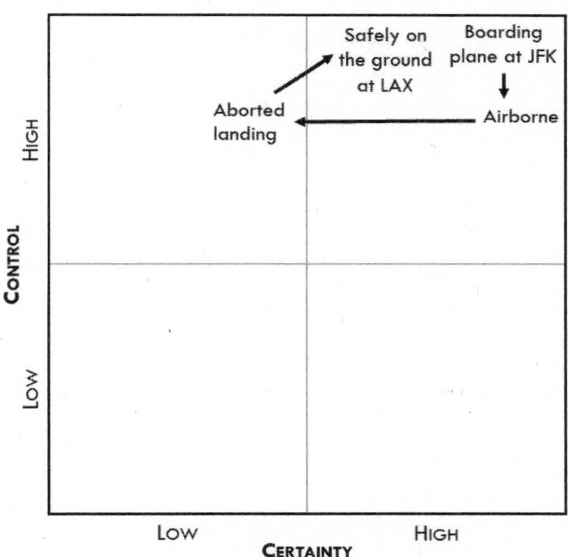

FIGURE 1.13: Mapping a plane ride, pilot experience

While our aborted landing was out of the ordinary, it wasn't an emergency. It was a landing in heavy fog that became a go-around. Processes and procedures that were well understood and well rehearsed replaced others that were routine. As I described the experience, my friend saw nothing that would have created concern with respect to the certainty or the control he, as the pilot, would have felt during the flight.

Group mapping exercises like the one I just shared have taught me two important lessons: first, we do not all see the same experience in the same way, and second, frequently we don't even see the experience as it really is. Our level of confidence can distort our view of the world. When our confidence is high, we may believe we control things that we don't and can't, and we may see certainty that does not exist. And at lows in confidence, we experience the reverse.

Common experiences can be anything but that when mapped on the Quadrant.

Mapping and the Confidence Quadrant in Practice

When I first began using the Confidence Quadrant, three things surprised me.

First, I saw that, after a brief introduction like the one I just provided for you, users had little trouble plotting experiences. The ability to associate moments with feelings of certainty and control came quickly.

Second, I noticed that, after seeing their experiences mapped, users said the images helped explain the emotions they felt and the choices they made. Abstract feelings were organized on the Quadrant in a way that seemed logical. Moreover, as users looked more closely at clusters of dots within a specific box, they quickly understood why seemingly unrelated events, like a receiving a promotion at work and running a new personal best in a marathon, could generate such similar feelings and kinds of behaviors.

Finally, I found that users were comfortable discussing their experiences and sharing their Quadrant maps with others, even if that meant acknowledging their own shortcomings. Where they might have been reluctant to openly discuss a lack of confidence, users tended to be remarkably open expressing their level of certainty or control, even when it was low. Mapping specific experiences on the Quadrant seemed like a factual—almost true or false—determination: "*Of course*, I was in the Stress Center while I waited for my cancer diagnosis!" While highly subjective, dots on the map *felt* like objective data points. There was no judgment attached—no "right" or "wrong" answer.

Through mapping exercises, I've learned not only how much life routinely moves us around the Quadrant but how differently we all see the world around us.

I've also learned that satisfaction surveys and "average consumer" data often overlook or obscure important behavioral patterns that are obvious thanks to Quadrant mapping. Mapping lets me pinpoint exactly where individuals and groups see themselves at a particular moment in time and quickly uncover what is behind respondents' feelings of certainty and control, or lack of them.

For example, when COVID-19 first hit, in mid-March 2020, I asked all sorts of people to map how they felt on the Confidence Quadrant. No matter who I asked—doctors, students, parents, business owners—respondents all mapped their position in the very lower left corner of the Quadrant, deep in the Stress Center (Figure 1.14). On the composite

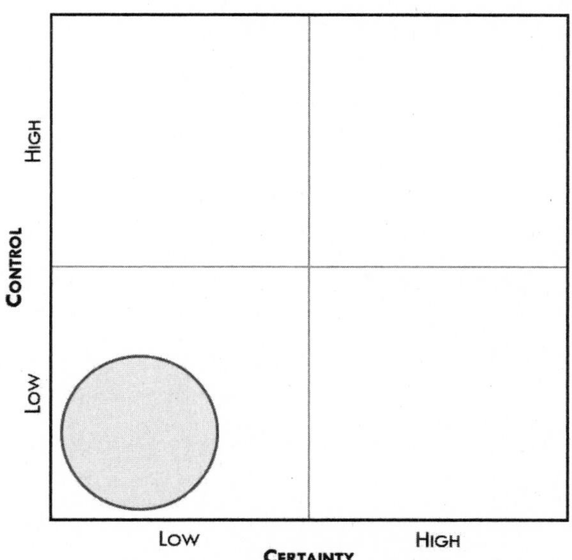

FIGURE 1.14: Mapping COVID, immediate crowd response

Quadrant where I plotted all their responses, the intense clustering of dots made it obvious that the pandemic had upended Americans' feelings of certainty and control. Everyone was intensely anxious.

But I noticed something significant when I surveyed these same people just a few weeks later: The cluster of dots had divided. One group had moved up and to the right on the Quadrant, while the other remained deep in the lower left corner of the Stress Center. Individuals who were able to work from home, order their groceries online, and isolate to form tight COVID bubbles began to feel higher levels of certainty and control in their lives than those who continued to work in hospitals, supermarkets, and other locations where they were less protected from the outbreak. What had been a common, shared pandemic experience just days earlier had now dramatically split in two (Figure 1.15).

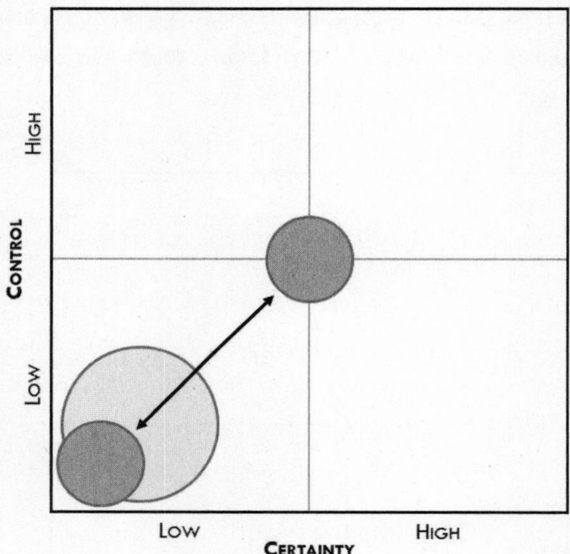

FIGURE 1.15: Mapping COVID, the K-shaped recovery

At the time, many economists and pundits were forecasting a V- or "swoosh"-shaped recovery from the COVID downturn.[3] Based on the extraordinary fiscal and monetary policy efforts put in place by the U.S.

federal government, they expected the coming rebound would benefit all.

The Quadrant maps I saw suggested otherwise. Based on the clear disparity in confidence levels illustrated by the two distinct clusters of dots I saw on the composite map, I predicted what I termed a "K-shaped" economic recovery—that those at the top end of the economic spectrum, who could work from home and more easily isolate themselves from the outbreak, would rebound from the pandemic far faster than low-income and "essential" workers.[4] The mapped pinpoints alerted me to what was likely to happen in the economy as the pandemic wore on.

The clear confidence divide that was evident on the Quadrant also alerted me to other possible concerns. Unless confidence improved for those at the bottom—and soon—income and wealth inequality would likely become much bigger social issues. Moreover, if the divide widened further, the feelings of fear and frustration felt by those clustered in the Stress Center would turn into anger and resentment. For employers, the wide divide suggested that they should expect to see an uptick in employee stress, a wave of resignations, labor strikes, calls for unionization, and demands for higher wages among low-wage workers. Policymakers would likewise be taken to task. And the wider the divide became, the more political pressure would mount to close it.

To be honest, I wasn't entirely surprised when my concept of the K-shaped recovery showed up in one of the 2020 U.S. presidential debates. The term resonated—it easily captured and reflected how people felt. Not only had my mapping efforts enabled me to clearly identify where there were shared feelings of powerlessness and uncertainty, they also helped me anticipate how those affected were likely to respond if those feelings didn't change.

Uncovering Issues Using the Quadrant

While I frequently use the Confidence Quadrant to better understand how feelings are driving consumer economic behavior, I use the Quadrant in all sorts of noneconomic ways, too. For example, a few years ago, I asked a group of high-performing college freshmen to map their senior year of high school. Based on their individual maps, I created the composite shown in Figure 1.16.

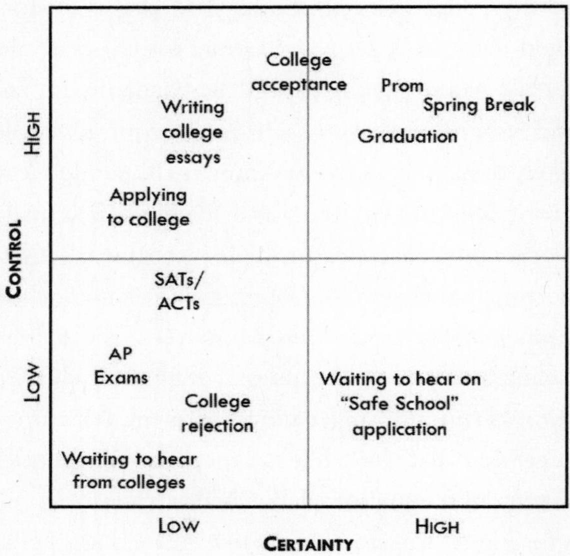

FIGURE 1.16: Senior year of high school composite map

While we parents frequently associate the senior year of high school with high confidence, that isn't what students' maps showed. For these students, most of their senior year had been spent on the left side of the Quadrant; they felt very uncertain. When I shared the composite with the parents of high school students and high school guidance counselors, many were shocked. While both groups knew the college application process was stressful, few fully appreciated how little certainty—and control—students felt. Students' senior years were spent largely outside the Comfort Zone, with much of their experience clustered in the Stress Center. When I shared that one student pinpointed on the Quadrant how she felt as she waited to hear from colleges right next to how she felt after breaking her ankle, I saw an audience of parents cringe. The idea that those two feelings were at all comparable was new and distressing to them.

While initially unwelcome news, the map opened the door to more honest communication and change. Individual students saw that they weren't the only ones who felt powerless and uncertain amid the application process and felt more comfortable talking about these feelings with their peers and family. Being in the lower left corner was no longer a sign of weakness—it was a widely shared experience. Moreover, armed with my maps, rising seniors and their parents went into the college admissions process with a better sense of what to expect. They had a useful guide for the year ahead that went well beyond application timelines and SAT test dates. So did guidance counselors and teachers. The maps caused them to rethink their ideas of how to be prepared for the most stress-filled moments of the year.

In my own classroom, as midterms and finals approach, I routinely remind my students that these moments invariably move them into the Stress Center. I encourage them to be nice to themselves and each other and to remember that once their tests are done, they will regain certainty and control in their lives.

Some of my favorite Confidence Quadrant maps are the ones that tell vivid stories in a single frame. Take a look at Figure 1.17, drawn by an emergency room doctor after I asked him to map his typical day.

Like most maps drawn by first responders, ER doctors' images reveal that their typical day involves quickly toggling back and forth between the upper right box and the lower left box of the Quadrant. Every time they've stabilized a patient and have established a sense of certainty and control, another ambulance or a medevac helicopter arrives, sending them right back into the lower left corner of the Stress Center. Back to work they go.

At their core, emergency room teams are in the business of restoring certainty and control. It's hardly surprising that burnout is a common issue for many emergency medical professionals when you see how much of their day is spent outside the upper right box of the Quadrant,

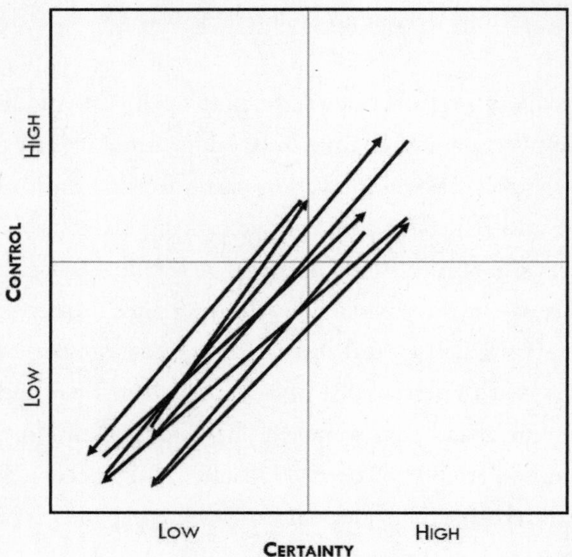

FIGURE 1.17: Emergency room physician map

struggling to get back in. At the same time, images like Figure 1.17 help explain why widely practiced emergency room procedures are vital. Knowing precisely how you will get out of the Stress Center is a must if you're certain you will be in it multiple times a day.

Sometimes Confidence Quadrant maps are deeply personal.

During the fall of my daughter's senior year of college, she wound up in the hospital for two weeks with unexplained gastrointestinal symptoms. She spent the winter and spring driving to specialists and undergoing diagnostic tests, all while trying to keep up with her classwork. By graduation, her medical team had figured out the cause of her distress and had a solution: dramatic, life-altering surgery.

Once the crisis abated, I asked her to map her medical experience. Since my wife and I had been on the journey with her, accompanying her to many of her doctor visits and hospital stays, I thought I had a good feel for what she would share and where she would put specific events from her experience.

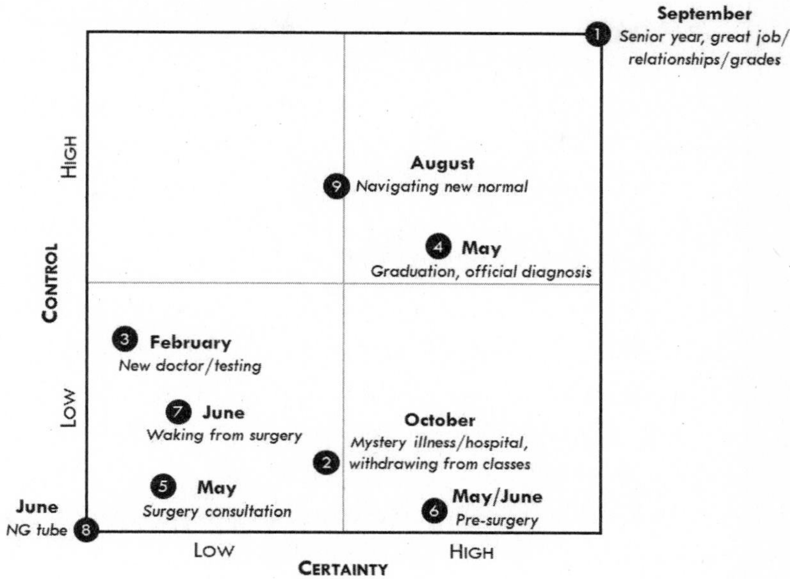

FIGURE 1.18: My daughter's medical experience map

Given the extreme nature of her surgery, I had expected to see dots in the lower left corner of the Quadrant marking the doctor's appointment when we learned the specific details of her treatment, or the evening before her surgery, when we learned that an unfamiliar surgeon would have to step in. To me, those seemed like the lowest points of her experience. They weren't; she had reserved that dire spot in the lower left corner for her post-surgical experience, when doctors inserted a nasogastric (NG) tube—a rubber tube with suction—to alleviate unexpected pressure in her stomach. As my daughter shared with me, she had been miserable living with constant abdominal pain, and as difficult as it would be, she had been optimistic the surgery would provide relief. But she had no preparation for the tube, and experienced more suffering from it than relief. With the NG tube in place, she felt as though she was constantly choking. She had a hard time swallowing, breathing, and speaking. She was in such emotional anguish from feeling so powerless that the doctors had to sedate her to prevent her from pulling the tube out.

When I shared her observations with her medical team, several members said they wished they had known how powerless she felt—that there were steps they could have taken before the procedure to mitigate her stress. This time, I was the one who cringed. How could they not have known patients felt powerless with an NG tube, especially since the treatment is so routine for patients with digestive issues? I was surprised they hadn't been proactive in addressing the potential anxiety.

I've used my daughter's story with medical workers and business leaders to challenge their thinking around the patient/customer experience and patient/customer satisfaction. If businesses don't know where their customers feel their greatest uncertainty and powerlessness, they have little hope of gaining trust. The same holds true with employees. Few employee satisfaction surveys ask employees to share suggestions that can improve a worker's sense of certainty and control in the workplace. Remarkably, simple steps often can be taken to address an organization's biggest sources of stress. In my daughter's case, she and her medical team now know that the NG tube insertion experience is much better with some throat-numbing spray and a wait of fifteen minutes for anti-anxiety medicine to kick in.

After listening to me discuss my daughter's experience, and considering the impact even a small decision can make in boosting feelings of certainty and control, a shift manager of a meat processing plant decided to follow my lead. She asked her employees to share their biggest sources of work-related stress, using questions that focused on where workers felt most uncertain and powerless on the job—topics that had never been raised before. Their responses surprised her. She discovered that many of the workplace challenges her employees identified were tied to minor problems *outside* of work. Employees felt powerless. They were embarrassed and afraid to ask for help when they needed the time to take care of unexpected obstacles like having a broken taillight on their car replaced or taking a sick child to the doctor. When she added flexibility to workers' schedules to enable them to handle small problems like these, not only did morale and productivity improve, workers missed less work overall. Because small issues were addressed before they became bigger problems, workers stayed out of the Stress Center.

Mapping also enables leaders to clearly see when their customers and employees are at the other end of the sentiment spectrum, feeling their most confident. By looking closely at what experiences respondents put in the upper right box, businesses can identify employees who should be celebrated and processes that deserve broader application—instances where things went well and conditions need to be replicated. The boosts to morale and the bottom line can be substantial as small actions result in significant improvements to customer and employee confidence.

Whether used to map a single moment in time or a longer-term experience, the Confidence Quadrant provides an easy-to-use tool to quickly uncover how groups and individuals feel and to identify opportunities for improvement.

•

As abstract as feelings of confidence, certainty, and control may seem, the Confidence Quadrant provides a framework to organize them and enables us to see why seemingly unrelated experiences—like an aborted plane landing and a broken ankle—can generate such comparable emotions and actions. In the next chapter, we'll explore how the Confidence Quadrant applies at work. As you'll see, business, too, can be all over the map.

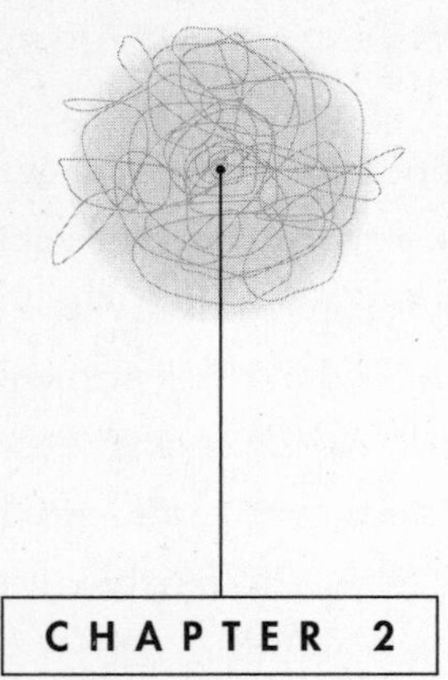

CHAPTER 2

The Confidence Quadrant at Work

IN THE LAST CHAPTER, I introduced you to the Confidence Quadrant, the tool we will use throughout the book to help visualize confidence. Through a few example maps, you saw that not only do our feelings of certainty and control change, in fact, they are constantly in motion. Real life routinely moves us around the Confidence Quadrant. In one moment, a game-winning soccer goal can propel us out of the Stress Center and into the Comfort Zone, and in the next, a victory dance that ends with a broken ankle can just as quickly return us there.

The same principle holds true in businesses. Whether leaders realize it or not, their organizations are constantly on the move on the Quadrant. Every day, their employees, their customers, their shareholders, their regulators, and their board members are moving from box to box—and rarely is everyone in the same place at once.

With this in mind, effective business leaders must know not only where precisely others are on the Quadrant and why, but where and how to move them next. After a major product defect sends customers into the Stress Center, a leader must respond like an emergency room doctor, quickly assembling a team focused on restoring confidence. Moments later, when a high-performing sales team has landed a big new client, the same leader must act like a professional basketball coach, celebrating success in the Comfort Zone while simultaneously working to prevent the team from becoming overconfident. Leaders must be agile, able to wear different hats depending on the circumstances and able to swap out one hat for another at a moment's notice. Their success, and their team's, depends on their ability to quickly read the confidence level of the room and respond accordingly.

Using the Quadrant to Assess the Confidence Level of Others

When I first speak with business executives about how to use the Confidence Quadrant to improve their leadership effectiveness, "event-driven" examples like a failed product launch or a major new client acquisition quickly come to mind. Leaders tend to believe that if they know what has just happened, and how those impacted are likely to feel about it, they can quickly locate on the Quadrant the spot that appropriately captures the feelings of certainty and control of those affected.

As a place to start, I agree with this approach—particularly when extreme events occur. Crises land *everyone* in the Stress Center, while unmitigated success propels us all far into the upper reaches of the Comfort Zone. After something major happens, it's not hard to map where customers and employees are likely to be on the Quadrant.

But waiting until extreme events take place to take a confidence inventory isn't leadership. Leaders are supposed to prevent crises and propel others toward success. Moreover, this reactive approach overlooks the fact that extreme events themselves often reflect the mood of others. Crises that shove everyone into the Stress Center often arise because some people were already there. Take the Arab Spring: While many think of the social unrest in early 2011 as causing confidence across

North Africa to fall, consumer sentiment there had already dropped precipitously due to high inflation in food prices and growing food scarcity. Those who participated in the wave of protests were already deep in the lower left corner of the Quadrant.[1]

Finally, how we feel after an event occurs often reflects how we felt beforehand. When we strike out, we react differently if it's our first time this season than we do if it is our eighth time of our last eight times at bat.

For these reasons, knowing in real time where key constituent groups are on the Quadrant matters. It is their mood *before* they show up in your store, in your office, and in your boardroom that will heavily influence not only their actions but their reactions to what unfolds next.

In my mapping work, I typically assess a group's feelings of certainty and control on three levels: a societal level, an environmental/circumstantial level, and a situational level. This may seem like a lot of work—it's actually not—but as you'll see, it is the accumulation of stressors in our lives, not just the presence of one stressor, that matters to the decisions we make.

1. SOCIETAL CONSUMER SENTIMENT

I find it easiest to assess social mood at a very macro level by checking broad measures of consumer sentiment. Every day, polling organizations like Gallup, the Conference Board, and Morning Consult ask thousands of consumers in the United States how they feel about the economy and their lives more broadly. While all these surveys ask slightly different questions and have slightly different names, their results reasonably align to paint a clear picture of our collective mood.

Companies spend millions of dollars every year on sentiment survey data, hoping to glean valuable insights into the feelings of their customers: one month, businesses learn that consumers are intensely worried about inflation, while the next, they read that falling prices at the gas pump have boosted spirits. By better understanding how consumers feel and the driving forces behind those feelings, businesses believe they can better anticipate their customers' behavior.

When it comes to broad consumer sentiment data, I care much more about *how* people feel than about *why* people feel the way they do. By focusing on the specific level of confidence reflected in the monthly survey results, I can get a sense of relative confidence—a measure of how America felt when we woke up this morning.

Because the major sentiment surveys have long time frames to them, charts like Figure 2.1, from Gallup, enable me to fit current sentiment figures into a broader context.[2] Do consumers feel as confident as they did in early 2000, at the peak of the dot-com bubble, or as hopeless as they did in late 2009, at the bottom of the financial crisis?

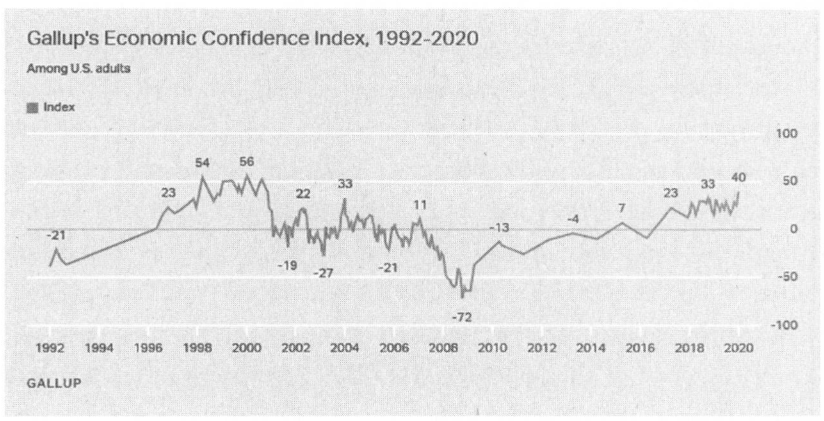

FIGURE 2.1: Confidence in the economy, 1992–2020. *Source: Gallup, Inc.*

The answer to that question quickly tells me where to plot consumers' mood on the Quadrant, in either the Comfort Zone or the Stress Center.

In my years of research, I have come to think of the broad consumer sentiment surveys as gauging our "pre-positioning"—our state of mind with respect to our feelings of certainty and control, and therefore our location on the Quadrant, *before* we do anything, or anything happens to us. It is the mood backdrop to the scenes of our lives. As a society, did we collectively sleep through our alarm, forget where we left our car keys, and hit every red light on our way to work? Or did we jump out of bed eager to tackle the new day, leaving enough time to pick up doughnuts for the office?

Visualizing where we are at a macro level on the Quadrant helps me better anticipate how we are likely to act generally. If we are in the Stress Center, as we were during the housing collapse in 2008 and 2009, I know the actions we are likely to take will focus on urgently eliminating vulnerability and doing whatever it takes to restore our lost certainty and/or control. When we are high up in the Comfort Zone, as we were at the peak of the dot-com bubble in 2000, I know we will do everything we can to remain there.

To help you see how this works in real time, let's map the first few months of 2020 on the Quadrant.

In January 2020, two months before COVID hit, most Americans felt a high level of certainty and control in their lives. Unemployment was near record lows, food and energy price inflation was low, and the stock market and home prices were near record highs. As Figure 2.1 shows, Americans' confidence in the U.S. economy then was higher than at any other point in about two decades.[3] As the year began, Americans were in the Comfort Zone, the upper right box of the Quadrant.

While news of the widening COVID-19 outbreak in China, and then Europe, caused a decline in American confidence into early March, sentiment surveys taken at the time suggest that we still felt a high level of certainty and control in our own lives.[4] We knew the outbreak was spreading, but we weren't bothered by it. COVID was a disease that was impacting people elsewhere; the threat didn't feel real to us. While not as confident as we had been in January, we were still well within the Comfort Zone.

But in mid-March, particularly during the week of March 9, COVID became a terrifying reality. Our feelings of certainty and control evaporated. In the span of seventy-two hours, our feelings of high confidence were upended. As a result, we collectively went from somewhere within the Comfort Zone to the depths of the Stress Center, in the lower left corner of the Quadrant. Working in real time, I mapped our sentiment migration in Figure 2.2.[5]

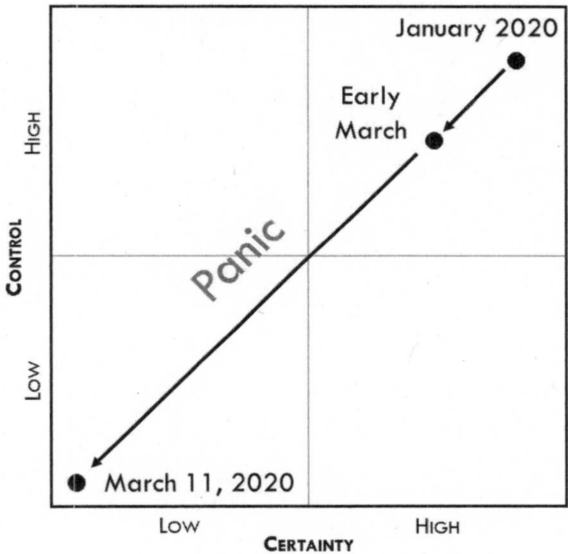

FIGURE 2.2: Mapping COVID, panic

When Gallup shared its early April 2020 survey results, it noted that confidence (as they measure it) had experienced its largest one-month decline in results dating back to 1992 (Figure 2.3).[6]

Where just two months earlier, more than 60 percent of Americans felt things were getting better, by April, the survey reported that 74 percent of Americans polled said things were getting worse.

Looking at COVID's immediate impact mapped on the Quadrant, it's clear Americans felt the way many of the passengers on my flight to Los Angeles felt when the pilot unexpectedly aborted the landing. Both experiences caused intense feelings of uncertainty and powerlessness. What the spring 2020 survey figures suggested to me was that given how low mood was and how universally people felt shaken, our response

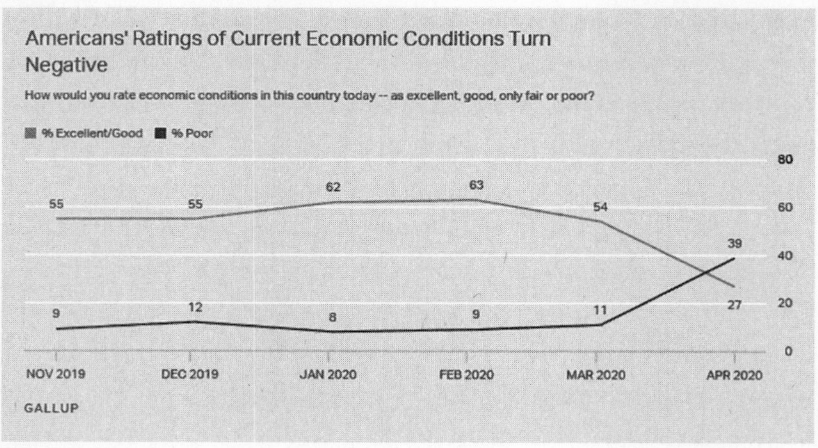

FIGURE 2.3: Impact of COVID on economic confidence.
Source: Gallup, Inc.

to the outbreak was all but certain to be extreme. Deep in the Stress Center, Americans of all walks of life would work to restore confidence in whatever way they could. Our dire shared sentiment backdrop framed our response.

2. ENVIRONMENTAL SENTIMENT

The early pandemic journey I mapped in Figure 2.2 is what sentiment data and polls like Gallup's suggest "we" experienced. I aimed to map the "average American"—but, of course, we all didn't experience the same pandemic. Some, such as the unemployed, likely began 2020 already deep in the Stress Center, in the lower left box. The same was probably true for those who were already experiencing chronic health issues, or, say, for those in the throes of a messy divorce. For them, the pandemic simply put a cherry on top of a heaping stress sundae.

On the other hand, those at the top of the economic spectrum or those who did not perceive the pandemic as a threat at all may have been completely unfazed as others panicked around them. If they experienced uncertainty or powerlessness, it was likely momentary, and they remained safe and secure within the limits of the Comfort Zone.

To think these two groups share similar memories of the pandemic would be silly. Measured in terms of vulnerability, they had no shared experience.

As much as popular-sentiment composites and averages may tell a story, they never tell the full story, especially when it comes to confidence. My map is not your map, and it is also not your neighbor's map. As I showed earlier, mapped on the Quadrant in terms of certainty and control, that nervous passenger sitting next to me on the way to LA had a completely different flight than I did—a different start, journey, and landing.

For all these reasons, leaders need to appreciate that other factors have a significant impact on our feelings of certainty and control. Leaders may want to consider their constituents' age, gender, income, race, relative education, employment, and even prior experiences before they map others' confidence on the Quadrant. The same innovative technology that brings an enthusiastic response from young workers can instill fear in older employees who see it as a career threat.

Then there are subtler environmental factors—like the time of day. As the Google Trends chart in Figure 2.4 shows, searches for terms like

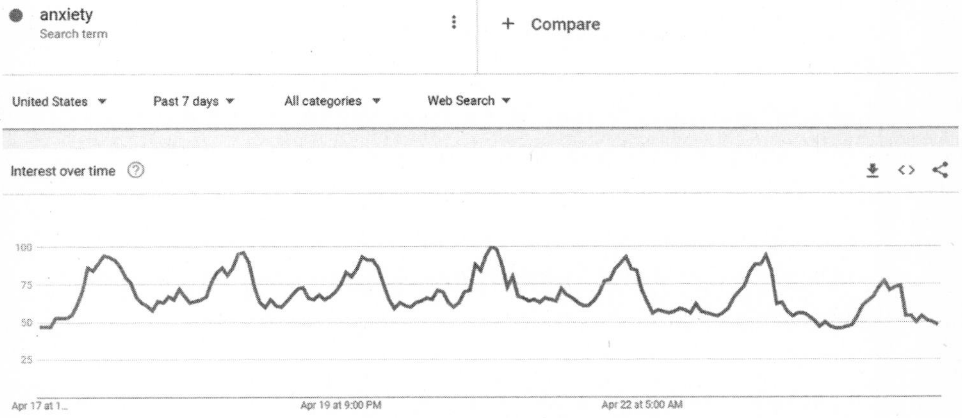

FIGURE 2.4: One week Google Trends chart for "anxiety." *Source: Google*

"anxiety" peak between two and three every morning, suggesting that late at night, our confidence naturally declines.

If I am a late-night first responder or a hospital emergency room worker, I need to remember that this heightened level of stress—naturally lower feelings of certainty and control—will factor into the behaviors of those I encounter, as well as my own.

Environmental sentiment analysis forces us to consider more thoughtfully the pre-positioning of those we are most likely to interact with, whether they are customers, employees, or any other important constituent group.

3. SITUATIONAL SENTIMENT

I began this chapter discussing "event-driven" sentiment and where feelings arising from distinct experiences tend to naturally map on the Quadrant. We saw that with little effort, we can reasonably approximate where on the Quadrant we might place everything from an emergency room visit to a major promotion. Common experiences are defined by the common feelings of certainty and control they generate.

If businesses operated in a mood vacuum, those placements—our "situational sentiment," as it were—would be enough to predict our collective confidence. But as I've shown, broad consumer and environmental sentiments impact our mood, too. Whether we realize it or not, we bring both with us as we head into a grocery store or a client meeting. Our pre-positioning plays a pivotal role in our preferences, decisions, and actions.

In my work, I've come to think of our pre-positioning as a "feeling amplifier." Where we are on the Quadrant *before* something happens will intensify or dampen our feelings of certainty and control and, in turn, our actions and reactions. When a customer enters a fast-food drive-through in a great mood, high in the Comfort Zone, she may overlook that it took a long time to be served and that the wrong dipping sauce for her chicken strips ended up in her bag. On the other hand, the same customer, when already in the Stress Center and in a bad mood, may impatiently honk her horn in line and then chew out the manager when she discovers the oversight. The alignment of situational, environmental, and broad consumer sentiment determines our behavior in everything from a drive-through meal experience to a home purchase to a conversation with our boss.

As you might imagine, strong consumer sentiment can provide an enormous tailwind to businesses, particularly as it is often accompanied by strong economic growth that boosts the environmental sentiment of many demographic groups at once. Strong, positive sentiment alignment propels our feelings of certainty and control up and to the right in the Quadrant; what might otherwise have felt good now feels *great*. Like the confident passenger on my flight, in this box we overlook turbulent moments.

Of course, the reverse also holds true: strong negative sentiment alignment propels our feelings down and to the left. What was otherwise bad now feels especially terrible. The slightest bump sends us spiraling.

Business leaders frequently overlook the amplification and dampening impacts of sentiment alignment. They seem surprised when sales growth unexpectedly exceeds forecasts and are perplexed when low-level employees who seemed happy yesterday are forming unions today. While they are glad to take credit for the former, leaders are quick to blame "factors beyond their control" for the latter. They (and their boards of directors) fail to appreciate not only the power of customer and employee sentiment but also the need to factor it into business decision-making.

While specific amplifiers can affect individual behavior, we see their greatest impact when strong feelings are widely shared. These feelings become the unseen force behind popular culture—for example, as when a crowd embraces a nascent trend and drives it to mania. When amplifiers align, powerful social movements evolve.

At peaks in sentiment, you can see the amplification effect at work in the stock market as investors speculate wildly. For those involved, the backdrop feels like certainty and control cubed. High consumer sentiment paired with a soaring wealth effect and markets that seem to only go up naturally drives investors deeper and deeper into the upper reaches of the Comfort Zone. This was the backdrop of investor feelings and experiences at the peaks of the dot-com bubble and the housing boom.

At the other end of the sentiment spectrum, the result of layered feelings of uncertainty and powerlessness will often make headlines. Take the Black Lives Matter, Arab Spring, and Tea Party movements. All three arose at extreme lows in consumer sentiment among groups that were already experiencing low environmental sentiment. All it took was low situational sentiment—a spark, as it were—to ignite a dramatic, widespread, spontaneous response. Participants' pre-positioning deep in the Stress Center served as an enormous amplifier behind the behaviors that subsequently unfolded.

These are extreme examples, but the concept applies on a smaller scale every day in business. Pre-positioning impacts the patience of both call-center representatives and their customers when service issues arise. It also impacts the eagerness with which consumers will accept new products, new technologies, and new processes. Given that sentiment is such a powerful headwind or tailwind, businesses need to factor it into their tactical plans.

Mapping Your Business on the Quadrant

So far, we've seen how the changing sentiment backdrop can impact the behavior of key constituent groups and their location on the Quadrant. Before moving forward, though, we need to pause to appreciate that businesses don't all share the same natural sentiment environments. There is no single "Business" box of the Quadrant; when it comes to customers' feelings of control and certainty, a hospital emergency room is far different from a five-star restaurant.

When I ask successful large-business leaders to map the current position of their companies on the Quadrant, most put their company in the Comfort Zone. When I ask them to explain their reasoning, they often frame the placement in the upper right box based on how they feel in their own role. With sales and earnings growing, they are confident in their business's prospects ahead.

While the Comfort Zone may be an accurate characterization for these business leaders' own confidence and for that of some company employees, it isn't typically where customers map companies. In fact, it's not where most business takes place. At their core, corporations are in the business of solving problems—addressing a customer's perceived shortcoming in certainty and/or control. Until the customer is satisfied and confidence is restored, she is anywhere but in the Comfort Zone.

Viewed through a customer's eyes and feelings of certainty and control, most service businesses operate in the lower right box, the Passenger Seat. Customers routinely turn to a business to solve a problem that they don't have the expertise or tools to solve themselves. When we call the plumber, rush to an urgent care facility, or even reserve an Uber, we are often somewhere in or near the Stress Center, seeking to address a situation where we feel like we have little certainty or control.

Knowing that we can't eliminate our vulnerability on our own, we deliberately enter into a relationship in which we cede control to someone else, hoping that with that we will regain our confidence—that we will have fully functional plumbing again, our broken finger will be set, and we will arrive safely at our destination. As noted earlier, the Passenger Seat is an environment where others have the agency. In this context, we hire someone to act on our behalf—to do something for us. In all cases, we hope that whatever the action is, it is a temporary step toward our eventual return to the Comfort Zone (Figure 2.5).

Successful business leaders often lose sight of how customers' maps differ from their own, especially as the gap between their own feelings, in the Comfort Zone, and the customer's, in the Stress Center, increases. As some leaders reach the executive level, they forget that the high level

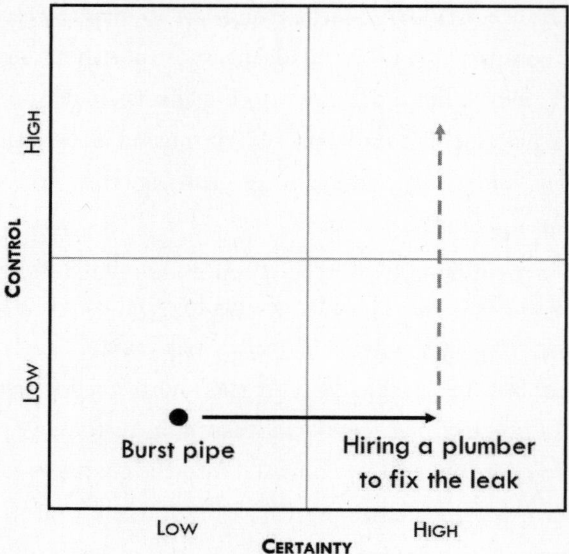

FIGURE 2.5: Mapping a burst pipe, hiring a plumber

of control they feel amid their wood-paneled C-suites and plush boardrooms isn't always shared by their customers.

Customers, too, underappreciate that as good as the Passenger Seat may look when we are deep in the Stress Center amid a crisis, it is still an environment of little or no control. In that lower right box, we have hired someone to do something for us.

When the certainty we were looking for isn't provided—the leak isn't repaired, the X-ray machine is down, or the Uber driver doesn't show—rather than moving successfully from the Stress Center through the Passenger Seat back to the Comfort Zone, we find ourselves completing a round trip out of the Stress Center, over to the Passenger Seat, and back again. Not surprisingly, that return is frequently accompanied by anger and frustration. Trust has been broken.

In most cases, our return to the Stress Center results in a new course of action. We fire our plumber and find a new service provider, hoping this time the replacement will deliver us successfully back to the Comfort Zone. In some cases, though, we may take a different path altogether to restore our confidence. Faced with a plumbing leak, we may turn to YouTube videos and then run to Home Depot or Lowe's in search of the necessary parts and tools, figuring we can repair the leak ourselves.

Home Depot and Lowe's, along with a sea of other do-it-yourself businesses, operate in the upper left box. These "Launch Pad" businesses are where we head to start projects we control. Rather than ceding control to others and exiting the Stress Center laterally, via the Passenger Seat, we say, "I will do it myself." In DIY mode, we proceed vertically from the Stress Center to the Launch Pad, experiencing "thrill of victory/agony of defeat" emotions comparable to those of a rock climber (Figure 2.6).

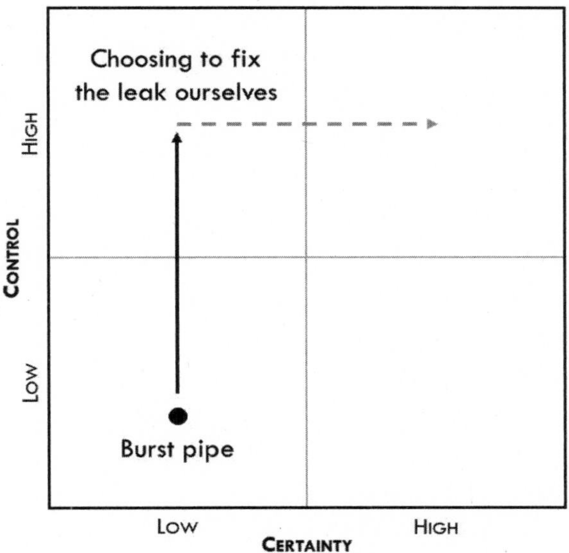

FIGURE 2.6: Mapping a burst pipe, DIY repair

If we succeed, we celebrate the installation of a new bathroom showerhead as though it was one of Hercules's twelve labors. If we fail, we yet again experience feelings of blame, shame, and embarrassment as we fall back into the Stress Center. We concede defeat and call the plumber we probably should have called in the first place.

As you likely sense already, businesses that operate in the Launch Pad have a completely different feel from those in the Passenger Seat (Figure 2.7). At their core, they are designed to satisfy a different customer need. As a Launch Pad business, Lowe's is focused on satisfying its customers' need for control. It seeks to empower others. It strives to have all the tools and parts customers need to complete a project in stock and logically displayed for fast pickup. It doesn't guarantee customers' success; it simply supplies them with the means to achieve it on their own.

On the other hand, your plumber, as a Passenger Seat business operator, is focused on delivering certainty. He seeks to serve others. You count on him to be responsive, skilled, and experienced in handling your problem. Easily finding the right part in his cluttered van is his problem, not yours.

During the early days of the pandemic, it was fascinating to watch restaurant owners as they tried to pivot from their well-oiled dine-in business models in the Passenger Seat to providing takeout in the Launch Pad. Few appreciated that with respect to customers' feelings of certainty and control, the two models are direct opposites; many learned the hard way that customers have far different expectations of the two environments. They failed to appreciate that speed and reliability of selection—vital demands for the grab-and-go consumer—mattered far more than attentive service and a flawless experience. Providing certainty to those who want control isn't the same as taking control on behalf of those demanding certainty (Figure 2.7).

It should come as no surprise, then, that companies routinely struggle as they attempt to leverage their successful experience operating in the Launch Pad or the Passenger Seat when they launch a new venture in the opposite box. Delivering services is different from delivering products. Gaining customer satisfaction when selling a car requires a different process than when servicing a car.

Most businesses find the most success when they stick to one box or

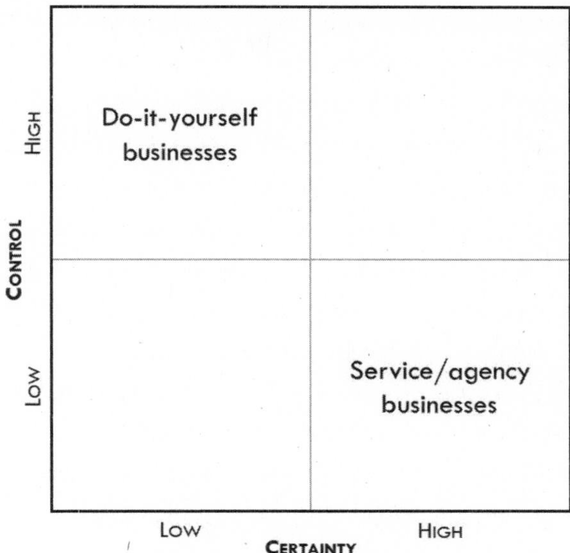

FIGURE 2.7: Mapping business types

the other—helping customers in the Passenger Seat *or* the Launch Pad. That's why companies like Best Buy are notable. Best Buy succeeds in running large-scale businesses in the Launch Pad and the Passenger Seat at the same time—its core electronics retailing business and Geek Squad, respectively. But it is an exception to the rule. As the management and shareholders of Zillow experienced firsthand, providing market information to real estate buyers is not the same as buying real estate and serving as a landlord to others.

Worse than businesses that try to serve customers in both the Passenger Seat and the Launch Pad, though, are the businesses that are unclear about the box in which they operate in the first place. In attempting to gain clients, service businesses in the Passenger Seat will sometimes try to accommodate Launch Pad DIY customers by agreeing to complex and expensive customization that is rife with opportunities for disappointment. They cede control to the customer in the belief that they can retake it over time when the customer is satisfied. With a control-craving customer, that rarely happens. The result is a driver's-ed-car experience in which it feels like there are two brakes, two gas pedals, and one steering wheel that both parties are trying to reach for at once. The division of control isn't clear. Mass customization sounds great to the client, but as Gateway, Dell, and other early computer companies found out the hard way, its complexity and cost can quickly outpace its revenue benefits.

Another reason businesses tend to be more successful sticking to just one box is that the risks and regulatory environment of the two boxes are significantly different. Businesses in the Passenger Seat often must submit to considerably greater government oversight as policymakers try to limit the risks consumers face in experiences where they don't have control.

And when the consequences of failure are especially worrisome, the licensing and compliance requirements can be intense. On our own, we can't easily identify a deteriorating jet engine or contaminated food; nor are we as consumers entirely comfortable that the private sector will always look out for our best interest, given its inherent profit motive. As a result, federal agencies like the Federal Aviation Administration (FAA) and the Food and Drug Administration (FDA) exist to ensure that there is high certainty to airline travel and food safety.

In the aftermath of the 9/11 attacks, we saw what happens when a high-consequence activity operating in the Passenger Seat, like air travel, fails. Following the armed plane hijackings, policymakers established the Transportation Services Administration (TSA) to oversee passenger screening and other transportation security processes in an effort to quickly restore confidence in the American air transportation system.

We routinely rely on government experts to provide the oversight and control that we can't on our own. When we get on an elevator and see the sticker on the wall with the word INSPECTED stamped on it in big, bold type, accompanied by a recent date, we take comfort knowing that professional engineers have just done their job. (It should come as no surprise, then, that the job of regulators isn't just to undertake their inspection role but to make sure signs of its successful execution are on full display, too.)

As experiences like 9/11 show, failures in the Passenger Seat Quadrant can be perilous not only for customers but for businesses, too. Given the underlying powerlessness of customers and the extraordinary demands for extreme certainty, even a small decline can trigger a collapse in consumer confidence. Unless a company can quickly restore the extreme certainty required by customers and regulators, it can quickly go out of business. If you run a business that requires an extreme level of certainty to survive—that is required to hug the far-right edge of the Passenger Seat box—then processes and procedures must be designed and followed to fulfill that mandate and communicate it to customers and critical stakeholders alike.

•

When most businesses think about confidence, they tend to paint with a very broad brush—they focus on consumer confidence and the well-known, widely shared measures of it. Not only is that often insufficient with respect to customers and the customer experience, it draws focus away from the business at hand. Stress Center companies are far different from Passenger Seat and Launch Pad companies. (Servpro, which comes to our aid after fire or water damages our home, and Boots & Coots, the oil-well firefighting company, are two such companies. Like other crisis-management companies, they presume their customers are deep in the Stress Center as they answer the phone.) When a company opens its doors for business, it needs to know where in the Quadrant it operates.

In the next chapter, we'll explore where leadership, employee, and customer confidence often collide: panic. As you will see, nothing can violently shove us from the upper reaches of the Comfort Zone deep into the Stress Center quite like a crisis.

CHAPTER 3

The Confidence Spectrum: Invincible to Defeated

HAVING INTRODUCED THE Confidence Quadrant and shared some preliminary thoughts on how business leaders can use the mapping process to improve their companies' effectiveness, I think it will be helpful now to offer a case study using a real-life experience: the COVID outbreak.

While on the surface every crisis is different, these types of experiences, and the panic they foster, share a common trajectory when mapped on the Confidence Quadrant. Moreover, if we look at the approach taken by those who have been highly successful in managing environments of extreme vulnerability, we can understand not only why their approach worked but how it can be applied by others to manage crises more effectively.

Sentiment Cycles and the Confidence Spectrum

When economists and CEOs speak about the variability of corporate profitability and consumer spending, they routinely do so in terms of the booms and busts of economic cycles. Eras of ease and prosperity are regularly followed by periods filled with challenges and hardship. As charts like Figure 3.1 show, these performance cycles are mirrored by rising and falling sentiment. Economic activity is a natural consequence of how individuals, businesses, and policymakers feel.

Cycles of confidence can be mapped easily on the Quadrant. Rather than flowing up and down like a wave along sine-shaped curves, however, our feelings can be plotted along what I refer to as a "Confidence Spectrum," which runs from the lower left corner of the Quadrant to the upper right corner. As confidence rises, we move up and to the right. Then, when we reach the upper right corner, we reverse, moving down and to the left until we reach the opposite corner. There we reverse again, beginning a new cycle of rising confidence (Figure 3.1).

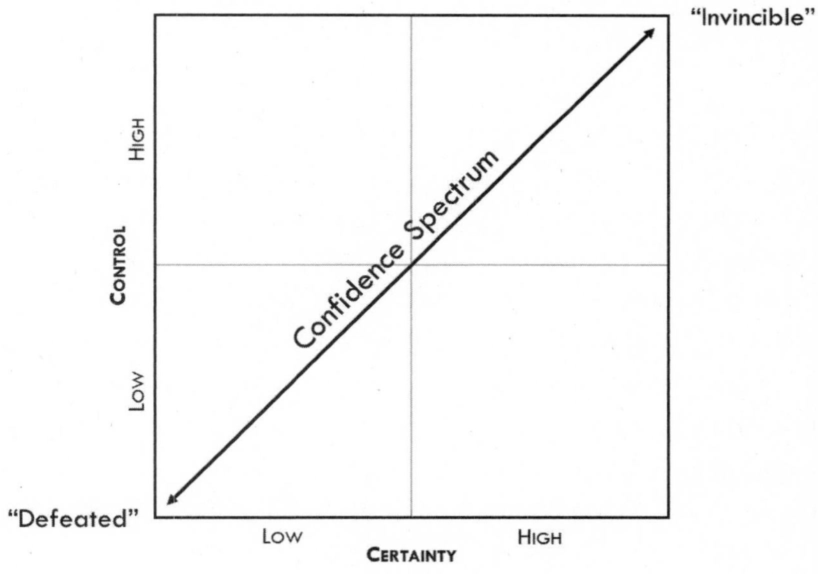

FIGURE 3.1: The Confidence Spectrum

While we don't typically think in these terms, our range of confidence is finite. When we feel that we have total control and certainty—when we feel invincible—we've unknowingly reached a terminal point. At a peak in sentiment, there is nothing more we can feel. Similarly, when we feel total powerlessness and uncertainty—when we feel defeated—we've arrived at the opposite end of the Confidence Spectrum. All certainty and control has been lost.

What causes economic and business cycles, then, is the choices we make as a result of our trolley-car-like behavior as we move back and forth, over and over, from one end of the Confidence Spectrum to the other. While we rarely realize it in real time, "Invincible" is the pride-filled moment before our fall, while "Defeated" is the ash from which we inevitably rise. At both ends of the Spectrum, just when we think this trend can't possibly end, it does. Ironically, the limitlessness we sense at the extremes is warning us of the Spectrum's true, finite length and that an abrupt reversal is imminent.

CONFIDENCE AND VULNERABILITY: OPPOSITES ON THE SAME TRACK

In the Introduction, I suggested that vulnerability is the opposite of confidence. Like "Bright" and "Dark" on a light's dimmer switch, confidence and vulnerability exist as extremes on the same spectrum—as one goes up, the other goes down. The "Confidence Spectrum" in Figure 3.1 could just as easily have been labeled the "Vulnerability Spectrum," with "Invulnerable" at one end and "Hopelessly Vulnerable" at the other.

While this half-empty take may seem needlessly pessimistic, it can be very useful when trying to plot where individuals and groups are at any given moment on the Confidence Spectrum. Fearlessness, for example, arises not so much from feelings of extremely high confidence as from feelings of extremely low vulnerability. When we are fearless, we feel that nothing can harm us. Conversely, as our confidence falls, it is our intensifying feelings of vulnerability that lead us to become more cautious. Feeling afraid, we naturally take fewer risks.

Our feelings of confidence and vulnerability may be two sides of the same coin, but they don't have the same weight. Vulnerability feels heavier; confidence feels lighter.

To get a feel for this phenomenon, I want to revisit the early days of the pandemic, which I mapped in Figure 2.2 (page 35). While I didn't describe it in these terms, Americans' migration from the upper right corner of the Quadrant to the lower left corner was a wild ride down the Confidence Spectrum.

When we go from feeling highly confident to feeling extremely vulnerable in a flash—when there is a sudden and precipitous drop in our feelings of certainty and control—that's panic. Panic is the extreme anxiety we feel and the behavior that occurs when we experience intensely accelerating powerlessness and uncertainty and our vulnerability skyrockets. "Panic" is simultaneously a noun and a verb.

And here is where things get interesting. *Why* we actually panic may surprise you.

Take COVID, for example.

THE FLOODGATES OPEN

It was Wednesday evening, March 11, 2020. Just moments after an oversized pink teddy bear removed its costume head to reveal former vice-presidential candidate Sarah Palin on *The Masked Singer*, Fox News cut in with an address from the White House in which President Donald Trump announced a hastily arranged travel ban between the United States and Europe. President Trump's action came shortly after the World Health Organization had declared the COVID-19 virus a global pandemic. By the time he finished his remarks, news was exploding on social media that one of America's most popular Hollywood actors, Tom Hanks, and his wife, actress Rita Wilson, had contracted the virus.[1]

At roughly the same time, moments before the tip-off of an NBA game between the Oklahoma City Thunder and the Utah Jazz at the Chesapeake Energy Arena, Donnie Strack, the team doctor for the Thunder, rushed onto the court to confer with game officials. After a few anxious moments, the two teams were suddenly ushered back to their respective locker rooms. The game was abruptly canceled and, in a flash, social media exploded once again—this time with reports that Jazz center Rudy Gobert had also contracted the virus.[2]

Over the next twenty-four hours, the entire NBA season was suspended, Disney World announced it was closing its gates, and a wave of American universities and colleges sent their students scrambling home for the remainder of the spring semester.[3] The day after the Hanks/Gobert news broke, the Dow Jones Industrial Average fell 2,352 points—almost 10 percent—its biggest one-day drop since 1987; some pundits even called for the financial markets to be closed outright to stop the sell-off.[4] Fear of the outbreak and its potential consequences ricocheted around the public consciousness, and by the end of that week, most schools and nonessential businesses across America closed indefinitely, and the term "social distancing" entered our vernacular.

Some I have spoken with describe feeling "mugged" by the outbreak on the evening of March 11—as if they were unexpectedly taken down by a force that seemed to jump out of the shadows. That is an accurate take: framed in terms of collapsing feelings of certainty and control, the two experiences share a violent suddenness in which lives are unexpectedly upended as individuals feel shoved from the upper right corner of the Comfort Zone to the lower left corner of the Stress Center.

Daily Beast senior entertainment reporter Kevin Fallon summarized March 11 this way: "It was, for so many Americans, the moment that shit just got real. I know this because if you search 'shit just got real' and 'Tom Hanks' on Twitter, a whole lot of people did indeed say just that."[5]

Jenni Carlson, a sports columnist for the *Oklahoman*, had similar observations about the significance and suddenness of the moment: "What happened Wednesday at that [Jazz–Thunder] NBA game changed the way Americans think about coronavirus. Average Janes and Joes didn't seem all that concerned about the pandemic before. Now, we see how close the danger is and how quickly the spread can happen."[6]

Seemingly overnight, what had been a slowly evolving crisis turned into a panic.

IT'S PSYCHOLOGICAL, NOT PHYSICAL, DISTANCE THAT MATTERS

What I just shared is how the events of March 11, 2020, came together to form the emotional tipping point of the COVID outbreak. But this recounting leaves unanswered several significant questions. For example, how could a nation of more than 330 million people go from feeling largely confident one moment to experiencing large-scale panic the next?

Tom Hanks was just one person—and a celebrity whose life, by all objective measures, is very different from that of the average American. Moreover, he wasn't even in the United States at the time; he was halfway around the world, filming on location in Australia. Based solely on objective evidence, Hanks's bearing on the welfare of everyday Americans seems at best tenuous. So, then, how do we account for the panic that ensued?

To fully appreciate how we arrived at our "Tom Hanks Moment," let's rewind the tape.

When the outbreak was first reported, at the end of 2019, it was said to be "contained" within China.[7] That simple, one-word description implied that the virus could be and was somehow being held back—that there was a substantial, opposing force holding it in place, far away from us, and preventing its potential spread.

With national leaders, policymakers, and other experts also labeling the outbreak "contained" within a place that is foreign to most Americans, we believed we had little reason to worry. The "halo effect"—a cognitive bias in which we tend to overvalue the opinions of influential people in our lives—was at work. There wasn't just *physical* distance between us and the outbreak; there was also enormous *psychological* distance. In every respect—geographically, relationally, even temporally (in time)—the outbreak felt very, very far away. We viewed the pandemic as a "remote" possibility.

Then came news reports that the outbreak had spread to Italy, England, and other parts of Europe. Now, the physical distance between

Americans and the outbreak began shrinking. More important, though, so, too, did the psychological distance. The outbreak *felt* closer. While still thousands of miles away, the virus was present in a region of the world that seemed more familiar to us.

As Matt Phillips, a business reporter for *The New York Times*, said in an interview, "Everyone knew the virus was spreading in China and compartmentalized it. But there was a psychological shift when the virus spread to Italy. A lot of Wall Street workers have been to Italy. This wasn't as 'foreign' as people thought."[8]

As well-known U.S. multinational firms, including Starbucks and Apple, started to disclose that their overseas operations had been affected, the psychological distance shrank even more.[9] Now *we* were beginning to be impacted. And there was a clear trajectory we believed the outbreak was on—one that the Trump administration was already trying to get ahead of with its travel ban.

What the Hanks and Gobert news did was to eliminate any remaining *psychological* distance between the outbreak and many Americans. That Hanks was physically situated in Australia was irrelevant to our mindset. *Where* he was mattered far less than *who* he was—a highly trusted, iconic American symbol. The same was true for Gobert. Psychologically, he was one of us. We had welcomed Hanks and Gobert into our homes and into our lives for years; we had followed their careers and their successes and failures. We admired and respected them. They were like family. And if they could get the coronavirus, then so could we.

EXTREME VULNERABILITY: INTENSE UNCERTAINTY PAIRED WITH POWERLESSNESS

As Americans went to bed that night, they felt under threat. The future seemed unknowable.

As we've discussed, having *certainty* about what's ahead—or at least imagining we know what's ahead—is foundational to confidence. And by "ahead," I mean temporally, geographically, and relationally, too. We need to feel we know what's out there, whether it is tomorrow, around the corner, or sitting next to us at the dinner table. When we say the future is unknown, we aren't talking about the time ahead as much as we are expressing alarm about the troubling things that might fill it—the people, events, and experiences that may be unfamiliar to us. Familiarity, habits, and routine all breed confidence because we feel we can project them into the future.

The COVID pandemic upended that idea. It created discontinuity among our past, present, and future. All prior experiences seemed irrelevant; we had nothing from which to extrapolate. COVID was an epidemiological mystery, too. Experts knew little about the virus, its transmission method, its infectiousness, or its deadliness. We did not know who had it nor who was most at risk of contracting it. The virus took a jackhammer and destroyed what had felt like a solid foundation for our everyday decision-making.

But our newfound uncertainty was only half the story. The pandemic also introduced a second feeling: a sense of powerlessness. We lost control. Not only had the world become uncertain but there was little consensus, at that point, about how best to protect ourselves. We felt like pinballs, with the outbreak in control of the flippers. It was chaos in which everyone, regardless of socioeconomic status, was impulsively reacting to the day's news. There was no time for thoughtful planning—and even if there was, what difference would it have made? Our future was written in sand, and everywhere we looked, the tide was rapidly approaching to wipe the beach clean.

Shoved from high confidence to extreme vulnerability, we panicked.

Panic Patterns

As much as we may like to use words like "unprecedented" when describing events like COVID, when viewed through the lens of confidence, they fit a familiar pattern. Indeed, the events of early 2020 were entirely consistent with other major crises in which we were suddenly and unexpectedly shoved down the Confidence Spectrum to the depths of the Stress Center.

For this reason, it is worth pausing to examine this "Panic Pattern." It plays out over and over again, in all aspects of our lives: across society, business, and in our daily lived experience.

SOCIETAL LEVEL

When historians write about panics, they tend to focus on societal panics, extraordinary moments arising amid epidemics, financial collapses, or war: Pearl Harbor, the 1929 stock market crash, 9/11. There is scale, audaciousness, an element of surprise, and feelings of discontinuity to the event. There is a clear sense of "before" and "after" to a moment in which our lives feel upended. Societal panics are a shared traumatic event in which large numbers of people have their feelings of certainty and control upended at once.

Today, we experience societal panics in ways that are different from in the past. During the 2008 banking crisis, I spent a lot of time researching prior financial crashes and looking for behavioral parallels, figuring they might come in handy. In my work, I stumbled across the Panic of 1857, a pre–Civil War financial crisis that followed a major boom in the U.S. economy that included the California Gold Rush.

When historians write about the Panic of 1857, one of the first things they routinely mention is that while it was not the first financial crisis in American history, it was the first in which panic spread rapidly throughout the country. Amid the Panic of 1837, the financial crisis that had occurred just twenty years earlier, news could travel only as fast as the postal service. Back then, news took weeks, sometimes months, to spread. In 1857, fourteen years after the invention of the telegraph, news spread much more rapidly, creating a confidence crisis for investors throughout the United States and Europe in just a matter of days.[10]

Since then, as communication technology has evolved—from telegraph to telephone to radio to television to the internet, cell phones, social media, and a twenty-four-hour news cycle—the speed at which news travels and the population it reaches has exploded. Just as changes in material fabrication and computer simulation and modeling capabilities have enabled amusement-park roller coasters with steeper and faster drops than ever, advances in communication technology have had a similar impact on the acceleration and scale of collapses in societal confidence.

Given this pattern's broader backdrop to confidence, it is worth highlighting, too, that the United States has now experienced three major societal panics since the turn of the millennium: the attacks of September 11, 2001, the banking crisis of 2008, and the COVID-19 pandemic starting in 2020. The 9/11 attacks sparked an extraordinary collapse in confidence that resonated across all sectors of society. The banking crisis moved more slowly, but when the subprime mortgage losses that policymakers had initially characterized, too, as "contained" spread to higher and higher quality loans and borrowers, panic raced through the financial system.[11] As the stock market swooned and home foreclosures soared, feelings of powerlessness and uncertainty quickly spread across America.

While it may be an overstatement to suggest that we are now "primed" for societal panic, this repetition matters. We no longer see a large-scale crisis as an exception or something from distant history. While a societal panic is still abstract, there is far less psychological distance today between us and the threat of one than there once was. Moreover, and as anyone who has experienced a panic attack knows, fear of another panic can be self-reinforcing. We need to appreciate that if a societal panic is triggered, the pace at which confidence may collapse could be blistering given today's technology tools paired with our extreme social interconnectedness.

BUSINESS LEVEL

The COVID-19 pandemic, 2008 financial crisis, and 9/11 attacks were all large-scale societal panics rooted in sudden collapses in confidence.

All three events brought with them immediate and collective existential dread. Smaller-scale panics, though, happen routinely in the business world, albeit often at the same blistering speed, thanks to social media. The Deepwater Horizon oil rig explosion in April 2010, the back-to-back Boeing 737 MAX jet crashes in the fall of 2018 and the spring of 2019, and the Colonial Pipeline ransomware attack in May 2021, which cut off gasoline supplies to parts of the east coast of the United States, are just three examples that readily come to mind. In all cases, the confidence of management, employees, customers, and shareholders was simultaneously upended. Leaders had but moments to respond before their crises were global news headlines, with millions demanding answers to the same question: "How could this happen?!"

Business panics don't always involve catastrophe and flaming headlines. Often overlooked are the panics that happen among rank-and-file employees in the wake of industry-consolidating mergers. As companies come together with promises to shareholders of major cost cutting, low-level-employee morale frequently collapses. Vulnerability skyrockets as workers feel powerless while they wait to hear news of their fate.

The introduction of new technology, particularly among older employees, can foster similar feelings of vulnerability. In the 1990s, the rise of computer-aided design and drafting (CADD) systems felt like an existential threat to long-tenured draftsmen as engineers took on the role of drafters and designers.

While far smaller in scale than our societal panics, business crises generate similar feelings for those involved—and, as we will explore, they also generate similar kinds of responses.

PERSONAL LEVEL

Lastly, there are the panics we all experience in our own lives—the sudden increase in vulnerability as a major deadline nears for a project, or as we await news of an important medical test result, or when we've unexpectedly suffered a major injury. Moments like these demonstrate that no matter the cause, panic is what we experience as feelings of intense powerlessness and uncertainty suddenly take hold.

Effective Panic Management

Given the frequency with which we experience panics, you would think we would be great at managing them.

We aren't.

Often, this difficulty stems from our belief that we can avoid panics in the first place—that if we are prudent, we can avoid a sudden drop into the Stress Center.

Instead of viewing crises as a routine part of our lives, with consistent behavioral and emotional characteristics, we view these events as unwelcome, one-off experiences—awful outliers. We put our energy into preventing them from happening in the first place, rather than preparing and training to tackle them. And who can blame us? Panics are inherently uncomfortable, and they don't happen all that frequently (we hope).

We also associate panics with failure. To plan and train for them seems like an admission of defeat—as if we are deliberately preparing for the consequences of our own poor decision-making. Not only does this kind of thinking make us reluctant to prepare, when crises do occur, the moments are filled with feelings of guilt, shame, and blame. We believe crises occur only because someone or something must have screwed up.

To be fair, when crises happen, we scour the landscape for clear causation and someone or something to blame. We rush to identify a deciding factor. What we overlook, though, is that at the heart of blame is our need for certainty. We abhor randomness, and clear causation—blame—eliminates that. Randomness suggests that things are inherently uncertain, a condition that leaves us perennially vulnerable. (Imagine how few would invest in the stock market if, after a down day, market experts reported that they didn't know why the dip occurred.) As a result, when bad things happen, we won't rest until we can clearly attribute blame or direct causation. Our feelings about this process can be intense, too, with the result that, rather than focusing on the problem at hand, we obsess instead over accountability for its existence.

That is bad enough when we blame others, but all too often we turn the blame inward, and inaccurately so. We beat ourselves up, believing it was somehow our fault that we were mugged or that we slipped on black ice. We relive, in our minds, what we could have or should have done differently, rather than readily accepting the randomness of the event and our poor luck, and moving on to address our broader feelings of extreme vulnerability.

Most businesses act in much the same way—only rather than putting the blame on themselves, they usually seek to minimize their accountability. When crises strike, CEOs often bring in waves of attorneys and PR professionals whose sole goal is to deflect and/or mitigate accountability. This can not only draw attention away from addressing the vulnerability at hand, it can compound the problem: employees and customers, already feeling powerless, then feel unheard, too, with their concerns dismissed as somehow irrational, too extreme, or outright wrong. Rather than expressing empathy to those affected, business leaders are coached today to remain emotionless and to stay on a highly scripted message, for fear that to do otherwise will only increase the expense of a crisis and put them at risk themselves.

In doing research for this book, I was struck by how few business case studies exist on brilliant panic management, wherein leaders are celebrated for taking immediate action to resolve the issue. The most recent notable example—which crisis management experts still tout—happened forty years ago, when seven people in the Chicago area died after taking Tylenol capsules poisoned with cyanide. Rather than attempting to mitigate accountability, Johnson & Johnson CEO James Burke pulled the product from every shelf. Burke took fast and decisive action to eliminate vulnerability.[12]

Interestingly, that was the same approach Ben Sliney took on what just happened to be his first day on the job as the FAA's national operations manager. On September 11, 2001, Sliney called for the immediate grounding of every plane in the air, an unprecedented act that the 9/11 Commission later highlighted as a decisive moment in that day's chain of events.[13]

Given the praise both men received for their crisis management, it is worth exploring why they were so effective. I think it had a lot to do with their "Vulnerability-First" mindset—something all of us should aim for when we find ourselves deep in the lower left corner of the Stress Center.

A VULNERABILITY-FIRST MINDSET

As uncomfortable as the unknown makes most of us feel, there are groups and organizations in our society who train for panics and who handle them well. Panics are a normal part of everyday life for firefighters, police, and other first responders; the lower left corner of the Stress Center is where they go to work every day. For these crisis workers, the goal of their training is to halt the decline in sentiment as it races down the Confidence Spectrum, stabilize it, and then reverse it as quickly as they can—to foster feelings of certainty and control through consistently applied processes and procedures that have been regularly, often intensely, practiced. Like pilots with their consistent and well-rehearsed "go-around" procedure, first responders seek to routinize anticipated experiences that would otherwise cause high stress and potentially lead to panic.

When COVID hit, I interviewed a group of emergency room doctors and learned firsthand just how important the consistency of their processes and procedures is to them. In fact, many of them highlighted that it wasn't the virus that was their greatest source of stress during the early days of the pandemic—it was the disruption and constant revisions to their daily processes, particularly with respect to their personal protective equipment (PPE).

I also learned that a "Vulnerability-First" mindset is at the core of successful emergency room team practices. The most effective teams don't just fix broken bones; they seek to restore the lost certainty and control in their patients' lives as quickly as they can. Interestingly, these doctors' take on how to best handle crises differs significantly from that suggested by most business crisis-management experts.

As you might expect, ER teams' first steps focus on *effective prioritization*—quickly identifying the greatest potential danger to a patient. A crucial element of that step is *accurate diagnosis*—attempting to identify the true source of vulnerability and, first and foremost, ruling out the most threatening diagnoses. Critical to this process is an openness, if not outright eagerness, to accept what is in front of them. There's no time for wishful thinking, denial, or blame. The team's entire focus is on the present and what could yet be if the team fails to act. The result is that there is often a candid, blunt matter-of-factness to their initial assessments that is communicated to the entire team. Rather than sugarcoating reality, teams go to work quickly to gain an understanding of the full scope of the challenge.

Emergency room teams are very careful not to mistake obvious symptoms for the source of the problem, too. They view all information as providing important clues. Testing and conversations with other team members are encouraged. *Collaboration*, with an open exchange of all information, is considered vital.

So, too, is *urgency*. ER teams move quickly to address what matters most. Moreover, there is *constant reassessment* to ensure a patient's condition is stable or improving. There is an appreciation for the dynamic, "still in motion" aspect of the situation. And when circumstances change, and deteriorating conditions require it, doctors aren't afraid to *change their course of action*.

Finally, effective ER teams show *empathy and respect* for the vulnerable patient and for each other. They recognize that trust is a cornerstone to their process and to a patient's recovery. Teams know a key aspect of trust is *clear communication* in which information is realistic, truthful, and plainly and compassionately presented.

While James Burke wasn't a doctor by training, his response to the Tylenol tampering crisis suggests that he thought like one. He quickly diagnosed the situation and recognized that his company's problem wasn't simply a few contaminated bottles of Tylenol but the far broader vulnerability customers felt. Consumers didn't know if they could trust that Tylenol was safe. Burke demanded that others accept the reality of this perception. The company couldn't sugarcoat things. To be effective, Johnson & Johnson had to eliminate the vulnerability; leaving bottles on the shelves would only open up the potential for further, and possibly even greater, feelings of customer powerlessness and uncertainty. With that understood, Burke led Johnson & Johnson to act immediately, pulling every bottle while simultaneously clearly and honestly communicating the rationale behind the company's actions. He forged a hard stop to the slide down the Confidence Spectrum. He eliminated any potential for consumer sentiment to fall farther.

Within days, Johnson & Johnson shares rose, and Burke went on to be named one of *Fortune* magazine's 10 Greatest CEOs of All Time. President Bill Clinton even awarded Burke a Presidential Medal of Freedom.[14] Rather than being wounded by the event, the company was praised for its response. Like patients being told that the cancer they once feared was gone, customers were relieved to know that Tylenol was safe again. With that, trust in Johnson & Johnson soared.

Americans, too, were relieved on 9/11, knowing that the risk of further attacks had been fully eliminated by the grounding of *all* planes. Once again, concerns about broader vulnerability, not just the specific problem at hand, drove the decision-making.

Far too often, business leaders respond to a crisis by seeking to downplay bad news. As a result, they too narrowly define their crises. They focus on the crashed plane, the sticking car accelerator, or the blazing oil rig. They focus solely on what happened, while discounting the feelings arising from what happened. They also under-communicate, withholding unflattering information in the hopes that things will blow over. Policymakers do the same, hoping to minimize the bad things that have happened on their watch. They, too, focus only on what is burning or broken.

While that focus is important, it is insufficient. Leaders must not just simultaneously address the vulnerability arising from those problems and the uncertainty and powerlessness being felt by those impacted by what has occurred, but also lead with it. Those feelings are the real drivers of the panic, and until they are resolved, confidence can't and won't be restored.

As we went to bed on March 11, 2020, prepared or not, business leaders and policymakers faced an enormous challenge. Like James Burke and Ben Sliney before them, leaders had to quickly address a panic before it further fueled a self-reinforcing vicious spiral in confidence. To be effective, business and policymaker actions had to address not just the virus but our intense feelings of vulnerability arising from it.

What defines panics and crises isn't what has failed, been broken, or been destroyed as much as it is our confidence response to it—our sudden, intense feelings of uncertainty and powerlessness. If leaders have any hope of becoming effective crisis managers, they need to better understand how intense vulnerability drives our preferences, decisions, and actions.

Simply put, effective crisis management means eliminating vulnerability.

PANIC: NATURAL TURNING POINTS IN CONFIDENCE

When panic occurs, it often feels as if the emotional trolley car we're on is racing down the Confidence Spectrum so fast that it's going to jump the tracks and fall beyond the limits of the Stress Center. The sense of foreboding is intense. As we approach the lower left corner of the Confidence Quadrant, we feel that things will only get worse.

What we miss in these moments is that panics often precede important turning points in confidence. Shaken from the experience, we overlook the fact that the extreme uncertainty and powerlessness we are feeling is telling us that we are rapidly approaching the lower terminus of the Confidence Spectrum. The collapse of Lehman Brothers, for example, marked the very low point in consumer confidence during the 2008 housing crisis. Lehman's failure didn't cause investors to panic; it was the consequence of investors already panicking. Bankruptcy is the business world's way of saying a company is defeated—that it, its debtholders, its customers, its shareholders, and its board of directors have all arrived in the lower left corner of the Quadrant. It was the end of the line, for both the bank and the Confidence Spectrum.

•

Amid crisis and panic, it is often very difficult to be hopeful. The sudden loss of certainty and control is intensely stressful. But we routinely misinterpret those feelings. Rather than appreciating that our intense feelings have arisen because something *has happened*, we conclude that our intense feelings are warning us that something bad is *about to happen*. We brace ourselves for what is already behind us. We fail to appreciate where we are on the Confidence Spectrum—rapidly approaching or already at its lower terminus.

We do something very similar at the other end of the Confidence Spectrum. When I discuss the Comfort Zone in the pages ahead, I will cover our sense of invincibility and the manic feelings that arise from it. Invincibility, too, represents a natural, albeit highly counterintuitive, turning point.

For now, though, I want you to simply remember that our range of confidence is finite, and if we can look at panic, powerlessness, and extreme uncertainty objectively, we can avoid getting caught up in the high emotions that accompany them. Rather than fearing what is next, we can prepare for the better times that are likely to be ahead. Moreover, if we can adopt a Vulnerability-First mindset, we can more effectively lead others through these challenging times.

Now that we have gone to the depths of the Stress Center to discuss panics and to introduce the Confidence Spectrum, it is time to explore each of the four environments of the Confidence Quadrant in more detail. Along the way, I will introduce additional concepts and tools to help us better navigate our emotional landscape and anticipate what's ahead.

As we are already in the lower left corner of the Quadrant, we'll start with the Stress Center.

SECTION II

The Stress Center

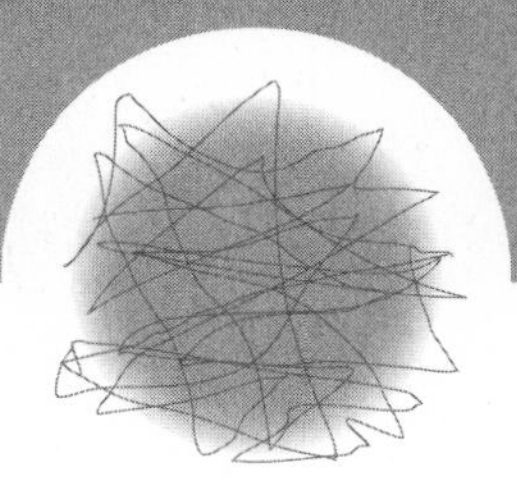

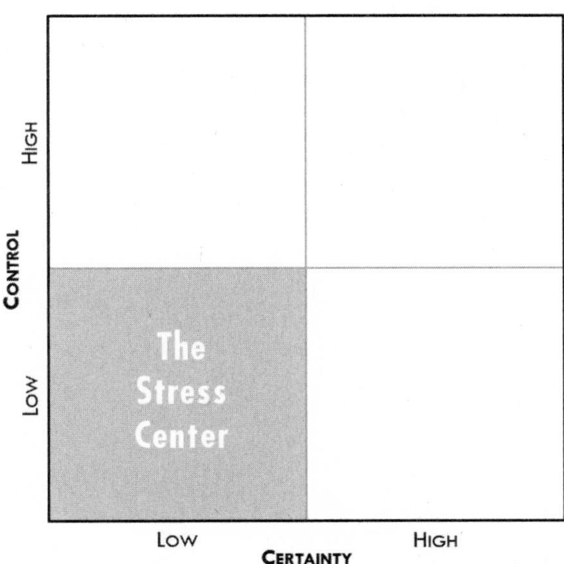

CHAPTER 4

The Stress Center and Environments of Low Confidence

MENTION VULNERABILITY TO many business leaders and you can all but watch their eyes roll. The term conjures up images of submissiveness and weakness. Great businesses and great leaders, they tend to believe, succeed at the expense of the vulnerable. Vulnerability means you've let your guard down, disappointed others, fallen behind, failed, and are at risk. No longer the predator, you are the prey.

Business leaders aren't alone in these thoughts, either. Few of us enjoy the discomfort that accompanies feelings of low certainty and control. They make us feel naked and exposed. And who can blame us? The question we are routinely asked when others see vulnerability in our eyes is "Is something wrong?" There is an implied incorrectness to our plight. Something is broken and must be fixed.

All these characterizations help explain why the Stress Center—where we feel our most vulnerable—is so filled with emotion and action. In the lower left box of the Confidence Quadrant, we feel threatened, and we know we must do something in response to address our sense of powerlessness and uncertainty.

What best defines the Stress Center is the nature of the decisions we are likely to make and the actions we are likely to take to eliminate vulnerability. The Stress Center is the land of impulse and emotion—and the farther we descend down the Confidence Spectrum, toward the very lower left corner of the Quadrant, the more urgent and intense our need for action becomes. That lower left corner is the land of the "fast and furious."

To get a feel for the extreme urgency and intensity of our behavior in that lower left corner of the Quadrant, I want to return to the COVID panic and revisit just a few of the thousands of decisions policymakers, business leaders, and individuals made in that time. They're wonderful examples of our natural fast and furious Stress Center response.

March 2020: A Case Study in Fast and Furious

General Motors CEO Mary Barra didn't wait to adapt her organization to the rapidly unfolding pandemic. On Friday, March 13, 2020, less than forty-eight hours after the Hanks-Gobert tipping point, she sent out an urgent message: "If the nature of your work allows for it, we are asking all GM employees and contract workers to work remotely."[1] As the head of America's largest automaker, she wasn't alone. Business leaders across the country directed employees to stay home wherever possible.

At McDonald's, management initiated a shift from counter sales to "contactless Drive-thru and Delivery."[2] Decades of well-established and highly refined processes and procedures were shredded and tossed aside, replaced by a completely new business model developed on the fly.

At American Airlines, flight schedules were eviscerated. Domestic capacity was reduced by 20 percent and international capacity slashed by 75 percent. Flights to Asia were all but eliminated.[3]

American business leaders took dramatic steps, bracing for the worst amid a storm of late-night Zoom meetings and conference calls. By the end of March, General Motors announced it had fully suspended its U.S. automobile production and would instead help supply critically needed ventilators and face masks. At the same time, it withdrew its earnings guidance for the year and drew down its revolving credit facilities by $16 billion.[4]

As Mary Barra put it in a press release, "We are aggressively pursuing austerity measures to preserve cash and are taking necessary steps in this changing and uncertain environment to manage our liquidity, ensure the ongoing viability of our operations, and protect our customers and stakeholders."[5]

Overnight, companies leaped into survival mode. Faced with intense uncertainty, business leaders across the United States and around the world once again reached for their crisis playbooks. They cut expenses, accelerated sales, dumped inventory, and raised cash wherever they could. Their goal was simple: retake control—move their organizations as quickly as possible from the depths of the Stress Center to the Launch Pad, hopefully en route to a quick return to the Comfort Zone.

Investors more broadly were also in survival mode, desperate for certainty and control. As sell orders flooded the equity and fixed-income markets, asset managers and brokerage firms tried to keep up with clients' soaring demands for cash.

Meanwhile, policymakers, too, reacted to the crisis. Uncertain of the pandemic's potential health impact, cities and states shut down bars, restaurants, and schools. The Centers for Disease Control and Prevention (CDC) recommended that gatherings of fifty people or more be prohibited for the next two months, one of the federal government's most sweeping efforts to slow the spread of the coronavirus pandemic.[6] In Washington, congressmen and central bankers fielded desperate pleas for help. Bankers and business leaders were terrified by what the financial market sell-off and the violent halt to the economy would mean for their organizations' survival. Policymakers needed to act, to do "whatever it takes," and fast, before things got worse.

And act they did. As historians have already recorded, the U.S. fiscal and monetary response to the pandemic was unprecedented.[7] Enormous in their scale and scope, the actions taken sought to shelter consumers and businesses from the pernicious impact of the outbreak and the economic damage left in its wake. Equally dramatic were efforts taken by most other policymakers around the globe. Given the extreme interconnectedness of today's financial markets and supply chains, the impacts of decisions made in one location quickly spread to others around the globe, creating a cascade of policymaker and corporate actions.

The COVID outbreak was a twenty-first-century crisis in size, breadth, and cost that left few untouched.

The Five Fs: Our Natural Stress Responses

On the surface, the collective, highly impulsive, and highly emotional response to the pandemic outbreak appears to be in a class by itself. No matter where you look, actions seem extreme: GM shut down *all* its U.S. operations. Fast-food restaurant drive-throughs handled *all* orders for *all* customers through contactless service at *all* locations. American Airlines and other air carriers grounded nearly *all* their international flights. Leaders painted with the widest brush possible as they tried to cover their vast canvas in a single stroke.

At the same time, the nature of our response was, well, predictable. Panicking, in the lower left corner of the Quadrant, we did what we always we do: we sought to restore certainty and control however we could—fast and furiously.

If we step back, we see that our pandemic responses were entirely consistent with our "normal" Stress Center behavior. They fit one of our five highly alliterative reactions. You are probably familiar with the first two: fight and flight. They are our automatic physiological reactions to any event we perceive as stressful or frightening.[8] But there are three other consistent Stress Center actions: follow, freeze, and—if you'll pardon my French—fuck it. I call them the "Five Fs."

On the "**fight**" front, we witnessed a synchronous take-control-to-combat-the-outbreak response from the public and private sectors. Just as we rush to Home Depot when a pipe bursts, leaders immediately went to work to tackle their most urgent challenges. Hospitals ordered vast quantities of PPE to protect their workers, as car dealers quickly sold off inventory to protect their bottom line. Overnight, leaders had to confront both the disease itself and its most immediate and pressing effects.

So, too, did individuals. After watching YouTube and TikTok videos, we made makeshift masks out of bandannas and T-shirts. We also tightly controlled where we went and with whom we interacted. Trips to the store were well planned, often frantically timed to a specific moment of the day or night when we anticipated the smallest crowds. And when we dared to socialize in person, we formed clearly defined "pods," limiting our interactions to the judiciously selected few individuals we trusted most.

When we are in the Stress Center, our fight response represents our attempt to move to the Launch Pad—to regain control in the hope that with it, we can regain our certainty as well.

Our "**flight**" response works in the same way, only rather than seeking to regain control through confrontation, we go to extremes to avoid confrontation at all costs. We run away, creating as much distance as we can from an imminent threat. Psychologically, we build a moat. Flight is what we do when we seek control by creating a barrier—in time and in physical distance—between ourselves and a threat.

Individuals were at the forefront of our flight response to the outbreak, with many already self-quarantining at home long before cities and states imposed lockdowns. Businesses and schools also contributed to the retreat, as workers and students fled office towers and college campuses. Kitchen tables replaced cubicle desks. First graders logged in to school from laptops and tablets, joining Zoom classrooms in which teachers struggled valiantly to hold their attention.

With today's communication technology, the ability to pivot to work from home, and delivery services like Amazon and Instacart, mass "flight" not only was possible but quickly became the norm for a large segment of the workforce. And for those with second homes in places like the Hamptons, self-isolation was never so well served. Remarkably, life at the top of the economic pyramid quickly returned to normal. Enabled by modern technology, and with food, shelter, and a host of support services already in place, the elite isolated in ease. As a result, those most financially able all but flew directly from the Stress Center back to the Comfort Zone.

Our third pandemic response was to "**follow**." When pipes burst, we quickly call the plumber, eagerly ceding control to someone we believe is more able to address the source of our stress. The act of following represents our attempt to leave the Stress Center via the Passenger Seat.

In the case of the pandemic, policymakers became "plumbers" for a nation. The Federal Reserve, the CDC, state governors, and local mayors all but grabbed bullhorns and waved brightly colored flags, acting like tour guides to encourage the crowd to follow their lead. They presented themselves as credible problem solvers offering to do whatever it took. Figures like Dr. Anthony Fauci, then director of the National Institute of Allergy and Infectious Diseases, and governors like New York State's Andrew Cuomo were widely praised for their leadership and crisis management skills.

Private sector companies like Pfizer and Moderna also played critical leadership roles in the pandemic response. "Follow the science" became a mantra as policymakers and drug company executives took to television, radio, and social media amid a record-time rollout of vaccines against the virus. Like their counterparts in the public sector, they hoped to end the outbreak crisis quickly by achieving herd immunity through high vaccination rates. A majority of Americans followed their lead.

At the same time, many Americans chose not to and instead followed other leaders, most notably popular television and radio celebrities or sources they found on the internet who offered compelling and competing recommendations. Many were stunned by the willingness of these Americans to not only consider but follow these non-establishment leaders. They shouldn't have been. When we are in the Stress Center, we routinely discount the advice of established experts, especially those from organizations that feel psychologically distant from us. We quickly swat away groups like the World Health Organization as "irrelevant," "conflicted," and "slow to act." Global institutions are so abstract to us that it takes little effort to poke holes in their credibility and to dismiss their relevance and expertise. In a moment when we crave certainty, they don't feel "real." And the same holds true for many national and even some state organizations.

Instead, we turn to those who are most familiar to us. Yet again, psychological distance and proximity matter. We naturally trust those closest to us. We *know* them to be real. We seek them out for advice, eagerly embracing their ideas even when they stray far from their perceived areas of expertise.

Still, it's worth appreciating that amid extreme uncertainty, anyone claiming expertise has the potential to be credible. With a burst pipe spraying in the background, we Google "plumber" and immediately start dialing the phone, never once pausing to ask about, let alone even consider, qualifications. "How fast can you be here?" is our only question.

With followership (as with flight), speed and ease are what matter most—and when they are provided by a familiar, trusted source, we quickly get in line. Moving laterally into the Passenger Seat is typically our fastest way out of the Stress Center. The alternative, taking control—and moving vertically into the Launch Pad from the Stress Center—requires more effort and often specific expertise. When we feel overwhelmed, both of those qualities seem in short supply.

Typically, we make good "follow" choices. But it would serve us well to be more deliberate. Impulsivity and ease—and, more specifically, our easiest narratives—can quickly get us into trouble. If you look at authoritarian regimes, sexual predators, grifters, con artists, cult figures, and even abusive business managers, you'll see that they have their greatest success in gaining followership in environments of high uncertainty and powerlessness. Masterful at providing compelling tales of certainty and appearing to be in full control, these figures make the Stress Center their feeding ground. When we are standing outside in a cold, driving rain and are offered a ride by someone who appears to have our best interests at heart and promises to return us quickly and safely to the Comfort Zone, it doesn't take much to convince us to get in the Passenger Seat. That appearance of certainty can be especially seductive when we feel defeated and hopeless.

Our fourth stress response is "**freeze.**" Extreme uncertainty and powerlessness can overwhelm us. We become paralyzed by fear; we feel as if we can't move forward physically, emotionally, or even cognitively. We're flooded by all the ways we feel vulnerable. The experience derails our ability to focus. At the same time, we overthink the consequences of our decisions, easily becoming exhausted.

Like soldiers on a battlefield, some were all but immobilized by the vulnerability they experienced arising from the pandemic. They didn't know what to do. Still others shut down, completely disassociating themselves from the experience. They may not have had the resources to flee physically, but they did so emotionally.

Finally, there were the highly successful leaders who had never experienced the Stress Center before—whose careers had landed them in positions of greater and greater responsibility crisis-free, due largely to luck. Many froze, embarrassed that they didn't know what to do and ashamed to ask for help. Unable to fight or flee and unwilling to follow, they wallowed in indecision, paralyzing their organizations.

Our final response to the pandemic outbreak—and to crises more broadly—is "**fuck it.**" I apologize for the vulgarity of the term, but its harsh, deliberate abruptness captures the nature of our response. We simply quit, believing the situation is meaningless and/or unwinnable, so why bother to fight?

Our fifth response is different from flight, and even freeze, in that while we stop trying to play the game as it is often defined by others, we remain actively in place. Instead, we play our own game, choosing to do things our own way, despite what others think—often to the detriment of others and ourselves. Unlike some of the other Five Fs, the fuck-it response is anything but passive.

During the pandemic, our Stress Center fuck-it response was on broad display. Some people, for example, became fatalistic. They did little to protect themselves from the outbreak, believing that contracting the virus was inevitable. They insisted on living their lives without alteration.

Meanwhile, in the financial markets, in what became labeled the "meme stock trade," informal groups of young, non-establishment investors came together via online message boards to target single, downtrodden stocks, like GameStop and AMC, in the hopes of "sticking it" to short sellers and other professional investors. Jeremy Grantham, a well-known institutional investor, described the phenomenon as "a totally nihilistic parody of actual investing."[9]

While Mr. Grantham was expressing his frustration with what he was witnessing, I suspect his words—coming from such a notable and longstanding establishment investor—brought a smile to many meme stock traders. They were not only winning their game but making other people angry in the process, too.

That is the nature of our fuck-it response. We equate disruption to victory, knowing full well we may never win in the end. We think, if we can't win, neither should others. Not surprisingly then, when confidence is very low, behaviors like terrorism and sabotage surge. They are extreme forms of our fuck-it response.

The Five Fs at Work

Extreme events, like the recent pandemic, provide clear examples of our natural Five F responses when we find ourselves deep in the lower left corner of the Stress Center. These moments showcase what we do in a crisis. But it doesn't always take a major panic to trigger these five reactions. Extreme feelings of uncertainty and powerlessness can arise in other ways.

Over my career, I have seen how the Five F responses have quickly taken hold of groups in the wake of a major merger or acquisition, or following a change in leadership at the top of an organization. When these events occur, it can be months before decisions are made that impact the lower levels of a company. Stranded in limbo in the Stress Center, and awash in uncertainty and powerlessness unfelt by those at the very top, rank-and-file employees choose their own paths. Some elect to leave (flight), while others jockey for position or forcibly resist the changes they perceive are coming (fight). Still others go along with corporate directives encouraging patience (follow), while some become paralyzed or preoccupied by the prospect of losing their jobs (freeze). Then there are those who openly work to undermine leadership (fuck it). Displeased with the outcome and/or believing they will soon be out of a job, they sabotage others—and themselves. They believe that if they're in the Stress Center, everyone else should be too.

Senior executives frequently fail to appreciate the widespread vulnerability they've just set in motion as they celebrate "groundbreaking," "transformational" corporate transactions—and their own career promotions—over champagne and passed hors d'oeuvres. With most employees focused on relieving their own Stress Center anxiety rather than the customer experience, it is no wonder most major corporate changes underperform expectations. Employees are too preoccupied with restoring their own lack of certainty and control to pay attention to new processes and procedures or to worry about new corporate goals. They are playing defense at a time when those at the top want them to be aggressively playing offense. When shoved involuntarily into the Stress Center, rank-and-file employees naturally put their own interests—and what they must do to get back to their individual Comfort Zones—ahead of the objectives set by management.

When major change occurs, the sooner leaders can restore employee confidence, the better. The same holds true with customers: acquisitions, divestitures, and leadership changes can easily upend customer confidence. If leaders don't think their clients are considering the same Five F options as their employees when major corporate changes take place, they are naive.

When business leaders first talk with me about the Stress Center, they typically associate it with major crises—moments, like the pandemic, when feelings of powerlessness and uncertainty are widespread and intense, when difficult decisions must be made and dramatic actions taken. Leaders quickly think of "crisis management" and the handling of a major, unexpected, disruptive threat, like a cyberattack, a product failure, or a political regime change impacting a foreign subsidiary. They view the Stress Center as an unwelcome outlier to their day-to-day job. It's the place where something went terribly wrong.

While memorable and highly emotional, these moments deep in the lower left corner of the Quadrant are, thankfully, rare. Businesses, though, routinely experience moments in the Stress Center. Somewhere, every day, customers or employees are experiencing feelings of powerlessness and uncertainty. And here is where things get interesting: while organizations have crisis management binders filled with processes and procedures for what to do when something goes terribly awry, and may even practice for it, few have thought through the practices and processes they want managers and rank-and-file employees to follow for the less intense experiences in the Stress Center. There's no process for a "go-around"; executives believe people will just know what to do when the time comes. Most businesses are like a medical system in which only emergency room doctors get trained (and, even then, for only a limited number of specific injuries). Few employees are taught basic business first-aid skills, and general practitioners and even urgent care teams (middle and senior management) are often left on their own. Leaders simply hope that when it comes to the small cuts and bruises, their employees will "do the right thing."

The problem with this approach is there is more than just one "right thing" we can do in the Stress Center. Those Five Fs are our natural responses to all stressful situations, not just crises. Running away from a problem, hoping it will just go away on its own, is a possible natural flight response in life—and at work, too.

Not surprisingly, if you look at major crises, they often evolve out of less significant Stress Center moments when employees felt ill-equipped or untrained to take control on their own, or when they didn't know who to reach out to for help (to follow) or the person they reached out to was unresponsive. The problem resolution process, if there was one in place at all, was flawed or insufficient. There was no clear, well-communicated path for how to get from the Stress Center back to the Comfort Zone. Even worse, in many cases, over time, employees began to believe there would *never* be an effective response. Resignation sets in.

Often, too, there was a culture of blame, shame, and regret with respect to Stress Center situations. Rather than accepting that Stress Center moments are a natural aspect of doing business, leaders considered them failures. Employees believed company leaders were more focused on either hiding these stressful experiences or laying blame at the feet of others. Flight and denial, rather than fight, were the organization's cultural responses to Stress Center experiences.

The Transparency of the Stress Center

What leaders routinely miss is that when a company slides down the Confidence Spectrum from the Comfort Zone into the Stress Center, they have no choice but to act. When employees and customers feel less certain about a company and its prospects and start to feel powerless, someone *must* respond. If employees can't respond, or don't know how to, that responsibility will inevitably rise to management. If managers can't or don't know how to respond, that responsibility will inevitably rise to the C-suite. And if they can't or don't know how to respond, it will ultimately rise to the board. The vulnerability escalates.

In the Stress Center, bad news doesn't get better with age. Left unaddressed, vulnerability spreads like an infection; with the passage of time, more people will feel more powerlessness amid even greater uncertainty. Topographically, the Stress Center is sloped. There's a "Valley of Despair" in that lower left corner, and left unattended in the Stress Center, problems will accelerate toward it over time. This is why, when vulnerability reaches the board, it is always already a far bigger problem than the board first realizes. The uncertainty and powerlessness are extreme and widely shared, leaving directors little choice but to move fast and furiously.

While it may take a full-out crisis to finally expose the depth and breadth of the vulnerability, unresolved Stress Center environments always end poorly. Vulnerability is an unsustainable state. At least one of those Five F responses is going to happen. It is a question only of which one, and its timing and degree.

This is especially true when it comes to customers. Unlike employees, they aren't paid to endure stress. They won't tolerate being left in limbo and feeling vulnerable in the Stress Center. Action is required; leaders *must* do something to restore customer confidence. Moreover, "fast and furious" is the expected response. In the Stress Center, customers are naturally impatient. The same holds true for suppliers, lenders, and shareholders. While strong relationships may buy time, they won't sustain those in the Stress Center for long. *Everyone* wants out of the Stress Center. Powerlessness and uncertainty are a poor pairing when it comes to money.

They are also a poor pairing with today's 24-7, fully online world. Many business leaders fail to appreciate that there is remarkable transparency when it comes to their company's Stress Center environments. All it takes is a few clicks to uncover how rank-and-file employees feel about their difficult working conditions. Message boards and Reddit threads are filled with workers' unflattering Stress Center stories.

Customers, too, are remarkably transparent with their feelings. Vulnerability is routinely the topic of irate one-star Yelp reviews and angry tweets. Social media provides the perfect stage on which to express our impulsive Stress Center emotions.

Then there is shareholder and lender vulnerability. Today's financial markets can be ruthless when it comes to pricing in investors' deteriorating feelings. Markets are barometers of confidence—and when vulnerability soars, the related price declines can be fast and furious, indeed.

C-suites are often quick to dismiss unflattering employee and customer feelings as "unjustified," and frustrated CEOs routinely label investor behavior as "irrational" when their company's stock price falls. Leaders become outraged when others openly express their feelings of vulnerability, quickly dismissing the stories and challenging their veracity.

Executives would be far wiser to appreciate the message being sent: like it or not, they, as leaders, are now in the Stress Center—and there, action is required. Unless resolved, vulnerability will breed greater vulnerability. It's worth repeating: powerlessness and uncertainty don't resolve on their own. Those Five F responses will happen, and if managers want "follow" to be the choice of the crowd, they must step up and lead.

What many business leaders fail to appreciate is how easy it is to spot leadership vulnerability today. Not only can you see how it's being measured by investors in real time via a company's stock price, but when organizations are playing defense, it doesn't take long into quarterly earnings calls to assess what management is worried about.

As I was writing this book, I watched as one business leader after another discussed the vulnerability of their operations arising from "chip shortages," "supply-chain disruptions," "inflation," "rising commodity prices," and other threats. With this information out in the open and emphasized in press releases and earnings calls, it wasn't hard to imagine what company executives were then focused on—or the potential implications of their actions.

That second aspect tends to be woefully underappreciated—by customers, by competitors, by shareholders and lenders, and even by business leaders themselves. As businesses are forced to address vulnerability, they set in motion what is about to happen next.

And if the problem is big, it's going to be all about defense. Addressing major vulnerability, especially following a crisis, can become all-consuming. Businesses aren't like football teams, which have independent, dedicated groups for both defense and offense. Typically, management plays the entire field. This means that when organizations are playing defense, they cannot play offense. They are so focused on addressing their vulnerability—fixing what's broken—they don't have the capacity to take on new opportunities. Innovation, investment, and long-term strategy are sidelined, replaced by remediation and tactical decision-making. In the extreme, this can set up a vicious spiral in which a management team's preoccupation with problem solving allows competitors to gain ground at their expense.

I see this a lot when extremely overconfident organizations begin to stumble. As their problems mount—and years of underappreciated risks come to the surface—managers become overwhelmed by all that is broken. Some organizations, like Lehman Brothers, fail quickly, while others, like General Electric, spend years playing defense as their industry peers excel around them. As businesses struggle in the Stress Center, they become fertile ground from which nimble competitors can reap new customers and talent.

There are other implications to a failure to address vulnerability, too. The more we see businesses simultaneously working to address the same vulnerabilities, the larger and more widespread the consequences. We witnessed this in real time in the spring of 2020, when many businesses overlooked the unintended consequences of the vast collective actions they and policymakers had taken in response to the COVID outbreak.

Leaders who were surprised by the supply shortages and inflation that occurred during the first twelve to twenty-four months after the pandemic hit shouldn't have been. In many cases, those same leaders were the ones whose extreme actions in March 2020 contributed to both phenomena. They fostered the "bullwhip effect." By shutting down production and canceling orders en masse in response to the outbreak, business leaders all but orchestrated the supply-chain-related challenges they later faced. The same can be said with respect to the fiscal and monetary policymakers and their extreme actions. Remember, as the crisis unfolded, no one was thinking about the long-term implications of their actions. Unknowingly, in resolving one problem, they laid the foundation for the next one: product shortages and price inflation.

This happens frequently, especially when groups of businesses within a single industry move in concert. If you look at the financial industry's collective response to the 2008 housing crisis, lenders rapidly made it all but impossible for new home buyers to obtain financing. Not only did this put downward pressure on prices, it set in motion the widespread purchase of homes by corporate buyers who had a far easier time accessing capital. Homes that would otherwise have been owned by individuals became corporate rental properties.

When there is a collective response to a shared vulnerability, not only is the impact magnified, the experience can be transformational. Just consider airline security before and after 9/11.

This raises an important consequence arising from our experiences in the Stress Center: Major vulnerability changes us. We never "go back to normal." Facing intense powerlessness and uncertainty, we are forced to respond. Still, even after we have resolved the immediate threat, our feelings of powerlessness and uncertainty linger. After collapse, our confidence is very slow to rebuild. We worry that our vulnerability may somehow return. As a result, we continue to work to ensure that we never feel vulnerable again. Unknowingly, we deliberately create a new normal, filled with processes and procedures specifically designed to protect us from returning to the Stress Center.

When I talked with ER doctors about their experience with COVID, I heard multiple references to the AIDS epidemic and how it was that experience of intense vulnerability that had transformed the treatment of epidemic viruses. From the use of latex gloves during patient exams to the use of sharps containers to dispose of used needles, specific processes and procedures were developed in the early 1980s to address the vulnerability hospital workers and patients experienced. Many of those changes are now routine in patient care.

The same kind of vulnerability-driven evolution happens routinely in business. The widespread financial vulnerability arising from volatile stock markets and high inflation during the 1970s, for example, led to a wave of change. Derivatives, passive investing, and even the principle of maximizing shareholder value—things we take for granted today—have their roots in the intense feelings of uncertainty and powerlessness investors experienced nearly a half century ago.

Finally, the same vulnerability-driven pattern of behavior is routinely mirrored in regulation. After a crisis, we adopt new behavior, and when we *really* want to ensure that we stay out of the Stress Center, we ask policymakers to take a major role. We don't just put up "Danger" signs; we hire security guards to make sure no one goes back.

In all cases, what is clear about the Stress Center is that it forces and fuels change. It is the ash out of which something new is born.

•

When we are in the Stress Center, we have one goal: get out. Action is required. And then, once we are successful, the goal is to never return. The impact of our vulnerability lingers.

But the Stress Center changes us in other ways. It dramatically alters our preferences. That is where we will turn our attention next.

CHAPTER 5

Introducing Horizon Preference

MARK TWAIN IS reputed to have said, "History doesn't repeat itself, but it often rhymes." While our means may change from cycle to cycle thanks to progress in things like technology, our basic instincts don't appear to evolve. We act in similar ways, driven by how we feel—so similar, in fact, that these recurring patterns are noticeable and useful.

In the financial markets, for example, technical analysts study patterns of past investor behavior and count on them as they forecast future price action based on historical precedents. They make money when investor behavior and markets rhyme.

Then there are those investors who believe in and follow market-focused theories, like the "Hemline Index," which came to the fore in the 1920s. It suggests that skirt lengths (hemlines) rise or fall along with stock prices. To these believers, women's decision to wear short flapper dresses during the tail end of the Roaring Twenties was an unmistakable warning sign in plain sight, suggesting financial and economic troubles ahead. So, too, they believe, were the miniskirts of the 1960s. Still others see similar tea leaves in the building of skyscrapers. The Empire State Building, the World Trade Center, and the Burj Khalifa all coincided with extreme valuations in the financial market.[1]

For investors, rhymes matter.

In the wake of the 2008 financial crisis and in search of rhymes, I went down a deep rabbit hole, hoping to gain a better understanding of investor behaviors in prior boom and bust cycles. What I found was that they all followed a very similar pattern, in which innovative technology and grandiose "this time is different" thinking paired with rising confidence manifested in a period of mania followed by a sudden and unexpected collapse in valuations and investor confidence. The cycle in feelings and actions was so consistent, I saw that history not only rhymed but damned near repeated itself.

As I began to work with the Confidence Quadrant and had others map specific experiences using the tool, I noticed similarly clear patterns. Within each box (and at spots along the Confidence Spectrum), specific feelings aligned with similar kinds of actions. There were clusters in which behaviors rhymed.

While the patterns were interesting, I didn't find them especially useful. Knowing that when we experience intense feelings of powerlessness and uncertainty we turn to the Five Fs might make for an interesting class discussion, but it wouldn't necessarily help leaders do a better job in a crisis.

As I thought more about it, I realized I had inputs and outputs but no clear way to connect the two. I lacked an understanding of the transmission mechanism between our feelings and actions. I still couldn't explain why certain kinds of behaviors were tied to specific mixes of feelings.

Ironically, I found the answer at the top of a roller coaster.

Our "Me-Here-Now" Stress Center Preferences

I hate roller coasters. As a control freak, I see little difference between my feelings in the Passenger Seat on a roller coaster and in the Stress Center. It's why, when the time came, my wife was the preferred driver's-ed teacher with our children. She didn't wince, as I did, when the car passed every mailbox and telephone pole.

Put me on a roller coaster and then add in the click-click-click of the car as it slowly ascends skyward, and you will soon find me deep in the Stress Center. When the cars pause at the very, very top before they scream down the track, I can all but feel my heart beating out of my chest. It's pure panic for me. I am in the very lower left corner of the Confidence Quadrant.

It was atop a roller coaster, though, that it hit me. I found the connection I had been searching for that linked our feelings and actions: how it was that mood changed our preferences, what we naturally need/want based on how we feel. This was the missing link.

Atop the roller coaster, as I braced for what was about to happen next, the only thing that mattered to me was my own self-interest—precisely where I was and what was about to happen to me in the next few seconds of my life. Nothing else mattered—not the person sitting next to me, not what was happening elsewhere in the park (let alone elsewhere in the world), not what would happen next week, next month, or next year. My sole focus was "Me-Here-Now."

As I looked at different behaviors mapped by others in the lower left box of the Quadrant, I realized they, too, were driven by this same Me-Here-Now mindset, especially those in the very lower left corner. What became clear was that when we feel especially vulnerable, Me-Here-Now preferences dominate. Self-interest and intensely close physical and time proximity are what matter most to us. An imminent threat forces us to focus on ourselves—right then and right there. The Five Fs of survival mode are our natural response as our intense Me-Here-Now preferences unknowingly dictate our behavior in a crisis.

Just think back to March 2020 and you can see our Me-Here-Now preferences behind the wheel. As the COVID outbreak hit, we could not and, as a result, did not care about what was happening to others. We did not care about what was happening elsewhere. And we had no interest in even talking about the future. What was the point? If we didn't get through what we faced in that moment, we didn't have one. Our entire focus had to be, and was, on Me-Here-Now.

And it wasn't just each of us in our own lives. Corporate leaders and policymakers were driven by identical preferences. If you take a moment and revisit the first pages of Chapter 4, you will see one Me-Here-Now action after another taken as businesses and governments responded to the outbreak. Decisions were impulsive, focused on immediately addressing the intense vulnerability organizations experienced—other people, other places, and tomorrow be damned.

When framed by a crisis or as "survival mode," our Me-Here-Now preferences and our extremely narrow view of the world make perfect sense to us. How else would we respond when threatened than to focus on our own individual survival?

What we overlook is that Me-Here-Now preferences apply to any moment—no matter the cause—when we lack certainty and control in our lives. A car accident, a broken leg, a poorly received presentation, a bad breakup, a layoff, a college rejection letter, or any other experience that places us in the lower left corner of the Quadrant has the same impact: we immediately revert to Me-Here-Now mode. It is a native trait of the Stress Center whose intensity is a function of our proximity to the lower left corner—the closer we get, the narrower our focus becomes.

Here is where it gets interesting. Our Me-Here-Now preferences then transcend all our decisions and actions at once. If we arrive in the office in Me-Here-Now mode because our car broke down on the way to work, we stay in that mindset on the job until we regain certainty and control in our lives. We remain preoccupied, far more focused on our own car problems than on the objectives of our manager. And there are other, more subtle consequences. In Me-Here-Now mode, we are likely to be less strategic at work. Our immediate car problem makes it difficult for us to consider time frames and even geographic distances that are far away. We are likely to be more xenophobic and nationalistic. Our mood is our mood, no matter where we are or what we are doing. We aren't good at compartmentalizing the certainty and control we feel in our lives.

When confidence falls, no matter the reason, I know Me-Here-Now preferences will likely drive the decision-making and actions that follow. With that information, it isn't hard to reasonably anticipate how people will then act.

And the ways are likely to surprise you.

For example, my students smiled knowingly when, in early March 2020, I showed them stock charts highlighting the dramatic rise in the stock price of Domino's Pizza Group as the pandemic outbreak took hold.[2] In our earlier class on confidence and food, students had shared their favorite "after a breakup" meals. Pizza and Chinese food—takeout meals that are routinely delivered right to our door within minutes—were just below Ben & Jerry's Chocolate Fudge Brownie ice cream at the top of the list. So were a long list of fatty snacks—which one student several years ago aptly tied back to the Five Fs and nihilism, labeling them all "fuck-it foods."

When our confidence falls, our diet naturally reflects our Me-Here-Now mindset. Healthy food choices and long-term diet plans get thrown overboard. Again, if the future is uncertain, what's the point?

Figure 5.1 shows a strong similarity in the fluctuations of Google search intensity for the terms "seasonal depression" and "comfort food." Comfort food, like the other low-confidence foods identified by my students, tends to be heavy in fats and carbohydrates. And with its clear connection to warm memories, nostalgia, tradition, and family, it is the ultimate Me-Here-Now cuisine. It is our least adventurous choice. In Me-Here-Now mode, we crave what is most familiar any way we can find it.

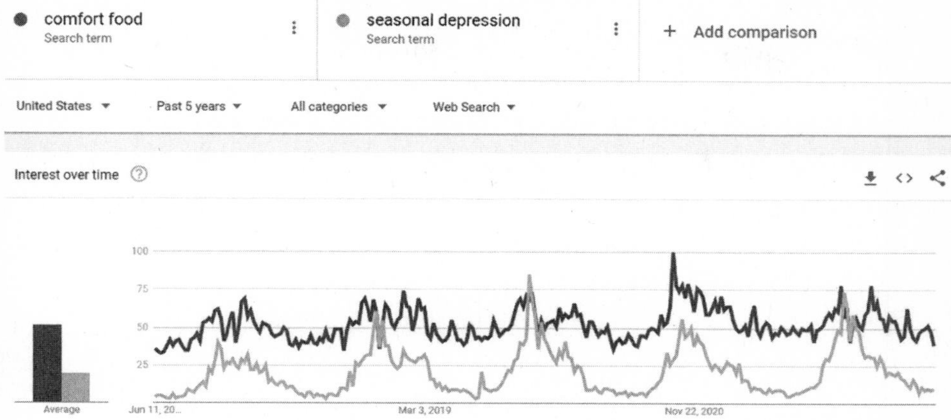

FIGURE 5.1: Google Trends chart for "seasonal depression" and "comfort food."
Source: Google

Our need for familiarity in our food choices plays out in ways that stretch well beyond our waistlines. The locavore and farm-to-table dining movements, too, tie to environments of low confidence. When Walmart launched its initiatives to increase the sales of local produce in the wake of the financial crisis, it couched the effort in economic terms: amid a backdrop of high diesel prices, trimming the number of "food miles" produce travels cuts fuel costs.[3] But it fit consumers' Me-Here-Now mood, too. When our confidence is low, closer equates to safer and better—both for us and for those who matter most to us, our local community. It should be no surprise, then, that the post–banking crisis era also brought with it a surge in growth of local craft breweries and artisan bakeries. These small-batch Me-Here-Now purveyors were the antithesis of the global behemoths like Anheuser-Busch InBev and Mondelēz International (the owner of Nabisco) that dominate alcohol and food sales.

When you stop to look at our low-confidence-related decision-making, it isn't hard to spot our Me-Here-Now preferences at work. Low-confidence eras are Me-Here-Now in 4-D—economically, politically, socially, and even culturally. The late 1960s to early 1980s was one of those Me-Here-Now eras, bringing major upheaval across every dimension. "Confidence" became "self-confidence" as the Polaroid camera and the Sony Walkman became enormously popular. More recently, this trend has continued with the iPhone, K-Cups, and even selfies.

It may seem to you that I have been cherry-picking examples over the past few pages, so I encourage you to consider your own preferences when your confidence is low. Moreover, the next time you are on an airplane and unexpected turbulence hits, pause to reflect on your focus. Socially, geographically, and temporally, how broad is it? Until the experience passes, you are highly likely to be focused on Me-Here-Now.

Introducing Horizon Preference

Deep in the Stress Center, our Me-Here-Now decisions and actions are impulsive reactions to the threat in front of us. That they are fast and furious shouldn't be surprising.

But consider what happens as we begin to relax—when the bear moves away from our tent, when we get off the roller coaster—as we begin to move up and to the right on the Confidence Quadrant, toward the Comfort Zone. Our preferences change. The urgency of our actions abates. The intense time pressure we just felt to do something falls away. We're less impulsive and more deliberate in our behavior.

Our focus broadens, too. Rather than thinking solely of ourselves, we ask others if they're OK and what they want to do next. We become more social and more interconnected. Shared interests arise. Similarly, our time horizon expands; we begin to think about what we are going to do next. Where just moments earlier we felt the future was unknowable, it now seems clearer. Finally, our physical horizon expands. We are open to considering more than just the few feet around us. Socially, geographically, and temporally, our preferences and focus expand. What I call our "Horizon Preference" broadens.

I believe Horizon Preference is the unnoticed natural transmission mechanism that connects our feelings and our actions at all levels of

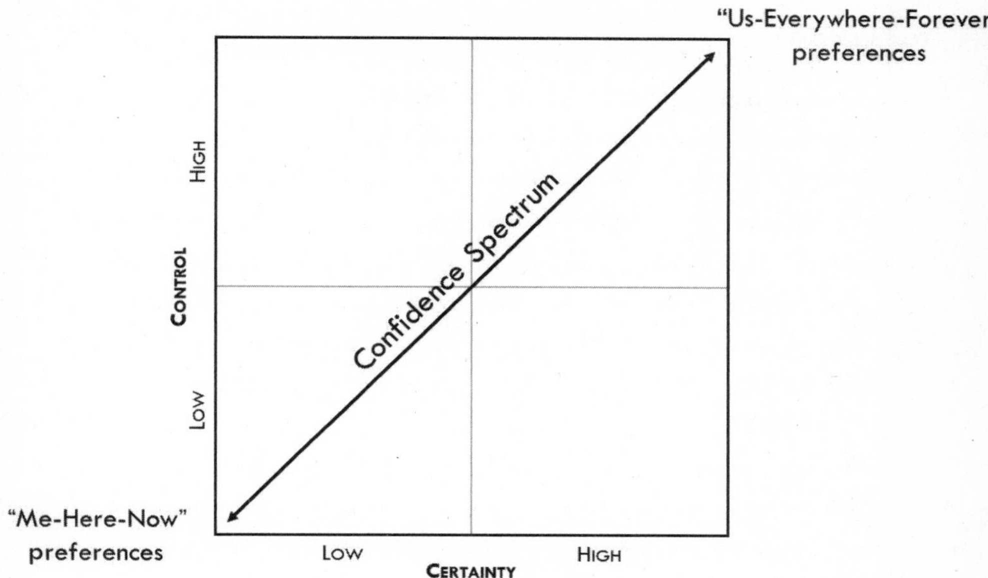

FIGURE 5.2: The Confidence Quadrant and Horizon Preference

confidence. Deep in the Stress Center, at the lower end of the Confidence Spectrum, we experience extreme Me-Here-Now preferences. At the other end of the Spectrum, in the far reaches of the Comfort Zone, we experience extreme "Us-Everywhere-Forever" preferences.

At peaks in confidence, we eagerly embrace collective interest, expansive geography, and long-term time frames. Extremely confident, we are generous, collaborative, and cooperative as we work together on ambitious long-term strategic goals that reach for targets far out into space. We go to the moon!

Unnoticed, Horizon Preference prescribes the actions we take based on how we feel. It feels as if we have been fitted with variable-lens goggles that automatically and naturally manage our peripheral vision based on how we feel in three dimensions at once: a social horizon, a physical horizon, and a time horizon. Our world shrinks and expands based on our mood. Vulnerability forces a narrow focus, while confidence allows for a broader, more expansive reach.

An easy way to understand Horizon Preference and see how its three dimensions simultaneously connect our feelings and actions is to consider our travel-planning decision-making.

At extreme lows in confidence, we stay home alone. Feeling powerless in an uncertain world, we don't venture off the porch. Moreover, we don't want to invite anyone in to join us. We turn inward and isolate ourselves. Too much is unclear—the people and the places around us and the future.

At peaks in confidence, though, we plan for elaborate trips years from now that take us to far-off places among people and cultures that are unfamiliar. Our high-confidence choices are driven by far more than wealth; they are grounded in the belief that well into the future, we will have high control and high certainty no matter where we land in the world—and, now, in space. At the top, the horizon is entirely clear—socially, geographically, and temporally. The world is flat. There is no fall-off in confidence—none. (And yes, Thomas Friedman's book *The World Is Flat* garnered widespread praise and popularity near a major peak in global consumer confidence.)[4]

And what I have just described with respect to travel planning for individuals applies to corporate planning more broadly. As you will see when we reach the Comfort Zone, at peaks in confidence, corporations (and their shareholders) believe the horizon is entirely clear, that anything is possible anywhere.

Abstraction Preference: The Fourth Dimension to Horizon Preference

To help you better appreciate this last point, I need to add an important fourth element to Horizon Preference: hypotheticality—or, more specifically, our relative preference for abstraction.[5]

As we stand on our porches and look out on the horizon, we quickly notice that objects in the distance are harder for us to see than those close by. Without binoculars, we struggle to make them out; they are more abstract. This same visualization principle applies to how we think of the future. We have more difficulty imagining what things will look like five years from now than we do imagining next week. Events we have planned for a year from now feel more abstract than those we've scheduled for this weekend. Finally, while we don't often think of it this way, the same principle also applies to our social interactions and relationships. We use the term "distant cousin," for example, to capture a relative's relative abstraction versus our "immediate family." We associate the principles of sight and geographic distance with far more than the physical world around us.

As shown in Figure 5.3, around each of us is an invisible series of concentric circles filled with people, places, and events in the future, all arranged by our perceptions of their relative abstraction—or, put differently, by the level of certainty and control we feel with respect to them.

The people, places, and things that we perceive to be more real—more tangible—are in the innermost rings, while those that are more abstract are farther out.

When we feel vulnerable and our confidence falls, it is because we feel threatened. Something unfamiliar and potentially dangerous has somehow penetrated our inner circle. Moreover, given its close psychological

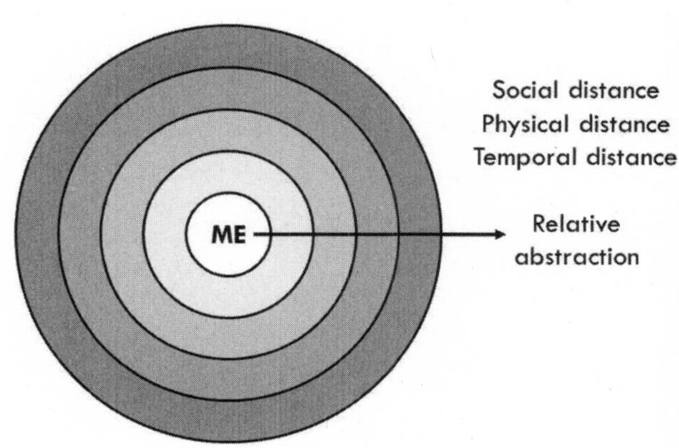

FIGURE 5.3: Relative proximity in four dimensions

proximity, the threat feels very real to us. Rather than feeling surrounded by the things that feel most familiar and that we trust most, we sense an intruder.

COVID was a great example. With the outbreak "contained" to China, it was a vague, hypothetical threat—somewhere out in one of our distant circles. As it spread to Europe, though, the threat began to feel closer and more real. Then, when the news hit that Tom Hanks and Rudy Gobert had been infected, COVID suddenly was real, immediate, and looming right next to us, ready to attack. A violent collapse in psychological distance had occurred; the outbreak went from being an abstract, psychologically distant threat to being real in a matter of moments.

Using the framework presented in Figure 5.3, I to visualize the change in our perception of the outbreak this way:

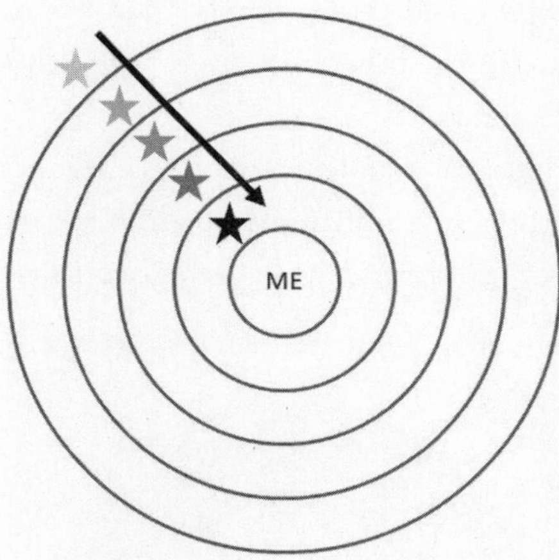

FIGURE 5.4: Our changing sense of the approaching pandemic

To succeed against the immediate threat we faced, we had to adapt. Without thinking about it, or even realizing it, we had to focus—on ourselves, on our own needs, on the present, and on the threat in front of us. It was our pre-programmed survival response. We had to use all our effort and energy on the only thing that mattered: the outbreak.

As a result, we were completely in the moment—socially, physically, and temporally. In a flash, the only thing that mattered was Me-Here-Now.

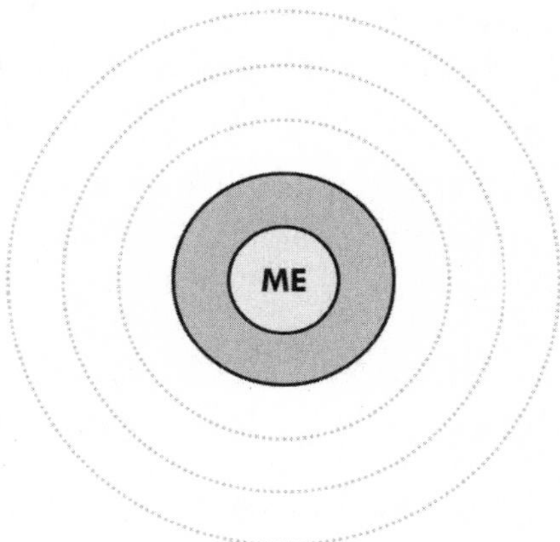

FIGURE 5.5: Our COVID focus response

As with all crises in the lower left corner of the Quadrant, with the outbreak, we impulsively dropped everything beyond the immediate, imminent threat. The outer rings of our lives became irrelevant; to have expended any energy there would have meant wasting valuable time and resources.

Before moving on, it is important to appreciate that while Me-Here-Now preferences may help us better respond to an immediate threat, they can have significant unintended consequences. As I shared earlier, impulsive short-term thinking aimed at addressing an intense vulnerability in one place can have long-lasting effects in others. Moreover, as Figure 5.5 makes clear, there is a lot we aren't paying attention to when we are focused on threats in the Stress Center—and in the case where others are struggling in the Stress Center, those things may include *you* as a leader. Executives of large organizations are inherently abstract. All those levels of management between the C-suite and frontline workers matter; each one makes a leader more psychologically distant. In the minds of employees, CEOs reside somewhere in one of those outer rings. And it isn't just individual leaders: as we saw firsthand during COVID with entities like the World Health Organization and other international agencies, psychologically distant leadership can't be effective when individuals have Me-Here-Now preferences.

To gain a better appreciation for why that is the case, and why the Stress Center can become so highly emotional, I need to introduce one final element of Horizon Preference. It is an intimidating mouthful: "Psychological Distance Distortion."

How Psychological Distance Distortion Impacts Decision-Making

In simpler terms, Psychological Distance Distortion means that our perceptions of social, geographic, and temporal distance are not fixed. They vary with how we feel.

Take our perception of time. When our confidence is high, and we are in the upper right box of the Confidence Quadrant, in the Comfort Zone, time moves quickly and effortlessly.[6] Time "flies" when we are having fun: our vacation days move faster than our best days in the office. When we are "in the zone," doing something we love, we suddenly realize that hours have passed, and we wonder how that could have happened. We lose all track of time.

On the other hand, when our confidence is low, and we are in the lower left box, in the Stress Center, time passes slowly. Minutes can seem like hours as we wait for the ski patrol to arrive after we have fallen on a steep, icy slope.[7]

While seconds, minutes, and hours may be standardized measures of time, how long they feel to us depends on our mood.

The consequence of this is a mood-driven accordion effect to the rings around us. With high confidence, the distance between the rings collapses. Those far-distant rings seem to be right next to us; ten years from now feels no different from tomorrow. Even strangers feel like close family members. Things that would otherwise be difficult for us to visualize—things that are abstract—seem vividly clear to us.

When confidence collapses, all this is reversed. The distance between each ring explodes. Suddenly, next week seems unknowable, and downtown feels as abstract and unfamiliar as a foreign country. It's no wonder time feels like it is moving slowly. What just felt very real to us now feels intensely abstract. We need the world to slow down simply in order for us to process what is immediately around us.

Hopefully, this explanation of Psychological Distance Distortion helps you appreciate why waiting for a critical diagnosis or waiting to be seen in the emergency room feels like it takes forever. We naturally become more impatient when our confidence falls. The fact that the Uber driver showed up at 10:02, not the 10:00 that the app suggested when we made our reservation, gets us worked up when we have a flight to catch. As we wait, we all but tick off each passing second. "One-thousand-and-one, one-thousand-and-two . . ." we count. Each moment is protracted.

Now, imagine how that must feel for a group of people. When a crowd's mood falls, the impact of collapsing time preference and the effects of time distortion become magnified as the group's impatience feeds upon itself. You can see this in real time when protestors take to the streets. Action is demanded *NOW!* as the crowd seeks immediate satisfaction. With our impatience soaring as time in the future feels like it is moving further and further away, delays become unacceptable, even when clear and consistent progress toward a goal has been demonstrated.

When internal projects are late, business leaders are frequently the ones experiencing Me-Here-Now time distortion. The impatience of those at the top can be palpable as action is demanded *NOW!* When the shoe is on the other foot, though, many leaders are caught off guard. They underestimate the urgency demanded amid low confidence by, say, striking workers. They dismiss requests for immediate pay increases as unreasonable.

When two groups operating with vastly different time preferences confront each other, tensions can quickly escalate. It is hard to reach agreement when one side sees an immediate need for action and the other believes that issues should be thought through thoroughly, with strategic plans developed and then implemented carefully over time. Leaders need to remember that anytime they are dealing with others who are experiencing vulnerability, that individual or group is almost certainly experiencing time preference distortion. As a result, responses need to be quick.

Time distortion, though, is but one of three distance distortions we experience. The same confidence-related variability occurs with our perceptions of social and physical distance, too.

Just ask marathon runners. They can quickly tell you which miles of a race felt longer or shorter than others. Miles aren't all the same; relative confidence often plays more of a role in how runners experience a race than the vertical ascent of the course. (Although, there, too, confidence plays a role. We perceive shallower hills when we are confident than when we are not.)[8] When we are tired and/or anxious, one mile can seem like ten. The same walk feels far longer in the rain than it does in bright sunshine.

Distance distortion, though, has broader implications. This phenomenon was behind all that toilet paper we hoarded during the pandemic: Just as we stuff cash in our mattress during a financial crisis, we need toilet paper and other critical supplies to be physically on hand because we are extremely anxious that we might run out. A store shelf just a few blocks away is too far for us, even though in the past we may have talked about the same supermarket as "nearby" and "extremely convenient."

What we really mean changes with how we feel.

Fears of a supply shortage, like other feelings of vulnerability, routinely collapse our distance preferences. We demand whatever we believe to be scarce to be stockpiled nearby.[9] We saw the same phenomenon in the 1970s, when the Middle East oil crisis manifested in a surge of home gas tank purchases (my own parents owned one) and the creation of the Strategic Petroleum Reserve. More recently, during COVID, we saw the same distortion-driven change in behavior as pandemic-related shortages forced the replacement of global sourcing and just-in-time supply-chain management with "near-sourcing," local warehouses, and just-in-case processes.[10] Even consumers got into the act, with many homeowners adding new walk-in pantries and/or making space for an extra freezer, as well as a home generator to provide Me-Here-Now electricity in case of a power failure.[11] Most recently of all, we saw a similar shift in physical distance preference with oil and gas when Russia invaded Ukraine. Overnight, European leaders began calling for national self-sufficiency and boosting domestic energy supply.

These responses draw in the last Psychological Distance Distortion: social distance. It is less obvious and might best be explained using the concept of trustworthiness: When our confidence is low, we trust others less. We see them as less dependable and more uncertain. As a result, when our confidence is low, sometimes even our closest family members can feel like strangers.

Many experienced this phenomenon firsthand during the pandemic, as vaccines and vaccination protocols became lines of social division. Once-homogeneous family members suddenly weren't all the same, and we felt socially distant from people we used to trust. Moreover, we questioned others' motives. Common ground became hard to find.

Amid crises, it is easy to see the impacts of Horizon Preference and Psychological Distance Distortion, but they are always at work. For businesses, it is vital to appreciate their impact. If customers and employees are feeling powerless and uncertain—whatever the reason—business leaders need to respond with Me-Here-Now solutions.

Horizon Preference and Confidence Correlation

Businesses spend a lot of time and money looking at how their results correlate to economic factors such as interest rates, inflation, and consumer spending. Some even look at the impact of changing sentiment and consumer confidence. Their focus, though, tends to be limited to the impacts these have on revenue; few look at their businesses broadly, through the lens of Horizon Preference. They overlook, and therefore don't plan for, the simultaneous impacts changing social, temporal, and geographic preferences have on their operations. However, with a comprehensive understanding of Horizon Preferences, organizations can adjust, prepare for, and even capitalize on the narrowing preferences accompanying the confidence downturns that often devastate an industry.

For example, let's say I run an international cruise line.

If I'm the head of a company like Carnival Cruise Line, Me-Here-Now thinking is the last thing I want to see during a downturn. Amid low confidence, not only are travelers likely to become more fearful of foreign cultures and far-off travel locations, they also won't consider, let alone plan for, future trips. To survive, I will have to scramble to offer cheaper, shorter, nearby journeys on smaller boats if possible and offer fully refundable fares just to attract customers. Every aspect of my product offering must be retailored to reflect Me-Here-Now thinking.

Then there are the challenges I will likely face internally, as my multicultural workforce naturally becomes more xenophobic. Infighting is likely to develop, often fueled by long-standing, inaccurate stereotypes. There are also likely to be issues arising from mounting nationalism in the destinations I serve. Challenging political environments will compound my problems both at home and abroad, with rules and regulations tightening as confidence falls. Even worse, all those policy changes will be far more inconsistent, as rule makers, too, exhibit their own Me-Here-Now/"My house my rules!" decision-making.

And if my business is struggling and my lenders and shareholders view bankruptcy as a real risk (after long believing it to be a remote possibility), they, too, are likely to be in Me-Here-Now mode. Equity capital will be all but impossible to raise, and what little credit may be available to me will come at a much higher cost, require immense amounts of collateral, include severely restrictive covenants, and be coupled with short-dated maturities.

My leadership team and I will be forced to fight battles on many fronts simultaneously. Needless to say, we might want to have a plan and be prepared for this. If we can anticipate some of these problems and prepare for them, we'll be steps ahead of our competition.

I don't mean to pick on the leadership team at Carnival Cruise Line, but they were woefully unprepared for the highly predictable, widespread devastation that collapsing Horizon Preference wreaked on their business when the pandemic hit. To be fair, though, they were hardly alone. After years of success, the leadership teams in most travel-related businesses naively thought they were immune from falling consumer confidence.

In September 2017, then American Airlines CEO Douglas Parker told analysts and reporters that the once-volatile industry had changed so radically amid the post–banking crisis recovery that his company would never lose money again. "Overtourism"—a word that became widely used before the pandemic hit to describe the condition of popular travel destinations overrun with tourists—would last forever.[12] Even in a bad year, Parker said, the world's biggest airline should earn about $3 billion in profit before taxes.[13]

In 2020, American Airlines lost $8.9 billion.[14]

With minor changes, I could recast what I just shared about the travel industry and capture what happened during the 2008 housing crisis. Collapsing Horizon Preference then, too, wreaked havoc among borrowers and lenders alike. As home prices collapsed and borrowers went underwater on outstanding mortgage loans, they quickly prioritized payments to Me-Here-Now credit card and auto lenders over those to distant, abstract, thirty-year-mortgage lenders.

And we saw a similar pivot in preferences during the Greek debt crisis, as intense Me-Here-Now feelings even led some Greeks to buy mattresses with built-in safes to hold the physical cash they had pulled from bank ATMs, just as some Americans had at the bottom of the financial crisis.[15]

What I've just shared are examples of the downsides to collapsing Horizon Preference. For the nimble, though, there are upsides. And this is what makes Horizon Preference so important: if your business can adjust and capitalize on it, Me-Here-Now thinking can represent opportunity.

An especially responsive plumber can have a successful career satisfying the Me-Here-Now demands of her clients. So, too, can emergency room doctors and nurses and other first responders. Some businesses and careers naturally entail interacting with individuals and businesses when they are in Me-Here-Now mode and require address of their urgent needs.

For most others, a Me-Here-Now climate means it's time to realign your products and services to the Me-Here-Now preferences of your clients, even when those occur for reasons unrelated to your line of business. Polaroid demonstrated that in the late 1960s; its instant camera was a perfect fit with the Me-Here-Now thinking of the time. Today, we are awash in Me-Here-Now products and services designed to give us what we want, when and where we want it. Streaming services like Netflix and Spotify are experts in Me-Here-Now, using algorithms to cater precisely to our individual current mood. Product delivery companies like Amazon, Instacart, Uber Eats, and DoorDash do the same. Then there is social media. Talk about Me-Here-Now thinking at work: Twitter, Instagram, Snapchat, TikTok, etc. now satisfy our every Me-Here-Now impulse, with few participants considering the long-term implications of a split-second decision to share an inappropriate message or image.

But consider that these companies have thrived in an environment that is also rife with political polarization, social movements, and a growing backlash to globalism. Me-Here-Now thinking is on display in far more than just our popular products and services. Moreover, today's backdrop "rhymes" with the political and social turbulence that accompanied Polaroid's wild success fifty years ago. What we are experiencing today isn't unique.

•

No matter how we feel, we have a natural Horizon Preference that accompanies it. Lows in confidence demand Me-Here-Now focus, while highs allow the reverse. When we feel vulnerable, we rebel against abstraction. We need things to be real.

The Stress Center, then, requires leaders adept at handling the Me-Here-Now needs of customers and other critical constituent groups. As you will see, the good news is that these skills can be easily identified and developed to better prepare us for the inevitable crises and moments in the Stress Center that lie ahead.

CHAPTER 6

Better Practices in the Stress Center

LIKE IT OR NOT, there is a crisis in your future. Whether it happens because of a defective product, poor customer service, a troublesome third party, or an economic downturn, it is a question only of *when* you and your business will end up in the Stress Center.

Most corporate crisis-management planning focuses on specific threats and what to do when threat avoidance fails. It's targeted on high-impact events, in which the financial and/or reputational consequences are especially punitive.

Often, the identified threats are based on peer pressure: they focus on widely shared concerns that other CEOs, board members, and/or regulators don't want to be caught unprepared for and flat-footed in the face of, say, a cyberattack. At other times, the focus of their preparation is backward-looking, a response to another organization's material misfortune or an industry's lack of prior readiness. Companies routinely draw up plans to fight the last war.

While I'm not saying these kinds of preparations aren't worthwhile and important, their high specificity leads organizations to think of each scenario as a one-off case. Crisis plans are highly customized and tailored to a single type of threat that appears on the surface to bear little resemblance to another. They are cause driven, arising from hurricanes, major product failures, and now pandemics. The result is that plans are built from the bottom up and in isolation around a given concern by experts most familiar with that specific concern's intricacies. While corporation-wide risk management and audit teams may oversee the process, typically their broad oversight role is to ensure a plan's existence and adequacy. The focus is compliance, in the hope that the experts consulted have the knowledge and skills to ensure the organization will recover from a crisis should one occur.

Better crisis management begins by recognizing that as unique as crises may seem, they share much in common. The 9/11 attacks, the COVID pandemic, and the 2008 housing crisis arose from vastly different causes, yet all fostered similar intense feelings of powerlessness, uncertainty, and extreme Me-Here-Now thinking. All three events upended confidence, shoving those impacted into the lower left corner of the Confidence Quadrant.

But note that in the moment, we didn't refer to any of these three crises as "problems." All were described as "threats." There is a difference, and it speaks to the reality inside every crisis. There are two challenges that must be addressed simultaneously: the source of the threat (the highly specific problem to be eliminated) and the feelings of vulnerability and other reactions arising from the threat (the common responses that come with every major Stress Center event).

While cause-specific crisis planning can be helpful, it leaves clear gaps. As history shows, not every corporate crisis can or will be planned for. Moreover, even if they are planned for, specific plans focus solely on problem elimination; they ignore the broader threat felt by an organization and other key constituent groups. As a result, feelings of uncertainty and powerlessness linger long after the storm has passed. Trust is slow to recover.

Improving Crisis Management

A better approach to crisis management would be to supplement specific event planning with processes and procedures that seek to address the feelings of uncertainty and powerlessness that arise amid crises, no matter the cause, and in real time rather than after the fact.

Earlier, I explained why it was important for leaders to take a vulnerability-driven approach in a crisis. I encourage you to go back to Chapter 3 and look at that process and its steps. As I shared, the process broadens participants' focus and shifts their mindset from simply eliminating a *problem* to include eliminating a *threat*. It demands that leaders immediately confront the reality of their dual challenges.

On the surface, this approach would appear to run counter to the fast and furious response most CEOs and boards of directors demand in a crisis. What emergency rooms routinely demonstrate, however, is that when rehearsed and followed, the approach not only can move fast but can better focus resources on what matters most. Moreover, it provides a structured framework that enables a crisis team to pivot as conditions require. The hardwiring is in the process of the approach to problem-solving, not in the specific application as with most crisis plans. As a result, it can be applied to *any* crisis.

For example, in October 2018, a Lion Air Boeing 737 MAX passenger jet crashed. Then, in March 2019—less than six months later—a second Boeing 737 MAX, operated by Ethiopian Airlines, crashed. Imagine if after the second incident, Boeing had taken a vulnerability-driven approach. The company would have gone into the experience already fully appreciating that it operates a business in which its customers are in the Passenger Seat. As a plane manufacturer, Boeing delivers a product that requires intense certainty because of the catastrophic consequences that accompany failure and the complete powerlessness of its ultimate client—airline passengers. When it comes to confidence, the normal operating environment for a passenger plane is inherently fragile, and sustainability requires the company to hug the right edge of the Confidence Quadrant.

Had Boeing taken a vulnerability-driven approach when its second plane crashed, it would have immediately broadened the organization's focus from a "foreign pilot problem" (its response after the first plane crash) and a very specific "737 MAX aircraft problem" (its response after the second plane crash) to an "aircraft problem *and* an extreme passenger, pilot, and carrier vulnerability experience."[1] The existential threat to its passenger aviation business would have been obvious. Moreover, that greater awareness likely would have caused the organization to shift its priorities and focus from the specific mechanical issues with its planes to the intense feelings of powerlessness and uncertainty felt by the air carriers it supplied, their pilots, and their passengers. The latter groups were Boeing's far bigger problems. Its reputation as a trustworthy aircraft manufacturer was on the line.

In response, for example, the company likely wouldn't have waited until regulators had grounded its planes. It would have done so itself immediately, appreciating that with confidence broken, and so widely, it was far better to be seen acting urgently and proactively, taking precautions rather than being slow and reactive. The greatest speed was needed not in repairing planes but in restoring trust.

It may feel as though I am Monday-morning quarterbacking Boeing's decisions, but it is remarkably straightforward to detail the kinds of actions companies should take when crises are recast from specific problems to extreme-vulnerability experiences. Crisis teams must determine how best to restore the sense of certainty and control in how others feel: customers, rank-and-file employees, shareholders, lenders. . . . Without their trust, there is no business.

In fairness, businesses have been coached to believe that solving the obvious problem and restoring confidence inside a business is the sole goal of crisis management. If there is a word that dominates crisis planning, it is "recovery." The objective is simple: get back to what *was* as quickly as possible. Leaders have been told repeatedly that success in a crisis comes from how quickly their organization can gain control over the problem and restore the status quo. Praise comes from taking "effective, decisive action" that enables their organization to get back to work immediately. In this analysis, speed is the critical crisis-recovery success factor.

With that being the case, "focused" and "fast" are the core tenets of most plans. There is little choice but to focus on the obvious problem (and, far too often, to quickly blame the obvious suspects for causing it). Thoughtful deliberation and comprehensiveness are off the table; they slow things down and add unnecessary complexity. Boards want an immediately satisfying response. The purpose of crisis planning is to ensure that people know what to do and can do it quickly should the need arise. Having a plan enables everyone to use the plan.

No one should be surprised, then, that most corporate leaders take an authoritarian approach to crisis management. Boards expect to see intense executive control of the situation. They believe that with both hands on the wheel, the CEO can get everyone else on board, drive the car fastest, and get to the desired destination. Moreover, boards want extraordinary certainty. Typically, having been surprised by a crisis, board members don't want any more shocks.

In fairness, what boards want in a crisis closely resembles what we all want when a pipe bursts at home: someone to respond immediately to our problem with the expertise to eliminate it.

But consider what this mandate looks like on the Confidence Quadrant when it is fulfilled in a corporate environment.

The good news is that if this approach is successful, certainty will be quickly restored; in fact, there will be *intense* certainty. In a crisis, CEOs typically leave nothing to chance. They all but drag businesses out of the Stress Center and across the Passenger Seat, landing them on the very far right edge of the Quadrant (Figure 6.1).

Unfortunately, rather than up in the Comfort Zone, where everyone can finally relax, the landing location is most frequently near the very bottom of the right edge of the Passenger Seat. Decision-making that was once spread through the organization ends up being tightly controlled in the C-suite. In the wake of the crisis, the business rests in the lower right corner of the Quadrant, a location shared by high-security prisons.

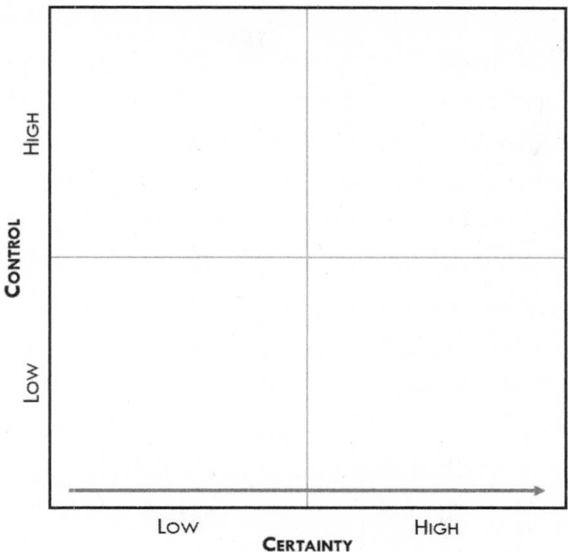

FIGURE 6.1: The authoritarian crisis response

For rank-and-file employees and even middle and senior managers, the environment feels like it, too. Worse, their relegation to the Passenger Seat feels like punishment for the crisis, whether deserved or not. Worst of all, it fosters an environment devoid of risk-taking. The lower right corner of the Passenger Seat is as far away from the Launch Pad as you can get. It's where everyone in an organization knows that authority rests with anyone but them.

Don't get me wrong: there are moments when this approach is warranted. Chaotic, violent unrest comes to mind—a situation where lives are at risk. In such a moment, leaving even a small amount of control with others can perpetuate a crisis. Total lockdowns occur for this reason. Too often, though, a lockdown is what "successful" crisis management looks like after the fact in business. Once the storm has passed, calm is celebrated, with leaders still holding a death grip on control for fear of another surprise tornado. Re-empowering employees and redistributing decision-making responsibility is the last thing on most C-suite leaders' minds.

To avoid this outcome, leaders must strive to preserve decision-making as deep into their organization as they can amid the crisis and appreciate that they will be more successful, in both the short term and the long term, when instilling a sense of certainty and control in those they lead. Demanding passive followership from employees doesn't accomplish that. In a crisis, leaders need others to share ownership of the outcome—to feel, when the storm has passed, that they helped resolve the threat.

Again, confidence in a business is restored when *others*, not just the C-suite, feel like they have certainty and control.

There is a second challenge inherent in the authoritarian response to crisis management. As much as executives may think otherwise, without trust, leaders can't drag customers from the Stress Center to the far-right side of the Passenger Seat as they can employees. Customers have a choice, and they can choose not to follow. That's a major problem when a business crisis impacts the customer. Then, trust in management tends to be in very short supply. When bad things happen, it is easy for clients to blame corporate leaders. Executives are supposed to prevent crises from happening in the first place. Given the opportunity, rather than being dragged out of the Stress Center and across the Passenger Seat, customers will flee altogether, seeking out another provider. Anyone looks better than the dangerous driver who tossed you around the front seat before dumping you unexpectedly at the curb.

Deliberately delegating authority in a crisis to those closest to the customer can go a long way toward calming frayed client nerves. Once again, psychological distance matters. Fancy executive titles mean little in a crisis—in fact, they only reinforce the vast psychological distance that exists between executive offices and the field. In the ER, we don't care who the president of the hospital is, let alone want to meet her. When confidence is low, customers—like the rest of us—want to deal with those who are most familiar with and sympathetic to our needs and best able to help us with our specific, individual Me-Here-Now concern. Business leaders are foolish to ignore this reality.

Evaluating Crisis Leadership Abilities

There's another reality businesses are foolish to ignore: a sudden decline into the Stress Center mandates tough leadership decisions. With confidence low and trust broken, boards and leaders themselves must consider whether a change at the top is required.

Put simply, leading in the Stress Center is far different from leading in the Comfort Zone that typically precedes a crisis. Most boards are slow to appreciate this and even slower to do something about it. They think they have successfully hired an "all-seasons" leader with the requisite skills and abilities for any environment; they fail to appreciate that few can successfully navigate all four boxes of the Confidence Quadrant. Too often, boards wait and watch as a struggling leader makes thing worse. Collective vulnerability builds—among coworkers, among customers, and among the board. When boards finally act, it is an act of capitulation, not unlike when investors sell and go to cash out at the bottom of a major stock market decline. Feelings of powerlessness and uncertainty mount until a board's "fuck-it" response finally kicks in. I've seen this so many times that it has become an important contrarian indicator for me—a sign that an organization is rapidly approaching the bottom of the Confidence Spectrum. You'd be surprised how many times a sudden CEO change marks a major low in the stock price of a company. By the time boards act, the feelings of powerlessness and uncertainty are widespread.

And here's the irony of it all: after waiting to act until an extreme low in confidence (a.k.a. the absolute peak of the crisis), boards then typically bring in a risk minimizer—someone with "safe hands" who the board knows won't take any risk whatsoever. The board deliberately hires someone to smother a fire that was already about to go out on its own.

Instead, before a crisis hits, boards need to ask three questions:

Does the CEO have the self-confidence to effectively lead in a crisis?
Do others have confidence in the CEO to effectively lead in a crisis?
Does the CEO have the skill set to effectively lead in the crisis?

To be clear, the answers to all three questions are feelings based. Trust is entirely subjective. That said, there are objective factors associated with each question that should be considered.

With respect to CEO self-confidence, if there is a mindset that gets in the way of getting out of the Stress Center, it is one filled with self-doubt—the one that naturally accompanies our feelings of powerlessness and uncertainty when we land in the lower left corner of the Stress Center, which is filled with blame, shame, and regret. We lament our arrival there and the cause that brought us to this point. We just want the problem to be over. Moreover, we want to go back to what was. Our desire is the past—yesterday looks far better than the uncertainty of today from which we are reeling. We overlook all the past's imperfections and challenges while we curse our current plight. If we could only go back to before!

Leaders are not immune to these feelings, especially those who innately hold themselves accountable for everything that happens under their watch. Those who believe they somehow allowed (or worse, caused) a crisis will have a difficult time resolving it. It's too personal. It is *their* failure, not the business's, and they can't address both at the same time. In Me-Here-Now mode, "Me" will always come first.

Then there are leaders who may be new to a role, especially following a major stretch promotion. They may not feel as though they know enough yet to lead—nor, typically, will those they must lead, nor will board members who were skeptical about the new leader in the first place, which won't help a new leader's self-confidence. Again, it is the curse of psychological distance and unfamiliarity. And those same feelings may apply to those who have never experienced the Stress Center before in a leadership role.

Whether true or not, the stories leaders tell themselves impact their behavior, and when a crisis hits, it is imperative for others to honestly assess who is at the helm. Does a leader think he can do the job or not? If he doesn't, he can't. He won't be effective.

Then there is the confidence of others. Far too often, this confidence is overestimated. Long, successful track records in the Comfort

Zone create a halo effect and a widely—and not infrequently, wildly—shared belief in the omnipotence of leaders. Everyone presumes that repeat victories adequately prepare leaders for crisis. Little attention is paid to where on the Quadrant prior success occurred—and often, it has been anywhere but the Stress Center.

Board members, too, fail to appreciate that while they may feel psychologically close to a leader, leaders are inherently psychologically distant to others. Executive relationships are far more fragile than they appear. Finally, boards also fail to recognize that as confidence in a leader falls, scrutiny and criticism of that leader will naturally rise. It isn't a question of *if* but *when* the dirt and the knives will come out. Foibles that were otherwise ignored or tolerated when confidence was high (and scrutiny nonexistent) will become front-page fodder.

And if that isn't bad enough, organizational cohesion will come under attack more broadly. With everyone in Me-Here-Now mode, leaders without a solid base of support don't stand a chance. If there was infighting before a crisis, it will all but become active combat. Boards should accept this and pull wounded leaders from the game. Leadership vulnerability doesn't get better on its own.

Rethinking Crisis-Leadership Skills

Finally, some leaders simply lack the required skill set for the Stress Center. A leader who may be wonderful when coaching a high-performing Super Bowl team in the upper reaches of the Comfort Zone might not have what it takes to successfully lead in a crisis. And by "what it takes," I don't just mean prior experience successfully navigating a business through a storm. There are other skills needed, and they likely aren't what you'd expect.

When Russia invaded Ukraine, many military experts and political pundits cringed. They had little faith that a former comedian turned politician would have the skill set to successfully face off against an aggressive, experienced, authoritarian leader like Vladimir Putin. To the experts, Volodymyr Zelenskyy was in way over his head.[2]

I disagreed.

Back in early 2013, during the European debt crisis, pundits offered a similar take when former Italian television comedian Beppe Grillo and the Five Star Movement he cofounded won a quarter of the votes in Italy's general election, more than any other party.[3] Experts then, too, were flummoxed that a comedian could generate that kind of popular response. Many political pundits felt the same way when in 2008, amid the depths of the banking crisis, former *Saturday Night Live* comedian Al Franken was elected to the U.S. Senate, representing the state of Minnesota.

A comedian?!

While admittedly a very small data set, the experiences of Beppe Grillo and Al Franken suggested that the leadership style of Volodymyr Zelenskyy would fare far better than expected. Zelenskyy had skills that mattered in a crisis. In fact, I'd go a step further and say that successful comedians have a tool kit of skills that can serve as a checklist for organizations as they evaluate the potential of leaders in a crisis.

To be successful, comedians need the following skills:

Communication and the ability to read and command a rapidly changing room;
Perseverance and the ability to overcome frequent rejection;
Creativity and the ability to think differently and on their toes;
Keen observation and the ability to see things others miss; and
Resonance and the ability to relate to others.

While we don't typically think of these as C-suite qualifications, every one of these skills will be demanded of a leader in a crisis.

Comedians, though, aren't the only ones who have a great crisis-leadership skill set. So, too, does another group that doesn't naturally come to mind for most boards of directors: individuals who struggle with mental illness. In his book *A First-Rate Madness*, psychiatrist and mood-disorder expert Nassir Ghaemi details how manic and depressive experiences provide valuable crisis-leadership skills.[4] Shortly after the

Russian invasion of Ukraine, he wrote in a column, "Mania is associated with resilience to trauma, and creativity. Depression increases empathy and a realistic assessment of one's environment. In a crisis, a leader needs to be, first and foremost, resilient. He can't cut and run; he can't be scared; he can't dither. Creativity helps too; he needs to find a way out in a situation that seems unsolvable."[5]

Inventors share similar skills. So do triage nurses and many hospice workers. My point is not to suggest that businesses should target those professions or individuals inside their organizations with specific prior experiences for elevation to leadership, but rather to emphasize that effective Stress Center leadership is not what corporate boards and C-suite leaders think it is. When a crisis hits, most boards assess incumbent leaders and their potential replacements using a leadership mold straight out of Hollywood. They focus on appearances—confidence theater—rather than the specific skills required to successfully navigate the Stress Center.

History suggests that in a crisis, organizations would be better led by those for whom environments of uncertainty and powerlessness are familiar—where individuals have a proven track record of successfully demonstrating skills like creativity, resilience, empathy, and action. Because today's corporations seek to avoid crisis environments at all costs, most businesses tend to be devoid of such qualified crisis leaders. Then, when a crisis hits, they have no idea what leadership skills they really need.

Effective Communication in the Stress Center

The same kind of shortcoming exists with respect to crisis communication. Much as the Stress Center requires a leader with specific skills suited to the environment, it also requires a specific style of communication.

To best mirror the Me-Here-Now preferences of those in the Stress Center, leaders should structure their messages with the following five points in mind. Communication should be:

Immediate—When we are in the Stress Center, our perception of time can become highly distorted. Seconds pass like hours. We become naturally impatient. Moreover, slow or infrequent communication is interpreted, in the Stress Center, as a leader withholding information. Delays only exacerbate feelings of powerlessness and uncertainty.

Immediate time frames should be the focus of all crisis messages, too, and the time frame for all directed actions. Until a crisis passes, leaders must remember that others are in Me-Here-Now mode, in a seemingly endless present. People want to know what to do *now*.

In a crisis, many confident leaders want to turn their attention to the future. They want to get back to what they were doing before, to turn strategic when everyone else is still mid-crisis. But that urgent present is what all messages must emphasize and address. Until the storm passes, leaders must leave tomorrow until tomorrow. If they don't, they will be seen as tone-deaf, or worse, completely out of touch with reality.

Complete—Low confidence also brings greater scrutiny. Scrutiny is one way we eliminate uncertainty; we seek to know more about what is happening and why. As a result, crisis leaders need to err on the side of providing more rather than less information, and to more people than they would when confidence is high. In a crisis, many leaders seek to do the opposite: they limit the dissemination of information and, at the same time, they shrink the group with whom they share it.

Leaders lose credibility when one group learns important information before another. In a crisis, not only is all information important (again, it provides certainty), a failure to include all stakeholders will be interpreted as a deliberate choice to exclude them. Leaders need to go out of their way to shrink psychological distance—to help others feel closer to the leader than ever before.

Realistic—In a crisis, we abhor abstraction. We don't have the time or interest to interpret information. We want the straight scoop—even when it is bad. Bad news that is true represents certainty. Moreover, if a leader doesn't deliver bad news in a crisis, others will presume the leader is hiding a reality that is worse than the one the leader has shared.

Thanks to informal social networks, people on the ground share reality with each other whether leaders want them to or not—and they share it to the press, to customers, to regulators, and to everyone else that leaders don't want them to share it with. When confidence is low and Me-Here-Now thinking takes hold, organizations are completely porous. Everyone has their own individual story that they must tell someone else.

Leaders shouldn't just anticipate but *expect* that the ugly truth will get out. And if they had the chance to deliver it first and didn't, they will later be accused of lying. When that happens, it is game over for a leader's credibility. With leaders who lie—and here I must emphasize that the *perception* of lying will win out over the fact every time—there is no basis for trust.

Simple—In a crisis, we likewise abhor complication. Complex messages confuse people at a time when cognitive bandwidth is already challenged. These messages reinforce the powerlessness and uncertainty we feel. To address this issue, leaders should strive to deliver messages that are tailored to the lowest common denominator, devoid of buzzwords, acronyms, and technical jargon. Leaders should think about how they would share their message with a middle school student or grandparent who knows nothing about the business and then structure their message just like that.

Authentic—A crisis is not the time for a leader to try out a new personality—to try to be what the crowd wants (or what a leader thinks they want) rather than being genuine. Whether it is in the tone of their message or their style of dress, in a crisis, leaders must be who they are. Familiarity matters: it creates a basis for trust. People need to hear you in your own voice and see you as you have always been. It is remarkable how many leaders think a crisis requires them to look, sound, and act like a Hollywood crisis leader. A crisis is no time for playacting.

Three Final Words of Advice

Before moving on to the Comfort Zone, I have three recommendations for leaders in the Stress Center to consider:

1. ANTICIPATE ZERO-SUM THINKING

First, never underestimate the zero-sum thinking that accompanies our feelings of powerlessness and uncertainty at the bottom of the Confidence Spectrum. The Stress Center is an environment of scarcity, where it feels like there isn't enough of what matters. At best, our world is finite. As a result, we measure success and failure differently: we believe someone else's gain is our loss, and our gain is their loss.

While we readily accept the notion of zero-sum thinking in the context of sports and politics, we tend to overlook it in business. As organizations move deeper and deeper into the Stress Center, you can see the impact of zero-sum thinking as tensions rise and as the interests of shareholders, managers, creditors, and employees conflict—what one wants must come at the expense of another.

Consensus-seeking leaders, who are used to working amid the "we can all win together" mindset of the Comfort Zone, often struggle to adapt to the reality of the Stress Center. There, when decisions must be made, compromise is unachievable. Someone invariably walks away with the feeling of having lost and is jealous and resentful of another's gain.

Rather than being surprised by zero-sum thinking, leaders should anticipate it and prepare for its impulsive and emotional consequences. Loss management—and how leaders empathetically handle the rising vulnerability of others—is a critical skill in the Stress Center.

2. AVOID COMPARISON WITH OTHERS

Highly competitive by nature, most leaders benchmark themselves and their organizations against others across a long list of metrics: profitability, operating margins, stock price performance, compensation . . .

While these comparisons can be motivating in the Comfort Zone, they can be debilitating in the Stress Center. Unless an entire industry is subject to the same downturn in confidence, those in the Stress Center will invariably come up short. The grass will always be greener elsewhere. Moreover, the farther into the Stress Center an organization falls, the more the disparity in relative prosperity will show. The data will reinforce the hopelessness being experienced.

If leaders want to make a comparison, it should be to only their own most recent performance as measured in very short time frames: today's sales versus yesterday's, for example. When time frames are kept immediate, energy and effort can be focused on goals that are tangible and achievable. They can begin to form a foundation in confidence as clear, specific progress is routinely tracked.

A small improvement in sales or debt costs may not seem like much to celebrate, but in the Stress Center, progress is typically slow and incremental. While easily shattered, trust takes a long time to rebuild. Rather than being discouraged by this, leaders can use daily metrics to objectively demonstrate progress. Moreover, as confidence builds and Horizon Preference expands, daily goals can be easily extended to annual objectives that once again motivate high-performing teams.

3. VOLUNTEER

This final suggestion may seem like one bit of advice too many for leaders in the Stress Center. But hear me out.

Volunteering is typically the last thing crisis leaders think they have time for. All energy and effort, they believe, must be focused on the vulnerability at hand and its consequences. While that may be the case,

I'd offer that few actions boost our own confidence like doing good for someone else. Service demonstrates that we have certainty and control—that we have skills and ability valued by others. Moreover, service with others and for others builds connection, reminding crisis leaders—many of whom express feelings of isolation—that they are not alone.

As leaders plan how they will recharge amid a crisis—something that should be considered well before a storm hits—they should add volunteering to their list of options. As counterintuitive as doing more for others may feel, service can provide a much-needed boost in self-confidence and connectedness.

•

The same principles that apply to business leaders apply to all of us. Since the Stress Center is an inevitable environment, rather than focusing all our energy on avoiding it, we should prepare for it, deliberately seeking out environments of uncertainty and powerlessness to increase our familiarity with them and to develop the skills we will need.

As I close every semester, I encourage my students to take an improv class in the college's theater department—not because I expect them to become great comedians but because it will force them into a short-term, low-risk Stress Center environment and help them gain experience taking control and establishing certainty on the fly. Many Outward Bound programs offer similar opportunities. Finally, I encourage my students to remember that they have been in the Stress Center before and have figured out how to get back to the Comfort Zone. When we are deep in the Stress Center, we tend to forget that.

Which brings me to one final thought: what builds resilience isn't just our repeated experiences in the Stress Center but also the memories we have to remind us that we have successfully recovered, every time.

With that, it's time to relax. Next stop: the Comfort Zone.

SECTION III

The Comfort Zone

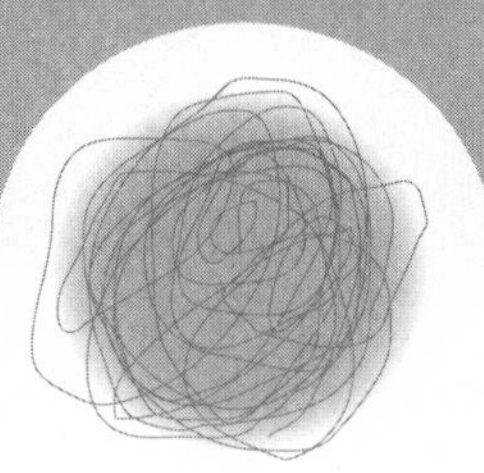

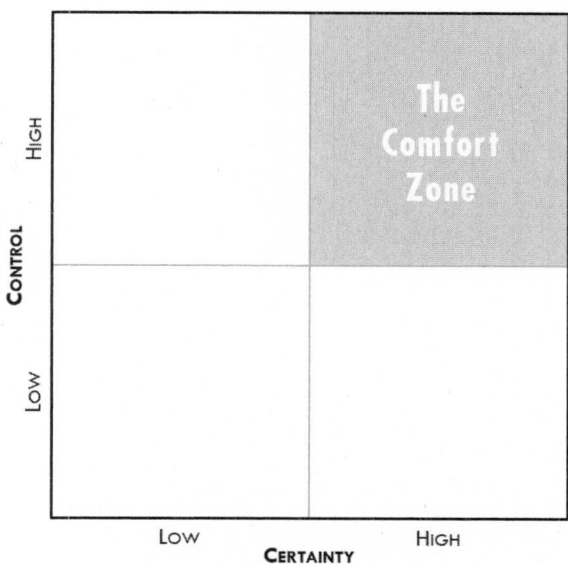

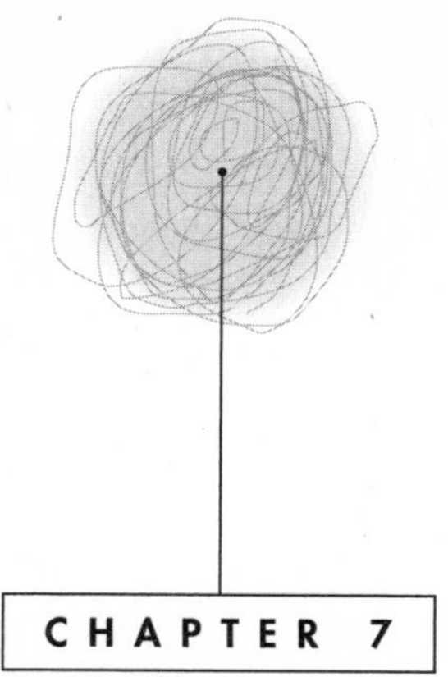

CHAPTER 7

The Comfort Zone and Environments of High Confidence

IN 1965, a Yale undergraduate named Fred Smith wrote a term paper for his economics class in which he laid out the logistical challenges facing firms in the nascent information technology industry. As he explained it, transporting urgently needed computer parts and electronic components was slow and expensive. The airfreight shippers the tech industry relied on to get them their parts the fastest owned few of their own aircraft; the carriers were almost exclusively agents—dependent on commercial passenger airlines that cared more about transporting people than cargo. Because of the system's shortcomings, Smith proposed another option—a system specifically designed to deliver time-sensitive shipments quickly and reliably—that offered far greater certainty and control to suppliers and manufacturers alike.[1]

Smith received an average grade from his professor, but what he outlined in his paper soon became the global delivery and logistics company he founded, now known as FedEx.

When I think about what it looks like to run a business in the upper right box of the Confidence Quadrant—the Comfort Zone—I picture Fred Smith and FedEx really hitting their stride, circa 1995. With the company rapidly approaching $10 billion in revenue and a private fleet of five hundred aircraft, Smith felt certain and in control at the helm. His confidence all but jumps off the page in his letter to shareholders that year:

> After years of aggressively building and carefully refining the world's most far-reaching express distribution infrastructure, FedEx employees, customers and stockholders are well-positioned for future benefits.
>
> Looking ahead, we're convinced that by continuing to strategically reinvest in our network, FedEx can remain the unrivaled leader in the fast-growing global express distribution industry, serving more customers, in more places, more quickly, reliably and cost-effectively.
>
> We call it delivering "The World On Time."[2]

When you look at FedEx's history, you see a living and breathing case study in rising confidence and the impact that rapidly expanding Horizon Preference can have on an industry. Starting with a single hub in Memphis, Tennessee, FedEx began flying a small number of carefully selected domestic routes—to places like Rochester, New York, the headquarters of Xerox—aimed at satisfying the needs of a few customers. By focusing on and controlling the entire shipping process, FedEx delivered not just parts but its promise of reliable overnight delivery. It reduced delays and lowered costs for clients, upending existing expectations in the process. FedEx became synonymous with overnight delivery and became a service that manufacturers and their customers could, and would soon, take for granted.

As consumer confidence took off in the 1980s, FedEx's operations mirrored society's rise out of the Stress Center and into the Comfort Zone. As the company moved up along the Confidence Spectrum, its

Horizon Preference broadened; the Me-Here-Now thinking that naturally characterized the company as a start-up was replaced by more expansive and strategic Us-Everywhere-Forever planning and execution. FedEx's fleet grew, as did the size and reach of its planes. As customer interest broadened, routes expanded globally, first to Canada, then Asia and Europe and, ultimately, the Middle East. Connections and interconnections boomed as the company added hubs in the Philippines and France. So, too, did complexity and interdependence, as the company later added retail consumers to its client list through its acquisition of Kinko's.

When FedEx launched its 1995 slogan "Absolutely, Positively Anytime," it was mirroring back to consumers and businesses the certainty and control everyone at the time felt, not only about the company but also about the world at large. With confidence soaring, we all believed we could get anything we wanted, from anywhere and at any time.

And it wasn't just goods: In the 1990s, global financial markets and international capital flows exploded in volume as Us-Everywhere-Forever thinking transcended the world economy more broadly. Just as high confidence brought "just-in-time" supply-chain management aimed at maximizing business efficiency and minimizing cost to the manufacturing sector, it also led to innovative financial products like securitization. Overnight, credit-card charges from customers in Wisconsin and Maine found their way to Wall Street, where they were bundled together to form enormous loan pools whose slices were then sold to investors from Hong Kong to Oslo. As the twentieth century came to a close, the world was a fast-moving and highly efficient system of interwoven conveyor belts that moved capital and goods just in time from one place to another.

Just as Fred Smith and FedEx benefited from and capitalized on our eager embrace of the Us-Everywhere-Forever Horizon Preference, so did many others. The 1990s are filled with examples: Jeff Bezos, who built Amazon from the ground up; Sandy Weill, who merged banks, insurers, and finance companies to form Citigroup; and Jack Welch, who transformed General Electric into an enormous financial-industrial conglomerate. All became iconic as they masterfully mirrored rapidly rising confidence with aggressive Us-Everywhere-Forever business strategies. Global scale, innovation, extreme efficiency, broad product breadth, and interdependence were hallmarks of successful organizations seizing the day.

Us-Everywhere-Forever Horizon Preference

Whereas low confidence brings our focus inward and erases our willingness to consider significant psychological distance, high confidence propels us in the opposite direction. Feeling increasingly secure, we abandon our timidity and become outgoing and expansive. Socially, geographically, and temporally, we embrace the unfamiliar. We feel emboldened and eagerly take more risks. We book exotic vacations. Businesses excitedly build or borrow manufacturing facilities overseas. Rather than fearing psychological distance, we see it as representing a vast, untapped opportunity. We "go west, young man!"

In extreme abstraction lies unlimited possibility.

Here's why:

Us—With mounting confidence and increasing perceptions of certainty and control comes a desire to connect with others, to broaden our circle. We are more social and inclusive, and more trusting of those who look and act differently. We naturally embrace diversity. In relation to others, we look for what we have in common rather than how we are different. Self-interest is replaced by social generousness—by a "one for all, all for one" mindset in which we believe we can *all* win if we work together. The Comfort Zone is an environment of abundance rather than scarcity, where we celebrate shared, collective success.

Everywhere—In addition to our willingness to branch out and our desire for connection, we also see a safer and more familiar world around us. When we are confident, we explore and travel eagerly and across farther distances. Physical distance is no longer seen as an impediment; we build bridges, lay railways, and launch ships and planes to connect us. With rising confidence, we believe that we can succeed just as easily in distant locations as we can right at home.

One of the classic behaviors of eras of high confidence is exploration. We go where no man has gone before. In the early 1960s, America committed to go to the moon, and more recently, we have seen those at the top—the extremely confident—fascinated by space tourism.

Forever—Finally, amid high confidence we perceive a backdrop of stability—and the more confident we are, the longer we believe that stability will last. In the same way that when we lack confidence, we can't see past today, when we are in the Comfort Zone, we imagine an expansive, forward-focused time horizon. We look ahead, as tomorrow represents endless possibility. As a result, we plan, think, and act strategically—ten-, twenty-, and even fifty-year time frames are common.

At the same time, we had better move fast. With time flying, urgency is the order of the day; if we don't act now, someone else will. The Comfort Zone is filled with FOMO—and that fear of missing out drives our decision-making. So, of course, we are willing to stand in a long line for the next new product at the Apple store and for the midnight premiere of a new movie. We don't intend to wait for our urgent wants to be satisfied.

•

Where low confidence confines us, high confidence liberates us socially, geographically, and temporally. Our psychological horizon is vast. Like Fred Smith and FedEx in 1995, we want to move as quickly as we can to embrace it all. Our world is awash in opportunity. We feel anything is possible.

When we are in the Comfort Zone, we feel relaxed and powerful. The world seems certain. We believe there is no better time to invest and grow a business, and to act on our feelings. We commit to building new factories in new locations, to adding new stores in new markets, and to adding new product lines to serve new customers. Our expansiveness is everywhere in everything.

In fast food, we see the impact of the Comfort Zone as restaurants add new menu items alongside a growing footprint of franchise locations. In retail clothing, we see new designers brought on to service new luxury lines aimed at tapping into an audience of more affluent consumers. Banks merge, adding capabilities and geography to serve more customers in more ways in more places. The focus is growth, growth, and more growth—in products and services, in manufacturing and distribution, in locations and customers.

With a surge in complex networks, we also need better infrastructure to move information, goods, capital, and people faster and more efficiently. The Comfort Zone is all about building and leveraging connections.

Playing Offense and Risk-Taking

If survival in the Stress Center is accomplished by loss avoidance and how well we eliminate vulnerability, success in the Comfort Zone is measured by how well we maximize our gains and how steadily we move farther and farther toward the upper right corner of the Confidence Quadrant. The Comfort Zone is all about playing offense—putting points on the board, booking revenue, adding new locations, and making sure we capitalize on every opportunity, real and imagined. Rather than seeing big, hairy, audacious goals as intimidating, we actively seek them out, with the expectation we will easily outperform those bold objectives. (Moreover, in the Comfort Zone, researchers like Jim Collins publish bestsellers like *Good to Great*, celebrating those who successfully do so.)[3] From organic growth to acquisitions, the Comfort Zone mantra is "Do whatever it takes to win."

With the high certainty and control we feel, we also "know" what to do. No instruction manual is needed. Our only question is: How do we do it faster, more efficiently, and in more places at once? Explosive growth isn't an objective so much as it is simply a required means to the end: Be first. Have enormous scale and unchallenged dominance that leaves others in the dust. And in the Comfort Zone, it is all about reward and recognition. He who has, does, earns, sells the most, wins.

"Success stories," like that of FedEx, quickly become inspirational corporate mythology when we are in the Comfort Zone, too. High-confidence eras are punctuated by magazine cover stories and CEO books filled with tales of bold risks taken and enormous rewards reaped, providing an endless library of playbooks to the era's eager business leaders.

Then there are all the buzzwords—terms like "blitzscaling," the "offense strategy" touted by LinkedIn cofounder Reid Hoffman. He encouraged start-up companies to grow at hyper speed and "take the market by surprise; build a long-term competitive advantage before anyone else; and get the attention of investors as the new market leader."[4] Comfort Zone eras are full of leadership shorthand and MBA case studies that excite our imagination and dare us to seize the day. And if those aren't enough, there are armies of consultants, recruiters, and investment bankers eager to satisfy enthusiastic leaders' need for growth and to capitalize on the energy and excitement of the times. Like shovel sellers in a gold rush, few groups do better in eras of high confidence than those who aid and accelerate the efforts of the most aggressive C-suite executives.

And therein lies Rule Number One for those at the top: bold risk-taking is expected.

Just think about how this mindset might play out as we consider buying a new home. In the Comfort Zone, we assume we have high job stability, with promotions and salary increases ahead. We can't imagine losing our job. With this backdrop, of course, we reach; we buy a bigger home at a higher price, with a bigger mortgage, imagining that our home's value, like our own compensation, will only grow in the future.

In the Comfort Zone, corporate leaders think the same way. They expand aggressively, often using high leverage as they and their lenders imagine record earnings ahead. Comfort Zone eras are filled with Hollywood imagery, all suggesting massive success. We are captivated by storytellers and the promise and possibility they extol. Moreover, we are captivated by those who tell it best. And the farther into the Comfort Zone we rise, the more fanciful and seductive their stories become. Given the vast potential imagined ahead, how can we not take the risk?

Perception Distortion in the Comfort Zone

As much as our risk-taking alignment with confidence may seem obvious, there are some important subtleties that go along with it.

One is the impact perception distortion has on our willingness to take risk. Again, how we *feel* impacts our perception of the world around us. Confident baseball players "see" a bigger and slower-moving ball. Field-goal kickers "see" wider uprights and a lower crossbar. Golfers "see" bigger cups, just as soccer players "see" bigger goals.[5]

With the consistency of these examples, it's not hard to imagine how the same kind of confidence-driven perception distortion can exist off the field, heavily influencing Comfort Zone decision-making in C-suites and corporate boardrooms. If athletes "see" that success can be more easily achieved when they are confident, why wouldn't executives and boards of directors? Why wouldn't they encourage a business to swing for the fences—to borrow more, to expand more aggressively, and to make acquisitions in larger scale and at higher prices?

Then there is the impact of high confidence on scrutiny. The two are inversely related: the better we feel, the less we focus. Feelings of high certainty and high control suggest that we have little to worry about—that we can relax and take it easy. Just like a straight, uncrowded highway on a clear day when we are behind the wheel, the Comfort Zone gives us little reason to pay attention—so we don't. Why would we expend the effort if it is unnecessary?

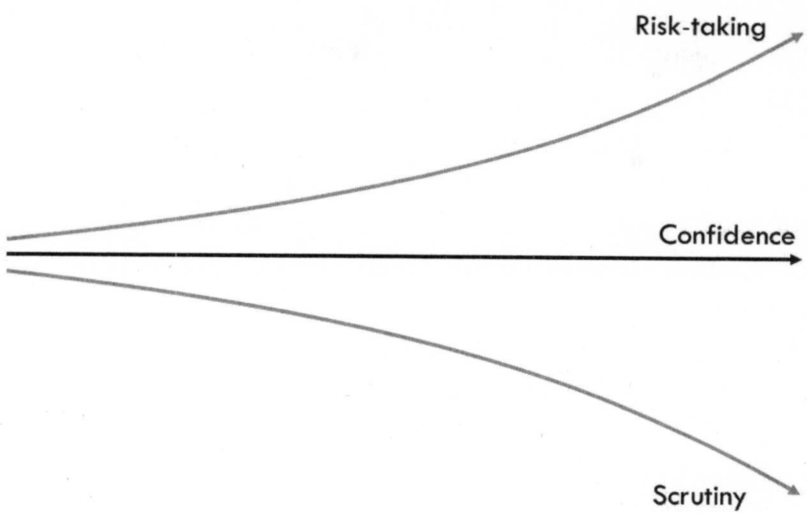

FIGURE 7.1: The impact of changing confidence on risk-taking and scrutiny

The net result is an extraordinary behavioral paradox: In the Comfort Zone, we boldly take our greatest risks, expecting the most favorable outcomes while paying the least attention to the potential dangers. Moreover, the farther we move toward the upper right corner of the Quadrant, the more extreme these behaviors become (Figure 7.1).

Just consider the mania in cryptocurrencies in late 2020. On the strength of rising confidence, investors stampeded into the market, with few understanding what exactly it was they were buying. Captivated by the potential returns they imagined, they eagerly overlooked the risk they were taking. As the 2022 collapse of FTX revealed, investors' due diligence was nonexistent.[6]

Financial history is filled with examples of similar behavior. From lenders extending credit to borrowers with no income and no job at the peak of the housing bubble to mid-nineteenth-century speculators eagerly buying up land in Poyais—a made-up country in Latin America—in the Comfort Zone, we take our biggest risks without batting an eye.[7]

Invulnerability and Mania

Earlier, I suggested that without intervention, our vulnerability in the Stress Center can easily increase. A vicious spiral can take hold in which our self-reinforcing negative feelings and actions push us deeper and deeper into despair. It is as if the plane of the Stress Center is sloped downward toward the lower left corner of the Quadrant.

The same concept holds true for the Comfort Zone, but in reverse. Rather than a vicious spiral, a virtuous spiral can easily develop in which our improving mood and more optimistic actions feed upon themselves. It's as if the Comfort Zone is sloped downward, too—unless interrupted, a virtuous spiral can easily propel us toward the upper right corner of the Quadrant.

After more than twenty years observing this pattern in investor behavior, I no longer view the Confidence Spectrum as a straight, flat line running from the upper right corner of the Comfort Zone to the lower left corner of the Stress Center but as more of an arc, with significant elevation at its midpoint at the center of the Quadrant. From either side of the center, we are naturally drawn toward the extreme. It's as if the two ends of the Confidence Spectrum are highly magnetized; the closer we get to them, the more powerless we are against their pull.

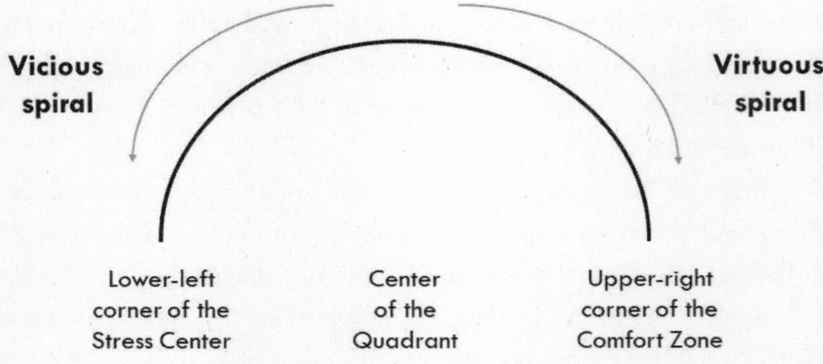

FIGURE 7.2: Virtuous and vicious spirals

Just consider our path out of the Stress Center. Deep in the lower left corner, it feels as though we are at the very bottom of a deep pit. We struggle as we first attempt to climb out; the energy necessary to make even small progress upward seems intense. It is exhausting, and we feel as though we could easily fall backward—be sucked down again, all but collapsing into despair.

That same steep slope also feels present when we leave the Comfort Zone and enter the Stress Center. Unless interrupted, a vicious spiral seems to accelerate, pulling us harder and faster toward the lower left corner of the Quadrant. The panic that we feel, as we approach that corner and our feelings of uncertainty and powerlessness soar, suggests that we race down a Confidence Spectrum whose grade becomes steeper and steeper until we are all but in free fall at the very end of it.

At the other end of the Confidence Spectrum, when we feel things are more and more certain and that we have greater and greater control, we accelerate, too—only rather than tumbling into free fall, it feels as though we are being propelled by an enormous tailwind of success whose increasing intensity moves us faster and harder toward the upper right corner of the Quadrant. It's like a downhill ending in a bike race, where we move with accelerating speed toward the finish line.

This dramatic acceleration in confidence near the upper right corner of the Comfort Zone can be easily observed in the financial markets. It is the natural opposing bookend to panic on the Confidence Spectrum—it's mania. Having experienced several manias over my career, I would describe them as social vortexes; between extreme confidence, jealousy, greed, and the fear of missing out, everyone gets sucked in. Investors can't resist the pull of the upper right corner of the Quadrant.

Nor, I would add, can business leaders. Those same factors—extreme confidence, jealousy, greed, and the fear of missing out—all come together at the top of the business cycle, leading companies to aggressively compete in bidding wars for supersized acquisitions.

While the financial media would suggest that manias occur when investors and business leaders feel invincible, I don't think the adjective fully captures the mood. At the extreme, everyone feels *invulnerable*. They believe no harm can come to them—none. And those feelings are widely shared.

Invulnerability doesn't get discussed much, but it is a much more useful lens than overconfidence through which to view and understand our behavior in the upper reaches of the Comfort Zone. "Overconfidence" suggests that we have too much of something—that we over-believe, especially in our own abilities. In fact, what drives our behavior is our under-beliefs. We underappreciate, and therefore overlook and/or dismiss, any and all threats. We underappreciate the potential downsides to our decision-making. We underappreciate the potential harm we may experience. All this underappreciation is why scrutiny tails off the more confident we become. In a thought-to-be-riskless environment, scrutiny feels like an unnecessary waste of time.

Many decision-making experts suggest that our choices in the upper right corner of the Comfort Zone are irrational. I disagree. When you consider the invulnerability we feel, they are completely reasonable and logical. They perfectly mirror the extreme certainty and control we feel.

Moreover, at our very peak in confidence, we believe those feelings will be permanent. What marks the top—whether for a market, a sports team, or a leader—is the extreme extrapolation of invulnerability. We believe we will stay unscathed forever. Not surprisingly, not only does our accompanying behavior look ridiculous in hindsight, it naturally sets up the precipitous collapse in confidence that follows thereafter.

While they appear unshakeable to the crowd, environments of invulnerability are extremely fragile. Systems and processes are designed around the belief that extreme certainty and control will exist in perpetuity and that nothing will ever go wrong. Everything is hyper-optimized for efficiency. Every safeguard is tossed aside.

When something begins to go wrong, as it inevitably does, and scrutiny then reintensifies, the ensuing collapse exposes the structural hollowness of the situation. With that, environments of invulnerability all but implode, collapsing under their own weight. Too much optimistic abstraction rests on far too little real substance.

The Five Fs of Extreme Confidence

Earlier, I identified five verbs that characterized extreme lows in confidence. For extreme highs, there are five adjectives:

Fantastic—Not only do things feel extraordinarily good in the Comfort Zone, the environment is extremely imaginative. Everything feels highly distanced, if not completely removed, from reality. No idea is too outlandish or too unexplainable to captivate the crowd.

Flashy—From celebrities to cars to fashion, the cultural symbols we embrace in the upper right corner of the Quadrant are ostentatiously attractive. Being bold and beautiful and standing out from others are widely shared goals.

Futuristic—All eyes are on possibility and the vast opportunity ahead. From technology to transportation to media to architecture and design, the focus is on extreme innovation unlike anything we've seen before.

Festive—Peaks in confidence are filled with large, jovial celebrations. There is overflowing abundance, gluttony, and debauchery. A good time is had by all—and, by all means, the more the merrier.

Frenetic—The pace of the upper right corner of the Quadrant is fast and energetic, often in a wild and uncontrolled way. Both extremes of the Confidence Spectrum are fast and furious environments—with one end filled with despair and an intense need for the stability of what was, and the other with unbridled enthusiasm and an insatiable want for what might be.

Which brings me to three bonus F-word adjectives for the upper reaches of the Comfort Zone: **fraudulent**, **fictitious**, and **fake**. Just like the depths of the Stress Center, the upper right corner of the Comfort Zone brings out the con men. With scrutiny all but nonexistent and the jovial crowd believing it is invulnerable, opportunities abound for the unscrupulous to profit.

You'd think we learn, but we don't. Every market mania provides examples. In the 1820s, it was Gregor MacGregor, who charmed the crowd into investing in Poyais. Amid the dot-com bubble, the leadership team at Enron duped investors and regulators with fraudulent accounting practices, a playbook followed more recently by Bernie Madoff and the folks at Wirecard.

And sometimes, at the very peak in manias, the scams are all but in plain sight. Just before the cryptocurrency bubble burst in 2021, investors were falling all over themselves to buy "shitcoins"—digital currencies with little to no value and/or no immediate, discernible purpose.[8]

That these currencies were then among the first to collapse in value after sentiment turned downward is hardly surprising. One thing we see, over and over, is that bubbles burst on a last in, first out (LIFO) basis. Those last to the party are always the first to leave, often violently so. Reckless risk-taking occurs only in the very upper right corner of the Comfort Zone—and once sentiment begins to drop, it then quickly evaporates.

In May 2007, when then-chairman of the Federal Reserve Ben Bernanke said that rising subprime mortgage defaults would not harm the economy, he underappreciated their LIFO significance.[9] "Ninja loans"—mortgages extended to a borrower with little or no attempt by the lender to verify the applicant's ability to repay them—became popular at the very peak of the housing bubble, when lenders and borrowers believed they were invulnerable to a market downturn and that home prices would only go up. Rising subprime mortgage delinquencies were the LIFO indicator that revealed that not only had the housing bubble peaked but, as confidence fell further, payments on less risky mortgages, too, would be jeopardized.

•

The upper right box of the Quadrant lives up to its "Comfort Zone" name; it is where everything feels easy and familiar. Given that backdrop, it is hardly surprising that it represents the best of times. Still, as much as we enjoy the Comfort Zone and strive never to leave it, leaders need to appreciate its inevitable downside. Intense feelings of invulnerability leave us ripe for painful surprises.

To gain a deeper understanding of why that is the case, we will next turn our attention to the impact of confidence on how we think. As you will see, confidence dramatically alters our basic cognitive processes.

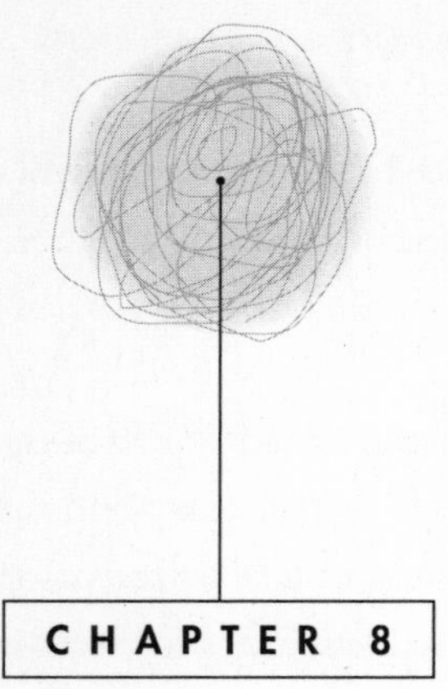

CHAPTER 8

Confidence and Cognitive Ease

To better appreciate why we act and feel the way we do in the Comfort Zone, we need to bust the myth that confidence is a function of how loudly we speak or whether we stand like Wonder Woman. At its core, confidence isn't so much an emotional or physical experience as it is a cognitive one. It is about what is happening in our head: when we are confident, our brain is relaxed.

Put simply, confidence = cognitive ease.

As the term "cognitive ease" suggests, things feel effortless when we are confident. We don't pause and strain as we think about what to do next—next just happens, as does the next event after that. It is as if we are on autopilot, where we know precisely how to handle things. Cognitive ease is what we experience behind the wheel of our car on an empty highway on a bright, sunny day. Afterward, as we pull into the garage, safely back at home, we have no clear recollection of how we got there. Sure, we drove, but we weren't really paying attention to the ride.

Psychologists use the term "fluency" to describe our experience of cognitive ease.[1] I like what the word brings to the conversation: the sense that our actions flow effortlessly when we're in this mental state. When we are fluent in a foreign language, we have an easy command of it. We have certainty and control in what we are saying, so much so that words and phrases come naturally, one right after another. We are no longer translating in real time; we're not thinking about how to conjugate a specific verb or how to make an irregular noun plural. The right words come out of our mouth before we realize we are speaking.

We don't use the term "fluent" to describe business leaders in the Comfort Zone, but we could. With high confidence, their actions appear effortless; they seem to know precisely what to say and to do next. They appear to exhibit cognitive ease at its best in every direction they turn. In environments from analyst calls to board presentations and sales meetings, leaders in the Comfort Zone seem at home as they quickly respond to questions and motivate others as they describe in detail the bright future they see ahead.

That same "at home" feeling captures star athletes on the playing field and entertainers on stage when they're in the Comfort Zone. They don't appear to break a sweat as they command the stadium.

In his book *Thinking, Fast and Slow*, psychologist Daniel Kahneman shares, "When you are in a state of cognitive ease, you are probably in a good mood, like what you see, believe what you hear, trust your intuitions and feel that the current situation is comfortably familiar." Those descriptions certainly capture the C-suite and the stadium when things are going well. Kahneman contrasts this to when we experience cognitive strain. Then, he suggests, "you are more likely to be vigilant and suspicious, invest more effort into what you are doing, feel less comfortable"[2]—which describes those tense board meetings when executives have missed their forecast and stumble as they try to explain why, or when an athlete fumbles the ball, or a performer trips over lyrics she has sung for years.

While he never intended it, both of Kahneman's descriptions fit how we act and feel when we are in the Comfort Zone and the Stress Center, respectively.

Fitting, too, are the labels of "System 1" and "System 2" thinking, coined by dual-process theorists Keith Stanovich and Richard West to describe the two processing systems of the mind, which are also discussed at length by Kahneman.[3]

System 1 is great when the task at hand is simple. It's quick and impulsive; it gets us to our answer efficiently. We use System 1 thinking to count by twos, moving effortlessly from "2, 4, 6, 8" all the way through to "96, 98, 100." On the other hand, we rely on System 2 thinking to count by seventeens. System 2 is deliberate, focused, labored, and slow. It provides the critical problem-solving tool we need when things don't make sense to us. System 2 is the all-wheel drive of our brain; we resort to it and put it in gear only when we are stuck.

Counting by seventeens kicks our brain into this all-wheel drive. We must tread carefully, moving slowly as we first visualize a piece of paper with two written "17"s stacked one atop the other and then use compound addition. We must first add seven and seven in the ones column to make fourteen, then remember to carry the one and add it to the other two ones in the tens column to come up with thirty-four as the answer. And that is just to arrive at the first summation!

In my class, I challenge pairs of students to pass a volleyball back and forth as quickly as they can as they count first by twos. Students smile and question whether they're really in a college class as the ball and the count move quickly. The exercise seems silly. The physical and cognitive effort are minimal with System 1 clearly in charge.

Then, when they are feeling confident, I ask them to repeat the ball toss, only this time counting by seventeens. The change in speed and effort is immediate. While the ball moves quickly back and forth as students count by twos using System 1 thinking, it remains painfully still as students kick their brains into System 2, some visibly sweating as they struggle to calculate thirty-four, fifty-one, then sixty-eight and eighty-five under pressure. Sometimes, students get so focused on the math, they forget to throw or catch the ball. Within moments, they realize that multitasking is a cognitive impossibility—and why texting and driving is such a toxic combination. As much as we may believe otherwise, when System 2 is triggered, we can focus only on one thing at a time.

When we are confident and in the Comfort Zone, we rely on our automatic and effortless System 1 thinking. Because we experience cognitive ease, there is no reason for us to have to think—and because our brain is inherently energy efficient (a.k.a. lazy), we don't. This state contrasts with the Stress Center, where our feelings of vulnerability demand problem-solving and our far slower and energy-zapping System 2 is what's thinking. Faced with uncertainty and powerlessness, we feel a need to respond. Our System 2 thinking helps us figure out what that response should be.

At the risk of oversimplification, I would offer that when overlaid on the full spectrum of confidence, our use of System 1 and System 2 thinking looks something like Figure 8.1.

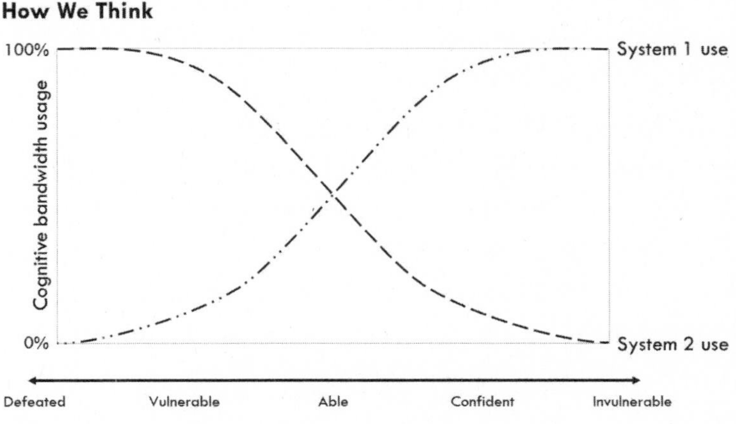

FIGURE 8.1: The impact of changing confidence on cognitive processing

The x-axis in this figure measures our relative confidence from low to high (left to right), while the y-axis measures how much of our cognitive bandwidth is being used by System 1 and System 2. Moving from left to right, you see that as our confidence increases, we require less and less System 2 thinking, and with less to worry about, System 1 takes over. It's as if the two systems operate on a pair of dimmer switches where when one rises, the other naturally declines.

When we feel vulnerable, as we do while first learning to ride a bike, we rely on System 2 thinking. We are exhausted as we struggle to maintain our balance while simultaneously paying attention to the road ahead. With so many things to focus on at once, we feel overwhelmed. Eventually, though, we experience an "Aha!" moment. We figure it out, gaining the fluency I described earlier. We go from experiencing intense cognitive strain and a heavy dependence on System 2 thinking to achieving cognitive ease and using System 1, often in a flash. We triumphantly shout, "I figured it out!" when we realize we no longer must think about balancing on our bicycle. From that point forward, unless something bad happens, we rely almost exclusively on System 1 while riding a bike.

While the time frame may be longer or shorter, learning new skills takes us on a journey from the left to the right side of Figure 8.1. Success reflects our migration from System 2 to System 1 thinking, with "Aha!" moments marking the tipping point where System 1 suddenly takes over.

The process works in the other direction (moving right to left), too, as we lose confidence. We experienced that phenomenon in March 2020 with the onset of COVID. Up until that point, with the outbreak "contained" within China, we used System 1 thinking to address the disease. We felt we had little to worry about, so we relied on our quick, lazy thinking to assess the situation. Then, when the outbreak suddenly felt real, we were forced to immediately focus and switch over to System 2 thinking. In a flash, we became overwhelmed by all the perilous possibilities that might arise and exhausted as we thought about them all; something as mundane as a trip to the grocery store suddenly felt as complicated as disarming a bomb. We went from underthinking COVID one moment to overthinking it the next. Underlying our panic was cognitive overload. Our brains couldn't process fast enough the increasing uncertainty and powerlessness we were experiencing.

When we think about our Five F responses to extreme low confidence, I think it is helpful to appreciate the overloaded cognitive backdrop to those actions. Our simplistic, highly emotional, and impulsive responses suggest that we reach a point where, after exhausting all of our System 2 ability, we suddenly shift back to System 1. Unable to come up with a plan, we resort to our most basic, primal behavioral processes.

Leveraging Cognitive Ease in Business

I believe that what truly defines tipping points is the sudden shift in our cognitive processing. As our confidence rises, our "Aha!" moments indicate that System 1 has taken charge from System 2—that intense focus is no longer required. And as our confidence drops, our "Oh, crap!" moments mark the reverse. With our feelings of certainty and control evaporating, we have no choice but to focus. We need System 2 to help us figure things out. When these tipping points happen, and the processing shift they entail happens simultaneously among large groups of people at once, the impact on behavior and decision-making can be dramatic.

Given this, business leaders can improve their results by paying closer attention to the cognitive processing of customers and employees. The following are just a few ideas for how.

ACCELERATING FAMILIARITY

I don't think it is a coincidence that the S-shaped trajectory of System 1 usage shown in Figure 8.1 mirrors the S-curve growth pattern most successful businesses experience. Both reflect the impact of rising confidence and the relative ease of doing things.

Like children learning to ride a bike, most new business ventures struggle at first to find their balance. Customers don't understand the product, or why they'd use it in the first place. Only after gaining acceptance and achieving cognitive ease can a business see its growth take off. As the customer base grows and more of that base becomes fluent in the product, sales explode. It becomes easier to sell more to more people than ever before, with sales ultimately peaking at a level that reflects the peak confidence of the crowd.

We witnessed this trajectory with the introduction of the iPhone. Apple experienced an unprecedented S-curve in growth. Worldwide adoption occurred all but overnight.[4] When people talk about the iPhone's highly intuitive interface, what they are describing is a product that enables the user to move almost instantaneously from System 2 to System 1 thinking. Cognitive ease was near immediate.

Given the importance of cognitive ease to confidence and success, it is striking to see how few organizations focus on it. Especially at the early stages of a business, cognitive ease needs to be front and center. If investors are going to provide capital and customers are going to buy a new product, both groups must feel at ease; they must first understand what is being sold. For leaders, this means marketing materials and product functionality must be System 1–centric. Borrowing again from Kahneman, to be successful, the customer experience must feel familiar, true, good, and effortless.[5]

For many inventors and entrepreneurs, the idea that their product must first feel familiar seems like an unnecessary speed bump, if not an outright contradiction. To them, innovation means bringing something deliberately new and different to market; they believe it's the novelty that matters. In fact, many pioneers go out of their way to withhold critical information, providing scant details about their new product to prospective customers, investors, and lenders for fear they will give potential competitors an edge. Boosting familiarity feels like the last thing they want to encourage.

Yet, consider how we typically introduce a friend to someone new. Immediately beforehand, we whisper in our friend's ear that the person is "just like" someone else they know well, or that the person shares our friend's career or interest in a hobby or sport. We deliberately associate the new, psychologically distant stranger with someone in our friend's closest circle or try to find something the two share in common. That clear, simple context speeds the introduction because the new person immediately feels somehow familiar. We do the same thing when we travel: we contextualize a new city in relation to those we already know. At the core of familiarity—and those people, places, and concepts that are psychologically close to us—is cognitive ease and our ability to use System 1 thinking in engaging with them.

The same holds true with new products and services. Acceptance begins with identifying what exists in common with other well-known items and broadening out from there. Whether one is attempting to establish confidence in a person, place, or thing, familiarity is a vital beachhead.

Consider the very first automobiles. Cars were first called "horseless carriages" for a reason; they were designed to feel like a familiar experience for the driver. It was only with time that the carriage itself was transformed from the old-school horse-and-buggy style seen in the 1800s to the futuristic cars on the road today. A similar design evolution took place as keyboards morphed from manual typewriters to electric typewriters to computer desktops. Mass adoption required familiarity and new users' ability to quickly become fluent in new technology. Just imagine how difficult it would have been for Apple to introduce the iPhone, with its broad functionality, had it not introduced the single-purpose iPod first. Because customers were already fluent in the iPod operating platform, it was easy for them to quickly figure out how to make calls, take pictures, and access the internet on the new device. The iPhone's highly intuitive functionality enabled users to keep using System 1 when they made the jump. They felt right at home.

There are additional benefits to familiarity, too. When customers can use System 1 thinking, new products and services feel true and good. We are less suspicious of them. This is an often-overlooked aspect of personal introductions and why those moments are so important and powerful. When we introduce a stranger, we signal that whoever it is can and should be trusted.

When we have successfully established familiarity and trust, conversations feel effortless for all involved. Vulnerability and System 2 thinking are replaced by confidence, cognitive ease, and System 1 thinking. Within moments, everyone is in the Comfort Zone. System 1 provides a cognitive seal of approval that then serves as a tailwind to broader acceptance.

If you look at the most successful businesses of this economic cycle—companies like Apple, Amazon, Facebook, and Netflix—what they have in common is that they enabled their users to immediately use System 1 thinking to interact with them. Their platforms were focused on providing cognitive ease wherever possible.

KEEPING IT SIMPLE

When businesses talk about customer effort, they often associate it with hard or complicated physical exertion. They think in terms of the number of clicks or assembly steps, processes that require us to move or to do something. While making those routines more efficient is helpful, companies too often overlook that the customer effort that matters most is cognitive—that if we are successful in managing it, others can feel confident and use System 1 thinking with a product.

Think of it this way: I can try to sell you a detailed, step-by-step solution for what to do in the event your clothes catch on fire, or I can show you how to "stop, drop, and roll." When your clothes are on fire, you don't have time to think through the details of fire suppression; it's much easier to remember the catchily named process that has three simple steps. Given a choice, that's the strategy you pick.

If this feels like I'm saying businesses must dumb things down, the answer is yes and no.

When we are stressed and relying heavily on System 2 thinking—as we naturally do when confronted with anything new—making things easier to understand, "dumbing things down," provides cognitive relief. And this is even more important in a crisis. Simplicity matters. From "stop, drop, and roll" to "ABCs of first aid" (airway, breathing, and circulation), emergency training is focused on fostering cognitive ease.

Experts know that encouraging us to sing "Stayin' Alive" if we are called upon to perform CPR makes it more likely we will perform the procedure correctly. "One hundred and three compressions per minute" isn't memorable, let alone anything we will be certain of without a metronome.[6]

ELIMINATING ABSTRACTION

Cognitive ease, though, goes beyond merely reducing complexity. It is about eliminating abstraction—making things absolute and, at the same time, intensely familiar. Whatever it is must feel true and real to us. Things must be concrete. We must remove hypotheticality.

In a crisis, EMTs do this immediately as they measure vital signs—pulse rate, temperature, respiration rate, and blood pressure. They obtain objective and necessary data that will inform their next action. Vital signs and medical-alert bracelets are how unconscious patients introduce themselves. They enable a first responder to quickly move a struggling patient with an unknown condition into a familiar category. Doctors recognize the issue; they have met the condition before. Vital signs help establish certainty.

While we immediately appreciate the need to eliminate uncertainty in the context of an EMT and a new patient, we forget that the same need applies to businesses when introducing new products.

And therein lies the rub for innovators. When bringing something new to market, many are captivated by the possibility. They want others to be just as excited about what a new product might do and to extol the potential that exists. Possibility excites the already confident. But for those in the Stress Center, it represents just more uncertainty. As a result, abstractness gets discounted in the best case, and dismissed outright in the worst, by a suspicious audience.

This is why prototypes, beta tests, and the proof-of-concept process are so important to confidence building. They help organizations eliminate the hypothetical from new ideas. Prototypes are tangible, "real" versions of a product (albeit not a fully functional version), while beta tests and the proof-of-concept process aim to demonstrate obvious feasibility. These efforts have the most success when they provide cognitive ease—when they eliminate abstraction and those involved see "*real* potential" for a project. Look up the television series *Shark Tank* and you can see this dynamic unfold as potential investors press aspiring entrepreneurs to be highly specific about the distinctive features of the products and services they are hawking.

Architectural firms go even further. They spend millions of dollars every year building detailed physical models of their projects so their clients can *see* what they are buying. Builders do much the same with model homes. Translating an abstract product into something that can be perceived—seen, heard, felt, smelled, tasted—is a critical step toward building confidence. Perception eliminates the hypothetical and provides context. It's why everything from deli meat to children's dolls is sold in clear containers; why perfume ads often come with a scratch-and-sniff sticker; and why car companies obsess over the sound a car door makes when it is shut. Manufacturers know that our perceptions matter—that we have a vast mental library of perception experiences that we use when we evaluate anything new. When we can use our senses, things seem real—even abstract concepts like car safety. Psychoacoustic experts know that engineering the right sound of a car door closing is their first opportunity "to make buyers feel the car's quality, craftsmanship, and safety and to justify a premium price tag."[7]

Whether it is for a building or a car door, modeling enables customers to know exactly where a new product fits in their mental library. When successful, it provides cognitive ease that speeds their acceptance and, in turn, the sales process.

Cognitive Ease Isn't Just for Start-Ups

It is easy to appreciate why eliminating abstraction and focusing on achieving cognitive ease make sense when launching and selling new products. But the introductory phase of a product isn't the only time when cognitive ease breeds confidence and brings customers into the Comfort Zone. It happens routinely in all facets of our lives. Well-trained emergency room personnel know that eliminating abstraction and creating familiarity are critical aspects of the job; they help lower patient anxiety. The same approach is true for other first responders—firefighters, ambulance drivers, and police officers do the same. At its core, crisis management is all about eliminating uncertainty and powerlessness. Reducing cognitive strain and helping others move from System 2 to System 1 thinking is a big part of that.

Sadly, few businesses see the parallels in their own operations. They miss that during recessions—and other moments when customer confidence is low—cognitive strain is a given. Not only do they miss out on opportunities to relate more effectively with their customers, they also unknowingly shoot themselves in the foot.

Imagine you were an executive of a fast-food chain at the beginning of March 2020. What if, amid the ensuing panic, you sought to make your restaurants a Comfort Zone for your customers—a place where they experienced certainty and control every time? What if you rethought your product offering and marketing strategy to better tailor them to customers' collapsing confidence and extreme System 2 thinking? Beyond an emphasis on curbside take out and delivery service, what else could you have done differently to better serve your customers by providing them with greater cognitive ease?

Well, you might have emphasized simple, "bundled" offerings of your most popular products. Picking a "Number 3" is far less complicated for a customer than choosing each of the meal's component parts separately.

You also could have halted new product offerings and told your team to bring longtime crowd favorites back to the menu. Novelty requires System 2 thinking. Selling nostalgia—a.k.a. selling intense familiarity—is a much safer bet when consumer confidence is low and everything around us already feels violently new. And in terms of marketing, you could have pulled anything that emphasized innovation and replaced it with well-loved images, icons, and messages from the past. You could have thought about how to make your offering feel more like comfort food to your customers.

At the same time, as CEO, you could have turned more decision-making over to those on the ground—to local operators and employees. Rather than headquarters leading a centralized response, you could have empowered those closest to the customer. From their successes and, as important, their failures, you could have learned the best practices for how to handle the new day-to-day operations of your business. You could have followed the ad hoc continuous-improvement model developed by healthcare workers, who shared in real time on social media and in group chats what was and wasn't working as they confronted the outbreak. They were at the forefront of establishing new norms for certainty and control for themselves and their patients. Much of what has become routine in handling COVID cases was crowdsourced. The most effective solutions rose from the bottom up.

Finally, you could have scaled back your menu, making it easier for team members to deliver meals more quickly to customers. We naturally become more impatient and irritable when we are under cognitive strain. Helping your team serve clients faster helps everyone when confidence is low.

With your clients in Me-Here-Now mode, desperately seeking cognitive ease, any of these solutions would have helped you meet your customers where they were.

In the wake of the housing crisis, Marie Kondo and her book publishers made a fortune doing just that. While her mission is couched in terms of "tidying things up," Kondo is in the business of transforming her readers' homes from Stress Centers to Comfort Zones by helping them throw out anything that doesn't "spark joy" and, in turn, gain greater certainty and control.[8]

Companies like the Container Store do the same. While we don't explicitly think of it this way, we purchase bins, baskets, and boxes to store similar stuff in the same place because they enable us to use System 1, rather than System 2, thinking.

If you pause to think about it, there are many businesses that, like emergency room teams, are really in the day-to-day business of providing cognitive ease to their customers. If clients don't have confidence, they won't buy.

Then there are those moments of service disruption, product failure, and other low customer confidence. Here, too, businesses forget to appreciate and to adapt to the cognitive strain and System 2 thinking that accompany these moments. Some organizations even compound the problem, believing that if they speak ambiguously or offer lengthy explanations, they can divert attention and accountability. They don't realize that by demanding even more System 2 thinking from their audience, they are adding to the stress and irritability of their clients. They overlook that at the core of trust is cognitive ease.

No matter the reason, when we are in the Stress Center and lack confidence, we experience cognitive strain. We have no choice but to use our exhausting System 2 thinking. Those individuals and organizations that can align best with our Me-Here-Now preferences and our need for simplicity have an enormous competitive advantage, especially when they help us feel their products are familiar, good, true, and effortless.

Overthinking, Underthinking, and the Perils of Cognitive Processing

When we are in the Stress Center, not only must we rely on System 2 thinking, often we can overthink things because of it. Awash in uncertainty and feeling powerless, we can easily imagine a long list of "what if?" concerns. Moreover, with time seeming to move very slowly in these moments, the environment is especially ripe for protracted, abstract thought. If you've ever awaited a major diagnosis, you've likely experienced this firsthand. Endless nights are filled wondering as every unexpected ache or pain sends you down a rabbit hole of worry after consulting "Dr. Google." We catastrophize.

This same overthinking phenomenon exists in the workplace. In the aftermath of a major merger, as employees wonder what it means for them individually, employee email messages and water cooler conversations are filled with "what if?" discussions. The more managers can eliminate abstraction (speculation) and provide concrete information (specifics), the sooner they can reduce the natural overthinking that goes on in the Stress Center.

At the other end of the Confidence Spectrum, there is an equivalent corporate danger, albeit one that gets far less attention: underthinking. When confidence is especially high and the workplace is awash in System 1 thinking, even major risks get but a cursory review. We experience grandiose thinking. And it is worth highlighting that in the upper right corner of the Comfort Zone, what companies are thinking least about are abstract concepts that, in a lower-confidence environment, would be subject to intense skepticism, deliberation, and investigation.

As investor confidence was cresting in early 2021, it was striking to see insatiable demand for extreme abstraction paired with extreme System 1 thinking. From special purpose acquisition companies (SPACs), whose specific line of business was still to be determined, to cryptocurrencies to NFTs to Web3 and the metaverse, what investors wanted most was things that were all but impossible to explain. Investors were plowing cash into dreams—opportunities at the far reaches of psychological distance, in time, in place, and in familiarity.[9]

Not long thereafter, many of these investments lost 90 percent of their value, with some quickly going bankrupt.

A similar phenomenon occurred at the peak of the dot-com bubble. Then, too, extreme cognitive ease and impulsive System 1 thinking were the order of the day—for both investors and corporate executives. Moreover, the peer pressure to play along was intense; those who resisted were labeled "too old" or "too dumb" to understand. In most cases, they were neither. By slowing down and applying System 2 thinking to the abstraction others were racing into, the doubters accurately concluded that the emperor had no clothes.

While this may seem obvious after the fact, in real time, the intense speed of decision-making and the obvious extreme use of System 1 thinking were warning signs in plain sight that were overlooked. The same was true at the opposite end of the Confidence Spectrum, in March 2020. The overthinking in response to the extreme uncertainty and powerlessness people were feeling was in everything. Americans' use of System 2 thinking was on overload.

•

When we think about confidence, we associate it with action and our many outward expressions of mood. We rarely consider what is happening inside the mind and confidence's connection to cognitive processing. When we do, not only can we improve the effectiveness of our own communication and marketing, we can gain critical insights into how we and others feel. Our cognitive processing, our confidence level, and our Horizon Preference exist in equilibrium. When we can identify one of these three elements, we can quickly deduce the other two.

In the next chapter, we will look at better practices for operating in the Comfort Zone. As you will see, there are steps we can take to maximize our success there and, as important, to preserve it, too.

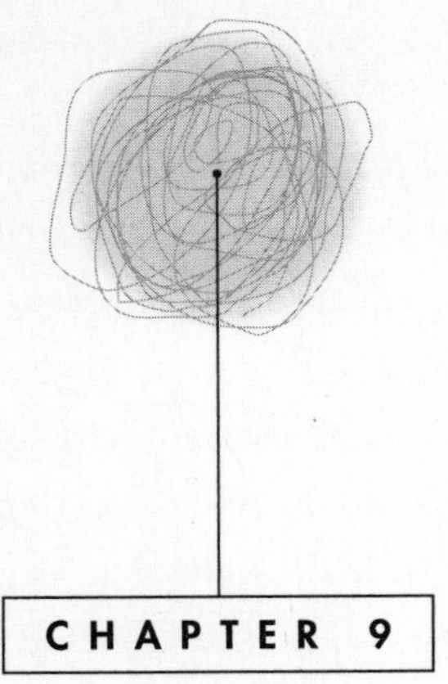

CHAPTER 9

Better Practices in the Comfort Zone

For most of us, the Comfort Zone lives up to its name. It's an environment of certainty and control where we feel relaxed and can thrive. It is where our training and experience feel most familiar and reliable. It's where we feel fully prepared and ready to go.

If we're business leaders, the Comfort Zone is where we bring all those business school cases we worked through, detailing how to successfully navigate complex, high-growth strategies. It's where we bring our years of on-the-job experience, the memories of what we did well, what we did poorly, and what we will do differently to make sure we don't fail again. It's where we bring all those executive memoirs that tell tales of how high confidence was harnessed to great advantage. We're like star athletes heading to the Super Bowl stadium and rock stars to Madison Square Garden. We have all the playbooks and set lists we need rolled into one. The Comfort Zone is the moment we have been waiting for, where all our hard work and effort will finally pay off.

But how we arrive in the Comfort Zone matters. If it is new to us—our first time in the ring—we are energized by it. It feels like a world of limitless opportunity. Untethered by doubt and feeling as though we are at last in control, we are ready to run and run hard.

If, on the other hand, we are an incumbent leader who has worked exhaustively to successfully guide an organization through an economic downturn or a crisis, entry into the Comfort Zone comes with a sense of relief. We feel as if we've fought a strong outgoing tide and have finally made it back to solid ground. At last, things feel familiar again. We have restored certainty and control. There is a tremendous sense of accomplishment and pride, in ourselves and in our team. We have finished a marathon and it is time for a well-earned victory lap. We made it!

Ironically, the Comfort Zone is where many established leaders and businesses end up getting lapped. As they breathe a sigh of relief that calm has been restored at last, they fail to appreciate that a new race has begun. With rising confidence comes a broader cultural need for speed and innovation. Many established leaders aren't prepared for that dramatic shift in preferences. While they want to celebrate a return to normal, the crowd has moved on. It wants novelty. Moreover, established leaders are overconfident that as battle-worn, experienced tortoises, they can outlast and outrun the young, nimble hares who suddenly seem to appear in large numbers out of nowhere.

"What do they know?" the tortoises ask.

The reality is that these established leaders and organizations can rarely outrun the hares. While their experienced, well-tested counterparts seek refuge in the Comfort Zone, those inexperienced new hares have a huge advantage. They bring to the table a brashness and a novelty that a now-confident crowd craves. They aren't bogged down by legacy.

Just look at the auto industry and the rise of electric vehicles (EVs). In the wake of the 2008 financial crisis, established car companies spent years working to restore confidence. When Mary Barra took over as CEO of General Motors (GM) in 2015, it was described as a "giant in decline." She was its fifth CEO in six years. For her, bringing GM into the Comfort Zone meant fixing the mistakes of the past. In her first year on the job, she had to deal with the company's largest product recall ever.[1]

Meanwhile, over at Tesla, an entire new generation of cars was taking hold. As weary, Me-Here-Now GM shareholders demanded specifics and clear tactical plans from Mary Barra, extremely confident, Us-Everywhere-Forever investors flooded Tesla with capital on the wild abstraction sold by Elon Musk. The precise nuts and bolts of large-scale car manufacturing that GM worked to deliver on lacked the sizzle of Musk's audacious cars of tomorrow. Tesla might as well have been called "Unlimited Possibility, Inc." given the potential that investors and customers saw in it. It comes as no surprise that Musk also positioned himself at the center of advances in space travel, solar energy, and cryptocurrencies; it simply speaks to his ability to intuitively grasp the crowd's clear desire for futuristic abstraction in the Comfort Zone and to capitalize on it. In a world awash in System 1 thinking, it was finally his time to shine.

As hard as GM worked to chase Tesla into the future of EVs, it faced an enormous confidence-related headwind. While Musk could do no wrong—with Tesla's stock price tripling in the three months following its widely ridiculed 2019 cybertruck launch—Barra and her team at GM had to contend with intense System 2 scrutiny.[2] For GM, EVs represented a radical shift from its past—a shift few believed would succeed. As I shared earlier, we struggle to believe organizations can successfully play defense and offense simultaneously, especially when they are of the size and scale of General Motors and the offense necessary to succeed represents such a radical departure from their reputation.

It's easy to single out Mary Barra and General Motors and the challenges they faced in competing head-to-head with Tesla. But they are hardly alone in business history. Comfort Zone eras are filled with David and Goliath examples, wherein longstanding incumbents go up against highly appealing, fast-moving, innovation-touting upstarts. Netflix, Airbnb, Uber, and other popular disruptive start-ups from the most recent economic cycle fit into a long history of Davids who took on well-entrenched Goliaths.

In the 1990s, the major, established U.S. financial institutions faced similar challenges as high-growth, "pure play," "monoline" upstarts like MBNA (in credit cards) and Countrywide (in mortgages) became crowd favorites at their expense. Just as with Tesla and EVs, these start-ups were touted as having distinct advantages because of their use of new, highly innovative technology. They weren't beholden to legacy systems or cultures. And we've seen the same behavioral pattern more recently with a wave of "fintech" companies.

But rapidly growing start-ups aren't the only new competitors in the Comfort Zone. The environment is also a breeding ground for dramatic industry consolidation. Here, companies leverage the crowd's optimism for growth, easily attracting capital for large-scale "roll-up" strategies in which individual members of a highly fragmented industry are quickly acquired, one on top of the next, forming massive enterprises. Businesses buy revenue and then slash expenses, using the mergers and acquisitions (M & A) market to grow their bottom line far faster than organic growth would ever allow. Rather than receiving praise for their innovation, acquiring companies are exalted as experts in consolidation—able to wring out every last penny of expense and quickly integrate disparate systems before they repeat the process at even greater scale.

In the 1990s, under the leadership of Hugh McColl Jr., North Carolina National Bank did just that—merging with one bank after another until it created the nationwide franchise we now know as Bank of America.[3]

Wayne Huizenga made a career of rolling up businesses. After buying up independent garbage-hauling companies to form Waste Management, he went on to create the movie-rental giant Blockbuster Video and then AutoNation, the country's largest car dealer.[4] When confidence is high and capital is freely available, those who can demonstrate success in effectively integrating businesses can form giants overnight.

Other businesses, like FedEx, deploy aggressive geographic expansion strategies in the Comfort Zone, using organic internal growth and/or leveraging the interest (and capital) of eager franchisees.

In all cases, the business objective in the Comfort Zone is clear: go big or go home. "Innovate," "merge," "acquire," "expand"—when you look at the verbs contained in Comfort Zone–era press releases, they all express the same goal: get big fast.

Rising Confidence Boosts All Boats

For Comfort Zone business leaders, then, the question isn't if but *how* they intend to accomplish this goal. They can't rest on their laurels. Yet that is exactly what M & A data and other measures of corporate activity suggest happens when it comes to large, established corporations: they wait far too long to act. They give their start-up competitors an especially long head start and then scramble to catch up. Worse, they then overcompensate for their belated start, taking on far too much risk just as the confidence cycle is about to turn downward. Unknowingly, they act like retail investors, who watch others make mountains of money before they act.

What these leaders miss is that there are enormous competitive advantages to acting sooner rather than later in the Comfort Zone.

THE UNNOTICED PERKS OF THE COMFORT ZONE

Earlier, I highlighted the many challenges businesses naturally encounter when operating in the Stress Center. Low confidence creates a strong headwind to growth. In the Comfort Zone, the direction of the wind reverses. With confidence and a migration from System 2 to System 1 thinking comes natural acceleration.

For example, when consumer confidence is rising, customers don't need to be sold. Thanks to improving cognitive ease, they have more bandwidth, leading them to buy faster while asking fewer questions. Customers are eager for what might be. All those customers who brought chairs, sleeping bags, and backpacks full of camping supplies to Apple stores ahead of iPhone launches wanted one thing: their new phone sooner than anyone else, no questions asked.[5] In the Comfort Zone, with customers eager for innovation and novelty, prototypes and proof-of-concept processes feel like—and in many cases are—unnecessary speed bumps to getting new products out the door.

There are other Comfort Zone benefits that accelerate the speed and volume of sales, too. Confident lenders provide more credit at lower rates and on looser terms—all while doing less due diligence. The supply of credit naturally rises with confidence; it is highly confidence elastic. Financing higher growth with higher leverage is never easier than in the Comfort Zone.

Then there's the supply of equity capital more broadly. It, too, is especially abundant in the Comfort Zone, particularly for those businesses offering limitless possibility. High-growth start-ups and innovative technology firms become crowd favorites in Comfort Zone eras. Moreover, because stock valuations mirror investor sentiment, the more confidence shareholders have in a business, the higher the stock price. As a result, high-confidence eras enable corporations of all shapes and sizes to access additional equity capital with the least dilution to existing shareholders. Comfort Zone eras are when founder wealth creation is often immediate and immense.

Confident suppliers, too, offer breaks to businesses, often partnering to maintain key positioning. Like investors, they don't want to miss out on even greater opportunities in the future.

Then comes the sea of benefits that flow from confident policymakers to businesses. From state and local tax incentives for business investment to reduced regulatory oversight, there are big breaks for businesses that come with Comfort Zone eras.

Consider the 1990s: Rising global confidence brought with it the integration of the eurozone and an era of extraordinary bipartisanship in Washington. Political centrism and compromise were front and center. So, too, were pro-business enthusiasm and business deregulation. Rules and regulations that were once thought to be nonnegotiable, like the

Depression-era policies that separated banks from brokerage firms, became seen as speed bumps hindering the pace of economic growth. Many were tossed aside as unwieldy and unnecessary. Monopolistic mergers and acquisitions faced little regulatory pushback, too, as organizations exploded in scale. Whether Republicans or Democrats were in charge, it was a time of high economic growth and strong financial markets.

Finally, there are the unappreciated cultural and social tailwinds that accompany Comfort Zone eras. There is greater harmony in the workplace and in the world more broadly, fostered by feelings of abundance and generosity. Feeling less vulnerable and less stressed, we are less violent, too. On their own, these factors may not seem significant, but they enable greater speed and intensity of investment and growth. If lows in confidence are marked by stacked vulnerabilities and a sense that there is sand in the engine that must be eliminated grain by grain, highs are marked by the reverse—a world that feels like a well-oiled machine.

As a result, for Comfort Zone business leaders, the tailwinds are strong, the seas are calm, and everyone wants to climb aboard a ship that all but steers itself at high speed as it travels from one exciting port to another.

Not surprisingly, Comfort Zone eras are environments where we commit to go to places like the moon and explore the far reaches of the universe. With our System 1 thinking in overdrive, we believe we can understand those people, places, and things that are most psychologically distant to us. The same is true with respect to time: the Comfort Zone is where we are naturally futuristic. We make plans filled with bold milestones that we won't celebrate for decades.

Amid the Comfort Zone, rather than demanding simplicity, we embrace complexity, recognizing that it is a necessary means to achieving our goal. Doing more—with more products delivered to more people in more places at once—is a requirement. We all but clamor for a company like FedEx to help make it happen. Again, between our confidence and the strong abstract processing skills that go along with it, we believe we can handle it all. We believe we *all* can be the next Fred Smith.

FOSTERING THE SPIRIT OF ENTREPRENEURSHIP

What business history shows over and over is that the Davids who act more quickly in the Comfort Zone reap enormous benefits in comparison to the Goliaths. If there is one vital "better practice" for leaders in the Comfort Zone, then, it is to be more entrepreneurial—to move faster and take more risks sooner. Leaders must avoid being underconfident. They must commit to pressing harder on the accelerator *before* the roadway appears clear and straight ahead. They must encourage those inside their organizations who want to innovate and expand; to lead, not follow, their industry peers.

Counterintuitively, for some companies, this means getting out of the way and giving high-potential, fast-growing business units the opportunity to run at full speed on their own, unencumbered by what is typically a slower-moving corporate culture.

Richmond, Virginia–based Signet Bank did just that in 1994, spinning off its rapidly growing credit card business. Over the next six years, the share price of what is now Capital One Financial Corporation rose thirteenfold! The remaining slower-growing regional bank then became an attractive takeover target that was acquired three years later at a substantial premium by First Union as part of that bank's national roll-up strategy. (First Union ultimately became part of Wells Fargo when the latter acquired Wachovia Corporation in the depths of the 2008 banking crisis.)[6]

In the Comfort Zone, few CEOs have the willingness that Signet CEO and chairman Robert Freeman had to carve up their organizations in order to maximize shareholder value. In fact, most leaders take the opposite tack, aggressively buying up bigger and bigger businesses at higher and higher prices. But more business leaders should follow Freeman's lead, especially because the Comfort Zone favors sellers far more than buyers. When confidence is high, demand always feels like it is outpacing supply. By spinning out operations and giving investors what they want earlier in the cycle, multiple expansions in the fastest-growing segments of a company can be fully realized.

Typically, C-suites don't consider corporate breakups until they have dropped deep into the Stress Center amid an economic or industry downturn, when financial pressures mount. Then, divestitures are made out of desperation. With valuations depressed and buyers sensing a clearly motivated seller, companies often end up exiting their peak Comfort Zone acquisitions at pennies on the dollar.

THE IMPORTANCE OF LEAVING THE PARTY EARLY

If success in the Comfort Zone can be maximized by stepping on the accelerator earlier than we think is prudent, it can be preserved by letting up on the gas and pumping on the brakes while others push the pedal to the metal as confidence approaches its peak.

To be clear, this is far easier said than done. As I shared earlier, there may be no siren's song more powerful than our own feelings of intense certainty and control. Pure cognitive ease is seductive, and so are all the trappings of the C-suite and the hype that comes with the upper right corner of the Comfort Zone. As economic rewards mount and accolades pile up, it's hard for many leaders not to believe their own press. Moreover, it is hard to convince others that caution is warranted when the environment feels fantastic, flashy, futuristic, festive, and frenetic. Amid a party-like atmosphere, deliberate, disciplined thinking is the last thing anyone wants.

Three Ways to Counter Invulnerability

Still, to counter feelings of invulnerability, there are steps leaders can take—and it is best if these steps are taken well before the party gets started.

1. CREATE A CULTURE OF CONTINUOUS IMPROVEMENT

One approach is to establish a corporate culture whose goal is "better" rather than "best." "Best" is a destination, and one inevitably focused on comparison with others. The challenge with best as a goal is that once it is achieved, everyone feels they've successfully finished the race. They're done. Moreover, they are likely to be overconfident, failing to appreciate that somewhere out there, there is another group eager to play King of the Mountain and one-up them.

"Better" suggests a never-ending journey. Asked in his eighties why he still practiced, the brilliant cellist Pablo Casals remarked, "I think I am making progress."[7] That attitude is a common one among many long-successful, world-class athletes, too. Their focus is constant improvement—like *kaizen*, the practice popularized by Japanese industry following the Second World War and celebrated in books like *The Toyota Way*.[8]

No matter what name you give to it, the mindset of constant improvement counters overconfidence by preserving an awareness of lingering vulnerability—that no matter where you are today and how much you have created so far, there is still more certainty and more control yet to be gained. Just when it feels as though you've reached the upper right corner of the Comfort Zone, objectives are again moved just out of reach.

Setting more audacious goals can have a similar effect, but there are real downsides to doing so during periods of high confidence. Wells Fargo experienced this firsthand. For years, management pushed what was called the "Gr-eight Initiative"—an internal goal to sell at least eight financial products per customer that was later determined to be unreasonable.[9] Unfortunately, that conclusion was not reached until confidence later fell and scrutiny revealed that a widespread culture of fraud had arisen inside the organization; employees had opened millions of fake accounts to meet management's goals. CEO John Stumpf, who had once graced the cover of *Forbes* magazine for "coining money," was exited, and the company ended up paying hundreds of millions of dollars in fines.[10]

Even with incremental goal setting and fostering a culture of "better," leaders must be especially careful in the Comfort Zone to ensure that they have adequate controls in place. Given the high financial and reputational rewards that accompany success in the Comfort Zone, executives and even corporate boards should not underestimate the lengths others will go to achieve them. In fact, I'd go one step further: given the volume of fraudulent, fictitious, and fake activity that is ultimately uncovered once peak Comfort Zone environments ebb, they should *expect* it. Sadly, as confidence becomes extreme, scruples all but go out the window.

2. CREATE AN OVERCONFIDENCE BINGO CARD

A second approach to counter overconfidence in the Comfort Zone is to objectively define what it might look like ahead of time, putting together a list of behaviors and actions that are likely to be seen—or, as I call it, creating an "Overconfidence Bingo Card" for your business.

Spaces on the card might include behaviors like these:

Audible applause/laughter on quarterly earnings calls
Analyst demands for strategic audaciousness
Record-high forward price-to-earnings ratio on company stock
Record-low borrowing spreads/record long-term debt maturities
Record-volume stock buybacks
Saturating "buy" recommendations on company stock with unprecedented price targets
Intense M & A courtship activity/business expansion initiatives
Industry "bidding wars," especially on supersized/trophy properties/companies
Intense urgency or board/peer pressure to undertake an acquisition, especially large scale/transformation etc.
Major industry deregulation/self-regulation initiatives
Record-high performance/stock awards and executive compensation
Long-term employment contract renewals focused on leadership retention
Board/executive meetings and retreats/sales conferences in luxurious foreign locations

A wave of new high-performance cars/vacation homes among executives
New corporate jets or a plush new corporate HQ
Corporate acquisitions of antiques, collectibles, art, etc.
Corporate purchase of professional sports stadium naming rights
Magazine cover stories/Harvard Business School case studies deifying company leadership; keynote speaking requests from the World Economic Forum; leadership TED talks
CEO memoir book publisher inquiries

Some of the examples above may seem farfetched, but it is well worth your time to create a list that picks up objective financial and operational measures, reputation-related actions, and specific industry traits, as well as social/cultural behaviors that would accompany an environment of invulnerability. The goal is not to create a checklist as much as it is to generate tiles for a mosaic. As comparable events inevitably unfold, you want a way to see that the bingo card is filling—that the confidence environment has reached an extreme where taking your foot off the gas and/or beginning to step on the brakes is appropriate.

Ultimately, the goal in the Comfort Zone is not to avoid overconfidence altogether but to steer clear of the worst of it. As I shared earlier, the greatest organizational missteps take place at the very peak in confidence. And often, these actions prove to be self-immolating. By avoiding the worst risk-taking at the peak of the confidence cycle, businesses are far more likely to become survivors at the bottom of the cycle—and to survivors in business come enormous benefits. Being the best house in a terrible neighborhood brings a flood of opportunity as customers flee failing competitors and industries are forced to consolidate.

While maximizing success in the Comfort Zone may get a company enormous media attention and shareholder accolades, doing so in the treacherous aftermath of that success is far more important. Avoiding the most tempting crowd-pleasing excesses at the top of a confidence cycle is critical: they all but doom you to failure.

In his especially ill-timed 2021 cryptocurrency ad, actor Matt Damon said, "Fortune favors the brave." That is not universally true. Timing matters. Fortune favors the brave early in the Comfort Zone. It is why acting more like an entrepreneur early on—and moving faster and more aggressively then—is so important. The rewards are greater for those who act earlier.

In the upper reaches of the Comfort Zone, fortune favors the cautious. Those who can recognize the environment and resist the siren song of the party-like atmosphere not only avoid the worst but position themselves best for the opportunities that, unbeknownst to many at the time, invariably lie ahead when confidence declines.

3. RETHINK LEADERSHIP AT PEAKS IN CONFIDENCE

Which brings me to one final point about peaks in confidence and the extreme upper right corner of the Comfort Zone.

As prescient leaders recognize the environment of overconfidence and begin to pull back on their organization's risk-taking appetite, they should also reassess the skill set of their leadership team. As I shared earlier, effective crisis management requires unique traits.

If there is a consistent résumé requirement for Comfort Zone C-suite leadership, it is demonstrated prior success. High-confidence environments are awash with highly optimistic leaders who have long, unblemished track records. These individuals have successfully capitalized on rising confidence financially, operationally, socially, and in many cases even culturally and politically. While they may have at one point been renegades, they are now establishment men and women who have mastered and exploited the system to their own and others' benefit. The Comfort Zone is the environment of rainmakers. It is led by those who are highly networked and revenue generating and who know how to turn high confidence into gold.

As invaluable as rainmakers are when times are good, they are useless when confidence falls sharply—which is all but assured after overconfidence peaks. Their ego, self-confidence, charisma, and big-picture focus, while invaluable in especially good times, aren't what businesses need to effectively confront a crisis. Worse, organizations whose C-suites and boards are rainmaker heavy—which many companies unknowingly are at peaks of confidence—are especially fragile.

One reason for that fragility is that the upper reach of the Comfort Zone is where organizations often provide stretch opportunities to young, high-performing leaders in whom they see great promise. Rather than lose talent to competitors, they ask a young, ambitious chief financial officer (CFO) to run a major line of business, or they move a top revenue producer into the chief technology officer or CFO role, hoping to round out their experience, promising even broader corporate responsibilities ahead.

Lehman Brothers did just that when the Wall Street bank promoted one of its top rainmakers, Erin Callan, to CFO in September 2007, just days before the stock market peaked. Callan was a *magna cum laude* graduate of Harvard, went to New York University Law School, and then worked for the international white-shoe law firm Simpson Thacher before moving into investment banking. Callan was the perfect peak-in-confidence choice. She had excelled at everything she encountered during an environment of rising confidence and seemed destined to even greater success ahead.

Nine months later, she was demoted. A year later, Lehman Brothers was bankrupt.[11]

To be fair, as much as Ms. Callan's ill fit with falling confidence and her inexperience as CFO may have contributed to Lehman's collapse, she, too, was arguably a victim. There was no worse moment to be named CFO of a Wall Street firm. Moreover, as she dug into her new role and expressed concerns about what she uncovered, she quickly found herself in conflict with her boss. She wasn't the only unfortunate peak-in-confidence leadership change at Lehman. Risk management chief Madelyn Antoncic was pushed aside at the same time "after repeatedly objecting to [CEO Dick] Fuld, [president Joseph] Gregory and investment banking boss Skip McGee routinely waiving aside risk limits on all manner of deals."[12]

Coming back-to-back, these two leadership changes should have had Lehman board members shouting, "Bingo!" Had they filled out their card early on in the confidence cycle, they would have grasped the significance of the two overconfidence-oozing changes and the clear abdication of risk management. They'd have known a Category 5 hurricane was about to make landfall. Instead, I suspect they simply nodded in agreement with these comments made by Fuld in the company's third quarter 2007 earnings release: "Despite challenging conditions in the markets, our results once again demonstrate the diversity and financial strength of the Lehman Brothers franchise, as well as our ability to perform across cycles."[13]

Nothing could have been further from the truth.

•

The Comfort Zone is the best of times, and the livin' is easy. Our feelings of high certainty and high control are mirrored by our eagerness for the future. We can't wait to see what happens next and are excited to capitalize on whatever it might be.

Supporting all that enthusiasm is cognitive ease. Our brain sees nothing ahead to require System 2 thinking. What the Comfort Zone reminds us is that at its core, confidence is a cognitive state. We are confident when our brain is relaxed. As wonderful as that feeling is, leaders should recognize its warning signs. If they're not careful, overconfidence is their future, and, if ignored, so is the inevitable peril that follows.

To effectively navigate the upper reaches of the Comfort Zone, then, leaders must risk unpopularity—being out of sync with the crowd. To better prepare for that moment, and to better prepare their leadership teams, leaders should consider not only the steps they can take to dampen overconfidence but how to recognize its many sentiment indicators in plain sight and prepare for far more challenging times ahead.

SECTION IV

The Passenger Seat

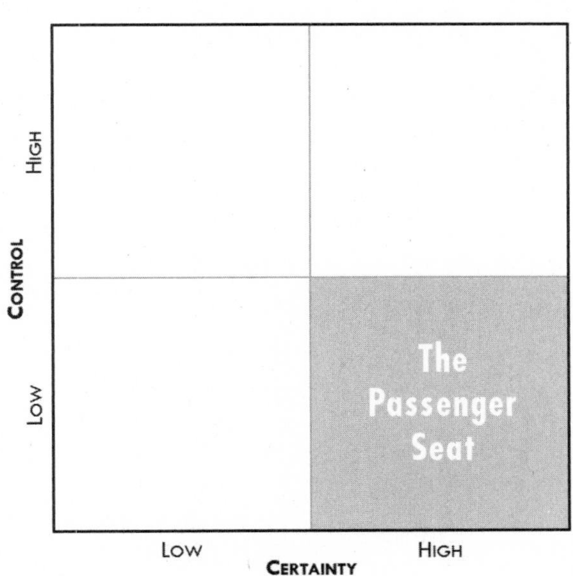

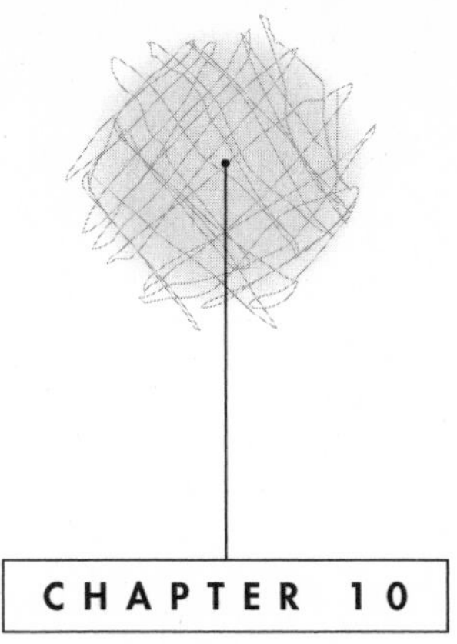

CHAPTER 10

The Passenger Seat and Environments of High Certainty and Low Control

In April 2021, President Joe Biden announced that after almost two decades of conflict and military presence, the United States would begin its withdrawal of all troops from Afghanistan. Two months later, a U.S. intelligence assessment projected that the Afghan government could fall within six months of the American withdrawal. While that time frame was shorter than prior forecasts suggested, policymakers took it as good news: Americans would be out of the country by September as planned, well ahead of a collapse.[1] The full withdrawal that President Biden had announced and had committed to could continue apace.

On August 15, just two months after the assessment was released, and amid the ongoing exodus of American armed forces, the Afghan capital of Kabul fell and fell quickly. Taliban fighters faced little resistance as they entered the city. Meanwhile, Afghan officials—including the country's president—fled.[2] The outcome stunned top U.S. officials, several of whom had been on vacation, having fully expected the pro-

Western government to hang on longer. Afghans were no less astonished by the speed with which their government crumbled. Even the Taliban was surprised.[3]

Environments of low control and high certainty are like that. With hindsight, everyone is surprised by their fragility and the speed with which calm is replaced by chaos.

In the case of Afghanistan, no one should have been caught off guard. Until just days before, the entire population of Afghanistan had been in the lower right box of the Confidence Quadrant. While U.S. policymakers on both sides of the aisle had avoided describing the country as an occupied state, when it came to the feelings of control of those within its border, it clearly was. From common citizens to national political leaders, everyone felt largely powerless. Control over the country rested in the hands of the U.S. military, and with that fact came a sense of certainty. When that control ceased to be absolute, it was replaced by the powerlessness that existed below the surface.

Afghanistan was the Passenger Seat in plain sight. In August 2021, the country was effectively an airplane from which the pilots chose to parachute out midflight, with no one ready and able to step in. The Taliban didn't take control as much as they scrambled to fill a power vacuum that swept the nation as Afghanis realized no one was in charge and the country was on the verge of collapse. Like it or not, without leadership of some sort, the Stress Center was next. With that possibility front of mind, some citizens chose to follow—to once again swap all-but-certain chaos for some level of certainty.

Our Paths to the Passenger Seat

If there is one word that captures the lower right box of the Quadrant—the Passenger Seat—it is "authoritarian." Someone or something else is in charge. The result is an environment not of confidence but of compliance and resignation—powerlessness. In the Passenger Seat, we do as we are told.

On the surface, you would think, then, that we would never choose to deliberately put ourselves in the Passenger Seat. That view disregards the way we imagine that environment based on our specific circumstances. As you'll see, whether we see ourselves as the beneficiary or the victim of our experience has a big impact on why we choose to move into the Passenger Seat—and how we feel once we've arrived.

ENTRY FROM THE STRESS CENTER

A common path into the Passenger Seat has its starting point in the Stress Center. As I shared earlier, one of the Five Fs of our natural stress responses is "follow." Amid panic, and already feeling powerless, we cede the potential for control to others in exchange for greater certainty. We gladly turn over our burst pipe to a plumber in the belief that he will take care of it and return us to the Comfort Zone.

When we are in the Stress Center, we frequently choose the Passenger Seat (rather than the Launch Pad) as our next stop. We call AAA when we have a flat tire, we rush to hire a CPA in early April to complete our annual 1040 filing, and we hire a lawyer to represent us in court after a DUI. In the Stress Center, we choose the Passenger Seat because we think someone else can solve our problem better or faster than we can on our own. We choose the Passenger Seat when we believe others have skills, tools, equipment, and/or aptitude we don't. We call in experts.

Groups more broadly follow the same pattern when they voluntarily follow authoritarian leaders—those who have or profess to have the know-how and forceful command to lead us back to the Comfort Zone. History shows that the shared feelings of extreme uncertainty and powerlessness that we experience in the Stress Center are the ashes from which most dictators and cult leaders rise. These leaders don't *take* power so much as have it bestowed on them by those who believe the leader will somehow save them and make things better. Hopeless crowds are often as happy to see an authoritarian leader as you or I are to see our plumber. The crowd all but meets them at the door, hoping the leader will solve all their problems.

Boards of troubled companies behave the same way. Desperate amid a crisis, they are thrilled to see a decisive, take-charge leader arrive on the scene. Most are even explicit about it, enthusiastically giving a new CEO "free rein" to do "whatever it takes" to right the ship. Hopeful of putting the worst behind them, directors are thrilled to hop in the Passenger Seat and let a new leader take the wheel.

Some troubled companies even add the confidence-boosting element of nostalgia to their leadership selection mix. To ensure a successful exit from the Stress Center, they bring back founders or prior CEOs who were wildly successful in their day—sometimes repeatedly. As I was writing this book, the Disney board called back recently retired longtime CEO Robert Iger, while Starbucks brought Howard Schultz, the company's founder, out of retirement for a second time.[4]

Nothing reveals a Passenger Seat corporate environment quite like the return of a "boomerang CEO"—and yes, there is such a term. It not only brings out into the open a failure in succession planning but also makes it clear that there were no internal candidates believed to be qualified to take the wheel.[5]

VOLUNTARY ENTRY FROM THE COMFORT ZONE

Our second path into the Passenger Seat typically feels less emotional. It occurs when we voluntarily drop down from the Comfort Zone above. Rather than a panicked Stress Center response, this move into the Passenger Seat is the result of a deliberate choice. It's what we do when we take an airplane flight across the country, get in the back seat of the car as a friend or a parent drives us to the movies, or ride on a roller coaster at an amusement park. In all these cases, we choose the Passenger Seat as a means to an end. Whether for transportation or a thrill, it's a temporary moment of powerlessness from which we expect we will soon return to the Comfort Zone.

Here's where the two scenarios I've just laid out are so different: In order for us to voluntarily leave the Comfort Zone and move to the Passenger Seat, we require extreme certainty. We expect to be the certain beneficiary, not the victim, of circumstance. The risk of a plane crash must be believed to be nonexistent. We must have complete trust in the friend or parent who is driving us and absolute confidence that the roller coaster will return us to the departure platform after several thrilling and terrifying minutes. Anything less than 99.9999 percent certainty—the very far right edge of the Passenger Seat box—is unacceptable. To voluntarily cede control, we must "know" we will return to safety.

That isn't the case when our starting point is the Stress Center. There, faced with neither certainty nor control, we demand far less certainty from those whom we follow than you might think. In despair, we seek "better," not "best" or "perfect," and will happily follow those who provide a compelling story of the future. Any port in the storm will do, not just the marina with hot showers. As a result, it takes far less effort and energy to move a crowd into the Passenger Seat from the Stress Center than it does to move them there from the Comfort Zone.

Consider, for example, how we hire a painter versus a plumber. Both experiences move us into the Passenger Seat. We *select* painters; we make a voluntary election while in the Comfort Zone. We deliberately ask around, look at the work they've done for others, and often negotiate on price. Our process is a thorough evaluation of the alternatives, and we'll wait, if necessary, to get just the person we want. Picking a painter frequently draws us to use slow, System 2 thinking.

On the other hand, when our basement is flooding, we all but *scream* for a plumber. We'll take anyone with a wrench who answers the phone. It's pure System 1 thinking. We don't have the time or the cognitive bandwidth to check references. We have a problem, and we want it fixed *now!* While our paths from the Comfort Zone and Stress Center arrive at the same destination, in the Passenger Seat, the two experiences couldn't be more different.

When we are coming from the Stress Center, our feelings of relief often begin to fade with the passing of time in the Passenger Seat. We realize and appreciate that while we may have regained some certainty, we still lack control. We aren't yet in the Comfort Zone, where we feel relaxed. The "better" we were once satisfied with begins to feel insufficient. Yes, it is great that a plumber has arrived, but after a few hours and a lunch break that feels like it has run too long and multiple trips back to the plumbing-supply store for parts, we become frustrated and wonder why our leak hasn't yet been repaired. We feel the same frustration as we check our watch while waiting for the AAA tow truck to arrive when we have a flat tire.

In these situations, if we don't soon regain control and advance to the Comfort Zone, we begin to feel trapped in the Passenger Seat. We wonder if we've made the right choice. Regret sets in; our feelings shift, moving from beneficiary to victim. We feel imprisoned and start to bristle at the control others have over us. Not surprisingly, we often then become less willing to comply, stating unequivocally to the plumber that, "No, I can't wait for you to come back tomorrow. Fix it now." Certainty without control leaves us hanging; we want and need both feelings. We begin to wonder whether we should bring in a new plumber—one who *can* get the job done.

Corporate boards behave similarly. After hiring a turnaround leader, they want to see immediate improvement. Crisis leaders who can't soon restore the confidence of shareholders, lenders, suppliers, and other key constituent groups quickly come under attack.

Bank of America CEO Brian Moynihan experienced this firsthand. Promoting him into the role at the bottom of the 2008 financial crisis, his board hoped he could quickly put the problems of his predecessor behind the bank. Instead, over the next two years, more issues were uncovered in the bank's loan portfolio and business practices. With that, the company's stock price fell by more than 50 percent. As the stock neared its low in the fall of 2011, *Bloomberg Businessweek* even ran a cover story with an image of a distressed Moynihan paired with the headline "Can This Man Save Bank of America?"[6]

Ironically, the cover proved to be a classic contrarian indicator of washed-out sentiment, with Bank of America stock trading almost tenfold higher when it peaked in early 2022.

More recently, Bed Bath & Beyond CEO Mark Tritton wasn't so lucky. Brought in with great fanfare in 2019 after serving as chief merchandising officer at Target, he was exited in July 2022 after the home goods chain delivered two consecutive quarters of "miserable sales," the company's share price had collapsed, and board confidence had evaporated.[7]

With impatient corporations and struggling crisis leaders, there is a clear process for removal. That isn't the case with social and political movements. There, tensions can erupt if the problems the crowd had hoped to see fixed aren't remedied quickly. Moreover, the more the crowd tries to take control back into its own hands from the leader it earlier followed, the more repressive those in control often become. Needless to say, things can quickly escalate. To quell an uprising, authoritarian leaders often seek to take even greater control, all but forcing mandatory compliance to even more rigid behavioral requirements.

And this is what a Stress Center crowd misses: to be sustained, an authoritarian regime must move those it commands farther and farther into the lower right corner of the Quadrant, where the crowd feels even more powerless against a force it is certain will be crushing. Conditions must resemble those in a maximum-security prison, where guards have total control and there are extreme consequences for a failure to follow the rules (Figure 10.1).

Sadly, what I have just described also characterizes many abusive relationships—both personal and on the job. Individuals in the Stress Center are often attracted to the confidence of their new partner; they are happy to follow. An authoritarian partner, though, wants to keep the other person in the relationship in the lower right corner of the box. They don't want to cede control to anyone, let alone see the other gain it. The result is that the more their partner seeks to reclaim or exert control, the more the abuser works to take it away.

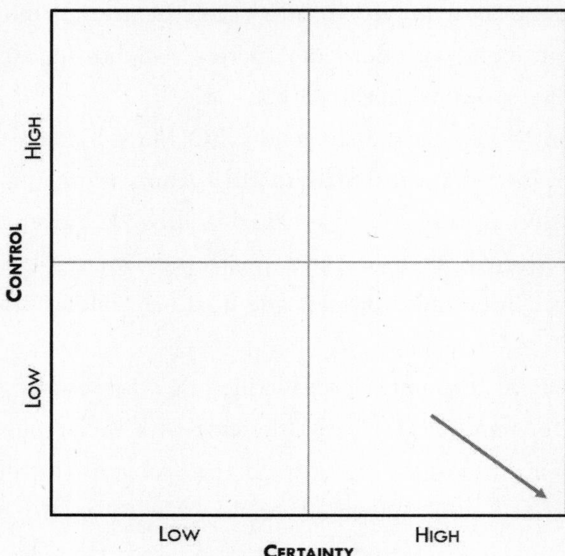

FIGURE 10.1: The authoritarian ideal, certainty and powerlessness

INVOLUNTARY ENTRY FROM THE COMFORT ZONE/IMPRISONMENT

Which brings me to the last common path into the lower right box: "imprisonment." Whether that means actual incarceration or an experience that involuntarily moves us from the Comfort Zone into the Passenger Seat—such as our sensation of being trapped when turbulence hits our flight, or when we're dragged by our friends onto a roller coaster, or when, late on Friday afternoon, our boss unexpectedly demands that we work the weekend—the lower right box of the Quadrant can be a high-stress environment, where suddenly we feel forced to do something against our will. When our need for control is repressed, the line that separates the Passenger Seat from the Stress Center disappears, and the two can seem indistinguishable.

That's what makes environments of low control/high certainty so unusual: Unlike our experiences in the Stress Center and the Comfort Zone, those in the Passenger Seat aren't consistent. They don't come with common feelings and actions; the path we take to arrive in the Passenger Seat, and whether we took that route voluntarily or involuntarily, frames how we feel.

To anticipate behavior, then, we need to appreciate the path and the mindset that accompanied our journey into the Passenger Seat. Finally, we need to appreciate that once we are in the lower right box, our feelings can change quickly. One moment, we can be quietly reading our book on our airplane flight, and the next we can be holding on for dear life. Unexpected turbulence changes everything.

Passenger Seat Environments in Business

For businesses that operate naturally in the Passenger Seat, like restaurants or law firms, it is imperative to appreciate their customers' feelings and pathways into the lower right box of the Quadrant. They need to know where their customers came from to best help them get to where they want to go—to consider, as an organization, whether they are a plumber or a painter. Sometimes, those roles can change moment by moment; law-firm clients have vastly different feelings when they're calling from the local police precinct after an arrest and in immediate need of representation than when they are looking to update their estate plan to cross off an item on their to-do list sometime in the next year.

If you are a plumber—an organization that specializes in crisis management and in the business of moving customers as quickly as possible from the Stress Center through the Passenger Seat to the Comfort Zone—strong diagnostic and technical skills are vital. So, too, is responsiveness. At its core, your product is rapid problem-solving. The less time your clients spend with you in the Passenger Seat, the better; you don't want to give them time to regret their decision or feel trapped working with you. Leaders running "on call" operations—whether a customer service center, a reservation center, or an urgent care—must appreciate that impatience is to be expected. Waiting on hold or standing in line only reinforces our feelings of powerlessness. Whatever our need, we want it addressed fast—and when it can't be, we want to know why. When we are on hold, letting us know where we are in the queue or allowing us to schedule a callback is incredibly helpful. Small steps like these provide greater certainty and leave the customer feeling more in control of their lives.

If instead you are an airline, an aircraft manufacturer, or an amusement park operator, you have different challenges. For companies like these, where nearly all interactions happen because your customer has voluntarily chosen to move into the Passenger Seat, sustaining extreme certainty is paramount. If your clients don't feel safe, you don't have a business.

The leadership team of ValuJet witnessed that in May 1996, after one of the airline's DC-9s crashed into the Florida Everglades, killing all 110 people on board.[8] A month later, the FAA grounded all the airline's planes, citing a long list of deficiencies ranging from training to maintenance.[9] While the airline did eventually resume flights, it never recovered and was quickly and quietly merged out of existence. After the crash, the company's reputation for cost cutting became incompatible with the expectation of extreme safety necessary to sustain an airline. With fallen confidence, passengers couldn't see how an airline could do both at the same time successfully.

Boeing faced a comparable challenge in the wake of its back-to-back 737 MAX jet crashes. In March 2019, just days after the second crash, global aviation regulators grounded all 387 MAX aircraft in service. The accidents and grounding cost Boeing an estimated $20 billion in fines, compensation, and legal fees, making it likely the most expensive disaster in business history.[10] Without the profits from the company's other lines of business to sustain it, it is doubtful Boeing would have avoided bankruptcy. The cost of the crisis—and the effort necessary to begin to rebuild trust with regulators, airlines, and passengers—was far higher than management and shareholders ever imagined.

Both experiences highlight the binary nature of Passenger Seat businesses. When the extreme certainty required to sustain activity in the

Passenger Seat fails to exist, confidence collapses. There is no middle ground. Cars driven by friends either are safe or they aren't. There is calm or chaos. Either we feel secure on the very right edge of the Passenger Seat or we are deep in the lower left corner of the Stress Center.

And here it is worth reiterating that especially for Passenger Seat businesses, facts don't matter. Safety, for example, is highly abstract. We have to imagine it will be there. What happened in the past may or may not be relevant to us. We must be able to imagine that our flight *will* be safe when we board the plane. Once again, the forward-looking nature of confidence plays a huge role in our decision-making.

Not surprisingly, the airline industry spends billions of dollars every year to help us feel safe in the air. From advertisements emphasizing regular maintenance to the preflight safety messages highlighting our plane's many exits, airlines take thousands of small, deliberate actions every day to make us *feel* safe. Then there is the work of regulators and policymakers. From TSA checkpoints to FAA plane inspections, travelers know extraordinary effort is taken every day to ensure certainty in air travel.

But even with all these practices in place, air travel comes down to *our* imagination and whether the safety we require to board a plane is sufficient as we subjectively assess it while we walk into the boarding area and down the jet bridge. Ultimately, neither the airlines nor the government determines whether we feel it is safe for us to fly—we do. It is *our* feelings of certainty and control, not just all their efforts, that matter.

Flying is an extreme example, but the same principles apply to all Passenger Seat businesses. Whether you are a lawyer, a barber, a restaurateur, or a hotel operator, your mandate is to foster an environment in which your clients feel relaxed yet have little control. Once they pick you, their fate rests in your hands.

Not surprisingly, then, most service businesses in the Passenger Seat live or die by reputation and word of mouth. How we feel about them—and the stories we then share with others that express those feelings—drives whether we go back. What ultimately determines a great haircut, meal, or overnight stay is whether or not we see ourselves back in the Comfort Zone when it is over. When we do, we post a glowing five-star review on Yelp. When we don't, we post a scathing no-star review detailing every little thing that went wrong. It's no coincidence that online reviews for Passenger Seat experiences tend to be at one extreme of the scale or the other. Outcomes in the Passenger Seat are binary: we are either confident in the result or we aren't.

Customer Confidence Is More Important Than Customer Satisfaction

With this in mind, it is surprising how few organizations solicit feedback on the issue of customer confidence and the certainty and control their clients feel in purchasing different products and services. Instead, organizations focus on customer satisfaction and whether expectations were met. They presume that if customers are doing business with them, their products and services must be trustworthy.

Satisfaction isn't the same as trustworthiness or confidence, though. I can be pleased with a meal but choose not to return to a restaurant because I don't believe my next experience will be consistent with what I just received. Satisfaction speaks to what *was*; customer confidence speaks to what *will be*. Again, confidence is inherently forward-looking, which, if I am a business owner, is what really matters.

Most company surveys also ignore those who were unwilling to buy in the first place—those consumers who weren't confident. Companies preach to the saved, as it were, rather than reaching out to the atheists. They ignore the feelings of those who won't and don't buy and, often, those who stopped buying. As a result, they frequently miss the early warning signs of a crisis.

Just imagine the difference in answers banks would have received during the 2008 financial crisis had they asked depositors to evaluate them not on customer satisfaction but on trustworthiness. With consumer confidence low, the answers to questions like "How certain are you that your money is safe in our bank?" or "Do you feel you have ready access to your money in our bank?" would have been telling. So, too, would answers to questions related to familiarity, such as "How well do you know your banker/does your banker know you?" We are much more likely to leave organizations that feel psychologically distant than those we think know us and to whom we feel an especially close attachment.

Imagine, too, the insights hospitals would gain by asking departing patients how confident they felt in their doctors or nurses or in their discharge plan, especially given the clear connection between confidence and lower physical and mental stress. Confidence improves our odds of recovery; we are more likely to take our prescribed medicines and follow a recovery plan if we are confident in them and their benefits to us.

Finally, what organizations miss with satisfaction surveys is that they demand participants be judgmental of others—that they ask, "Did they meet my expectations of them?" Confidence surveys, on the other hand, require respondents to look inward. These surveys ask participants to consider how the actions of others made them *feel*. Moreover, they do it in dimensions that are more specific, more actionable, and far less emotionally charged. Asking a customer what you need do to help them feel more empowered and more certain when they use your product or service is likely to yield far more useful and actionable information than asking what you need to do to make them more satisfied.

•

A surprising amount of our lives is spent in the Passenger Seat, where things seem certain yet someone else has control. Too often, though, those with control underestimate the fragility of the environment. They fail to appreciate that if we have a choice, we will look to have our needs met by those who can ensure we end up in the Comfort Zone. Then, sadly, there are those who purposely seek to hold us captive in the Passenger Seat.

Before turning our focus to better practices in the Passenger Seat, we are going to look more closely at how changes in confidence impact customer demand for different products and services. As you will see, especially for businesses that operate in the Passenger Seat, minor declines in confidence can bring about dramatic drops in demand.

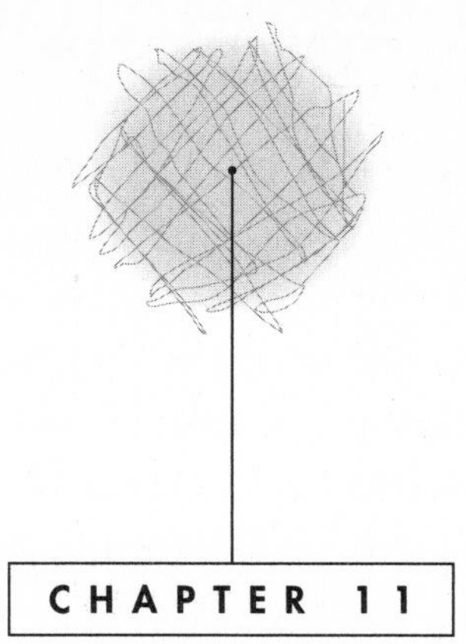

CHAPTER 11

Confidence Elasticity

BEFORE WE JUMP back into the role of confidence in decision-making, we need to take a quick detour to explore a concept straight from Economics 101: price elasticity and how sensitive demand for a product is to changes in price. While this may seem like a wild tangent, as you'll see in a moment, there is an important parallel: confidence elasticity.

For those unfamiliar with the topic, price-elasticity studies help companies know when it is better to heavily discount prices (so that, as a result, sales volume will increase substantially and more than make up for lower margins) and when it is better to just leave prices alone (because lowering prices will have little impact on customer demand). Sales of some products, like luxury goods, are highly sensitive to changes in price; they are what economists call "price elastic." If the price of a highly discretionary good, like champagne, increases, customers are less likely to be willing to buy it. Other products, such as gasoline and food staples, though, are not so price sensitive; they are "inelastic." Our demand for these items doesn't change based on what they cost—often because it can't. If we commute to work by car, we have little choice but to fill the gas tank every week, whether gas costs $2.50 a gallon or $5.00 a gallon.

Price inelasticity is why food and gas inflation weigh so heavily on consumer sentiment.[1] Inflation in these goods generates feelings of powerlessness and uncertainty. During the spring of 2022, as oil prices shot higher in the wake of Russia's invasion of Ukraine, you could see the devastating impact of higher prices at the pump on consumer confidence.[2]

Implicit in most price-elasticity analyses is the belief that price drives the volume of goods and services we buy—that we make economic decisions driven by purely economic factors. Moreover, these analyses presume there is stability to our demand sensitivity to price changes—that when the results from price-elasticity studies are applied in practice, in stores and online, the outcome is highly likely to reflect analysts' forecasts.

Finance department analysts spend hours looking at financial relationships, like the price elasticity of company products and how customer demand rises and falls with changes in price. With this information, businesses then set prices, hoping that the resulting change in sales volume maximizes the bottom line.

Quarterly earnings reports show that reality routinely upends price-elasticity projections. One moment, executives lament that volume fell short of expectations and look to attribute the gap to some unexpected factor; the next, they celebrate sales that exceeded expectations. And here is where it gets interesting: often, these same executives suggest that the better-than-expected outcome was attributable to higher customer confidence—that customers somehow "valued" their products more, were more "satisfied," or somehow suddenly "saw the quality in the service they received." With outperformance, leaders want to be recognized and rewarded for the achievement.

Using Confidence Elasticity to Improve Results

Given the frequency with which companies associate their performance results with changes in consumer confidence, you would think that rather than focusing on price elasticity, they would consider *confidence* elasticity instead.

Remarkably, few do. Moreover, even fewer realize they operate amid a variety of confidence-elasticity relationships. As you'll see, some of these relationships are tied to economic cycles and broad trends in consumer sentiment, some are tied to the specific products a company offers, and others are tied to the specifics of their industry and the implied contract—like the one for basic safety—that exists between a business and its customers. Again, satisfaction is different from trustworthiness. If consumers' confidence, and not price, carries the day, then maybe it is "confidence elasticity"—how sales rise and fall with changes in consumer sentiment—that corporations should analyze.

Here are four key dimensions of confidence elasticity:

DIMENSION 1: ELASTICITY TIED TO ECONOMIC CYCLES AND CONSUMER SENTIMENT

The first dimension ties elasticity to how most business leaders think of consumer confidence: how our broad feelings of relative optimism and pessimism (which are captured by sentiment surveys undertaken by the University of Michigan, Gallup, the Conference Board, and others) impact demand.

Confidence elasticity, framed this way, likely looks very similar to the price elasticity businesses are familiar with (Figure 11.1).

A supermarket chain, like Kroger, likely has high confidence inelasticity; it is unlikely that changes in society-wide consumer confidence are a big factor in aggregate demand. Typically, our demand for necessities, like milk, eggs, and paper towels, doesn't vary much based on how

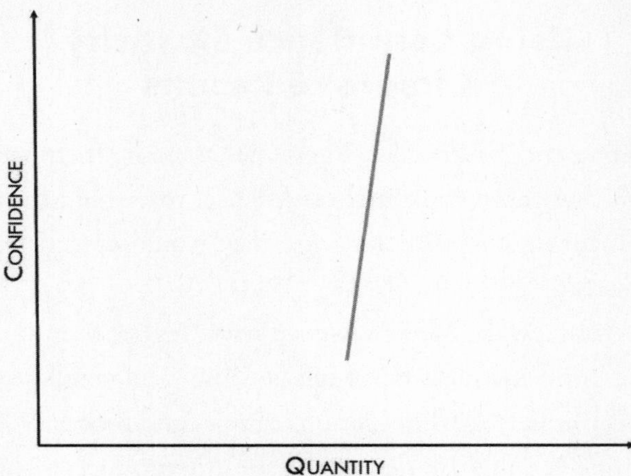

FIGURE 11.1: High confidence inelasticity

we feel. While we may be able to cut back a little when times are tough, what more often changes is the quality of the necessities we purchase rather than the quantity.

In contrast, there are companies like Boeing. Its commercial aircraft sales are likely to have a very high positive correlation to consumer confidence. The more confident we are, the more we and others travel, and the more planes airlines need to move us around. At the risk of oversimplification, the resulting demand/confidence relationship for Boeing aircraft likely looks something like Figure 11.2.

As discussed earlier, travel is an industry highly sensitive to changes in consumer confidence. Higher confidence means more interest in booking a European vacation, while lower confidence leads us to stay closer to home.

DIMENSION 2: SPECIFIC PRODUCT CONFIDENCE ELASTICITY

Confidence elasticity gets more interesting when consumer-sentiment data is applied to specific products. At the supermarket, demand for veal

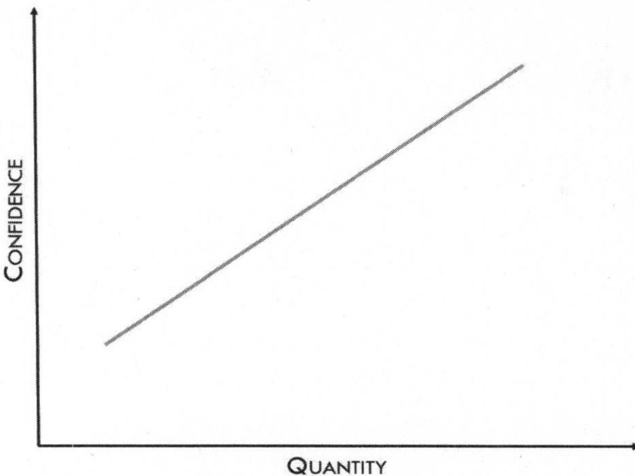

FIGURE 11.2: Moderate confidence elasticity

chops and other expensive cuts of meat, for example, likely rises with consumer confidence. At the same time, demand for store-brand canned goods may have negative confidence elasticity, rising in sales as confidence falls.

That was the case in the spring of 2022, when consumer sentiment fell sharply in the wake of higher gas prices. Kroger, for example, reported that sales of its store-brand products rose faster than national brands and that 92 percent of households purchased at least one of these products.[3]

The same concept applies to passenger planes. Airline demand for the biggest aircraft available, like the Boeing 777 and the Airbus 380, doesn't take off until global consumer confidence is especially high—when existing capacity on smaller planes is constrained and carriers believe that high passenger demand will only continue. For bigger planes to join the fleet, travelers and airlines need to be in Us-Everywhere-Forever mode.

The result is that the confidence elasticity for jumbo jets likely looks something like Figure 11.3.

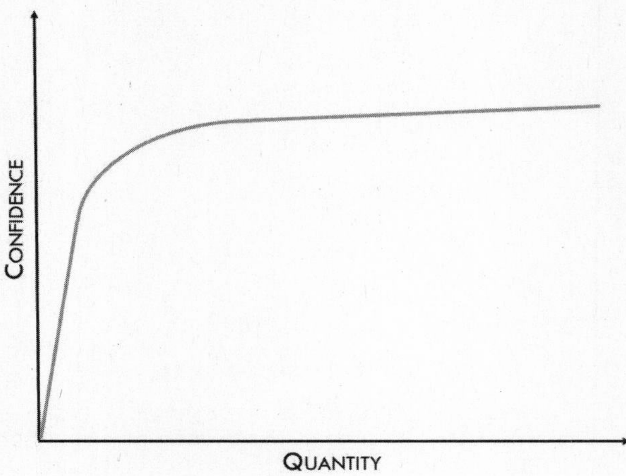

FIGURE 11.3: Confidence elasticity of high confidence goods

There is little demand for new jumbo aircraft until confidence is near an extreme, at which point airlines can't seem to get enough of them.

Ironically, we witnessed just the opposite scenario early in the pandemic, represented by the lower left corner of Figure 11.3, when airline after airline announced the grounding of their biggest planes and, in many cases, those planes' early retirement. Faced with neither the demand necessary to keep them in use nor the prospect of demand in the future, airlines dismantled entire fleets of Boeing 747s and sold the parts for scrap.[4]

The year 2020, though, wasn't the first time extreme low confidence grounded major fleets. Desert parking lots routinely become crowded with aged and jumbo-sized planes at lows in economic cycles. It is a predictable behavior that both manufacturers and airlines experience.

But there's a twist. Rather than becoming despondent over it, as they were in mid-2020, manufacturers and airlines should have been encouraged by it. Since industry-wide mothballing happens only around major lows in consumer confidence, all those parked planes were an important contrarian indicator. Ironically, they were harbingers of rising consumer confidence and a coming economic recovery—the ash, as it were, from which Phoenix and other popular travel destinations would soon rise.

As you might imagine, in real time it is hard for industry professionals and investors to imagine a recovery. But here is where confidence-elasticity studies can help. They help organizations better understand how sales and other behaviors ebb and flow over economic cycles. Important predictive patterns become obvious.

In my work, I pay close attention to the confidence elasticity of different goods and services, not just because of what they suggest in extreme events but what they indicate about consumer confidence more broadly.[5]

Intense demand for some products, like wide-body jumbo jets, appears only when consumer confidence is especially high, while demand for others, like nostalgic comfort food, surges only near lows. Ironically, the arrival of the Boeing 747 (and the futuristic, supersonic Concorde) in the late 1960s and, more recently, the Airbus A380 in 2005, signaled the end of an era. Both moments were manifestations of extreme high confidence and intense Us-Everywhere-Forever thinking. Had aircraft manufacturers and airline executives appreciated confidence elasticity and the implications of charts like Figure 11.3, they would have seen that confidence was rapidly approaching a peak and been better prepared for the downturn that followed.

Every industry has its own jumbo jets—those products that are sold only at peaks in confidence or whose sales volume skews heavily at the top. And there are many ways to cut sales data to find them. If you run a hotel chain like Ritz-Carlton, for example, changes in demand for specific room types, resort locations, stay lengths, and even amenity purchases would reveal important clues.

Industries also have their comfort foods that are most popular near lows, like the store-brand mac and cheese at many supermarkets. Then there are industries and companies whose entire sales structure has the confidence elasticity of jumbo jets or comfort food. Some businesses do best when we feel worst, while others thrive only at peaks in confidence.

I have a good friend who keeps track of the stock price divergence between Walmart and the luxury goods retailer Nordstrom. She believes it is one of the best real-time economic measures out there. Nordstrom far outperforms Walmart when consumer confidence is high, while the pattern reverses when confidence is low.

Which brings me to a broader point: nowhere is the product-confidence connection clearer than in the world of investing—although it is rarely presented that way.

In my Financial Economics class, I share Figure 11.4 early in the semester to introduce my students to the fundamental relationship between risk and reward in the financial markets.

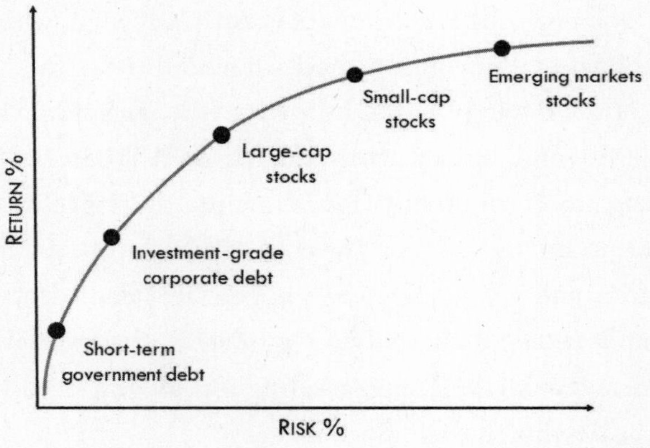

FIGURE 11.4: The relationship of risk and return in the financial markets

As the image shows, different investment options have different levels of risk and expected return. As you would imagine, investors demand a higher return when taking more risk. But ask yourself: When are investors naturally more willing to take more risk? The answer, likely, is when they feel more confident.

While the x-axis in Figure 11.4 focuses on risk, it could just as easily be replaced by the Confidence Spectrum. At the far left, at lows in confidence, when we are in Me-Here-Now mode, we want certainty to our investments. We naturally prefer cash and T-bills (the safest short-term debt of the U.S. government) over other alternatives. We gladly forsake the potential of a high return on our investments for the comfort of knowing we will get all our money back.

The confidence-elasticity graph for cash looks something like Figure 11.5.

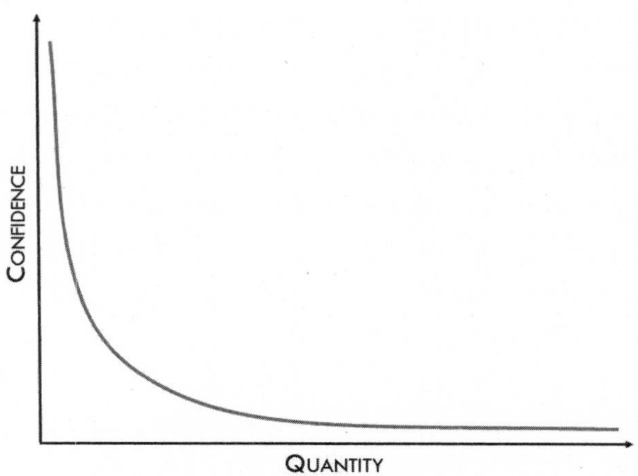

FIGURE 11.5: Confidence elasticity of low confidence goods

Investors typically have little interest in holding large amounts of cash until confidence collapses, at which point they can't hold enough.

At the other end of the Confidence Spectrum, though, when our confidence is high and we are in Us-Everywhere-Forever mode, holding cash seems silly, if not outright imprudent. We're "leaving money on the table." Instead, we opt for foreign, if not frontier, market alternatives. We eagerly embrace abstraction—unproven technology, extreme innovation, etc.—in search of the highest returns possible because we are certain higher-risk investments will pay off wildly for us. Rather than seeking to keep what we have, we want to maximize the potential gains on our invested capital.

As a researcher, I pay especially close attention to what investors are interested in and how they are allocating capital. What's "hot" expresses investors' risk appetite and speaks volumes about investor confidence.

When investors want to fill their mattresses with cash because they can imagine things only getting worse, it alerts me to anticipate a major market low ahead. Conversely, when the crowd has an appetite for the outlandish, I know a peak is near.

As retail investors piled into SPACs, NFTs, cryptocurrencies, and weekly out-of-the-money call options on highly speculative stocks in early 2021, I saw everything I needed to know that a major market peak was upon us.[6] There was reckless risk-taking by novice investors in extraordinary abstraction; moreover, the wildness appeared to come out of nowhere. Retail investors suddenly had an insatiable appetite for call options—highly speculative bets that the stock market would rise that offered enormous payoffs if it did but were worthless if it didn't. It was as if someone had yelled, "Open bar!" It was peak confidence elasticity at its very best. Demand looked like Figure 11.3.[7]

And it isn't just in the financial markets where the impact of changes in confidence on consumer preferences are in plain sight. As socionomics pioneer Robert Prechter first showed, demand for specific popular music styles follows our mood. Demand for slow, melancholy, minor-key ballads lush with lyrics of loneliness often accompany lows in consumer confidence while fast, bubblegum music fills the airwaves at peaks.[8] As I joke with my students, for investors, that observation suggests you want to buy Adele and sell Pharrell.

That comment may seem flip, but had you done so, you would have been rewarded handsomely. Moreover, the same concept applies to businesses more broadly. By better appreciating the confidence elasticity of specific products, services, and even elements of design, not only can leaders better anticipate changes in economic cycles, they can also better capitalize on trends in consumer demand.[9]

DIMENSION 3: EXOGENOUS EVENT CONFIDENCE ELASTICITY

What I shared earlier were examples of company- and product-specific confidence elasticity across the full breadth of the Confidence Spectrum. But there is a third application of confidence elasticity. Many industries also have "special circumstances" products for which soaring or collapsing confidence arising from an exogenous event creates especially high demand. We saw this firsthand in the early days of the pandemic, when demand for necessities like toilet paper, bottled water, and disinfectant wipes soared as confidence collapsed.

The confidence elasticity for these products looked something like Figure 11.6.

FIGURE 11.6: Confidence elasticity of crisis goods

Demand was highly inelastic until confidence collapsed. Then, as consumers hoarded all three products, it skyrocketed.

This is a pattern that is frequently repeated ahead of snowstorms, hurricanes, and other natural disasters, as stores experience runs on generators, tarps, milk, and other "crisis goods." We also saw this pattern with oil, wheat, and other commodities when Russia invaded Ukraine. As we all experienced, sudden concerns of scarcity can upend historical demand patterns.

Individual products have fascinating confidence-elasticity charts tied to exogenous events—with major implications for manufacturers, retailers, and policymakers. Thankfully, for many hurricane-related goods,

FEMA and retailers like Home Depot and Walmart have already figured that out. Ahead of major forecasted storms, they pre-position trucks and materials just out of harm's way in anticipation of strong demand. Utility companies do the same with repair crews and equipment.

Most organizations, though, don't think in terms of confidence elasticity when it comes to their preparation for exogenous events, especially when events occur infrequently. Just imagine how far ahead of the pack a hospital system might have been if it had undertaken scenario planning that had considered the confidence elasticity related to a pandemic. It would have had a much better idea of not only what supplies it needed but also what services it could quickly ramp up or curtail in response to the outbreak.

As much as businesses and organizations undertake scenario planning, few think of it in terms of confidence elasticity and how changing sentiment is likely to naturally change demand.

This concept applies to far more than just commercial product demand. There is enormous confidence elasticity to social, political, and even military decision-making. Demand for widespread social/political change surges when sentiment is low. These activities have a confidence elasticity like investor interest in cash (Figure 11.5); there's no demand until there is suddenly intense demand. The Yellow Vest, Black Lives Matter, and Occupy Wall Street movements all seemingly came out of nowhere at extreme lows in confidence. We see the same with aggressive military action: China's August 2022 encircling of Taiwan, in the wake of U.S. House Speaker Nancy Pelosi's visit to that country, came at a moment when Chinese consumer sentiment was at multiyear lows. An appreciation for confidence elasticity would also have helped the United States and Europe be better prepared ahead of not only Russia's invasion of Ukraine but also the invasion into Crimea that preceded it.[10] Those, too, came near lows in confidence.

The same holds true for terrorism—it's far less random than we believe. It is born out of powerlessness and extreme uncertainty; it's fight and fuck it combined. The bombing of the USS *Cole* and the 9/11 attacks, for example, both came near major lows in Middle Eastern financial markets.[11]

DIMENSION 4: CONFIDENCE ELASTICITY ARISING FROM CHANGES IN CUSTOMER TRUST

The final application of confidence elasticity is probably the one that is most important and yet most overlooked: it relates to what happens to demand for a product when trust in what matters most to customer confidence in that product changes.

Take safety in passenger planes, for example. The correlation between confidence and consumer demand for air travel, like the one I showed for Boeing in Figure 11.2, doesn't tell the full story. That confidence-elasticity chart presumes that no matter the level of overall consumer sentiment, passengers believe planes are safe and that there is underlying certainty to air travel.

Confidence elasticity has a vastly different image when we look at the relationship between consumer confidence and consumers' demand for air travel framed strictly in terms of the expectation of aircraft safety.

That confidence-elasticity chart looks more like Figure 11.7.

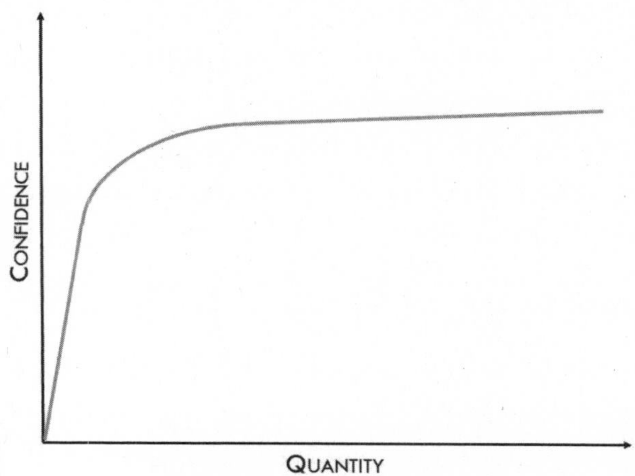

FIGURE 11.7: Confidence elasticity of goods requiring extreme safety

As I shared earlier, when we are in the Passenger Seat, we need extreme certainty to feel secure. Being "kind of confident" in the safety of the plane we are about to board isn't an option. We must be *sure*. The safety threshold that aircraft manufacturers must meet is extremely high, but once it reaches that point, we see little need to distinguish one plane from the next. When it comes to plane safety, it's all or nothing.

The same kind of confidence-elasticity curve applies to restaurants and meat-processing plants when framed in terms of food safety. The consequences of a small drop in our confidence that the food we are buying is safe to eat can have perilous consequences for demand.

Chipotle experienced this when a string of *E. coli* outbreaks hit the Mexican restaurant chain beginning in 2015. The company ended up running ads apologizing for sickening customers. One of its executives even acknowledged that people were afraid of their food.

Things didn't get better, though. The company had a norovirus outbreak in 2017, and then another in July 2018, in which nearly 650 people got food poisoning after dining at a Chipotle restaurant in Powell, Ohio.

Looking at the price chart of Chipotle stock, the impact on shareholders' confidence in management is clear. From 2015 to 2018, Chipotle stock lost two thirds of its value. Ultimately, the company paid a record $25 million fine to resolve criminal charges that it served tainted food that sickened more than 1,100 people.[12]

As I wrote this book, I watched a similar confidence crisis engulf Family Dollar stores with respect to pest control and basic sanitation.[13]

The Importance of Confidence Diversification

Early on in my banking career, I visited a client company that sold swimming-pool supplies and Christmas decorations. As I walked the floor of the warehouse with the CEO, he spoke proudly of his business's seasonal balance and how his effort to deliberately diversify the business had helped provide stable cash flow and earnings throughout the year.

CEOs spend a lot of time focused on diversification. They look to create a portfolio of businesses that provides consistent growth no matter the economic environment. Most business diversification strategies, though, might better be called extension strategies; they seek growth via products or geography that extend a company's reach. Management hopes to leverage existing customer, supplier, lender, and shareholder confidence into something new. The goal is to do more, in more places, with the hope that product/geographic breadth will provide a consistent rise in future earnings.

When analyzed in terms of confidence elasticity, though, most business extension strategies have few true diversification benefits. Within industries, adjacent products tend to have confidence-elasticity curves similar to those of existing products. Moreover, thanks to our highly interconnected global economy, even when spread across the globe, they tend to perform similarly. With few exceptions, global consumer confidence ebbs and flows in all but lockstep today. Not to say that can't and won't change, but geographic diversification doesn't provide the benefits it once did; we're largely mood synchronous.

If the goal of business diversification is to enable a company to better withstand fluctuations in the business cycle, it requires a different approach. Business and economic cycles are nothing more than confidence cycles delayed by the time it takes to implement the financial and economic decisions we make driven by the certainty and control we feel. To succeed across an economic cycle, then, companies must have a mix of products and services that do well across the full Confidence Spectrum.

As business leaders consider growth strategies, they should think about ways to pair highly confidence-elastic businesses with those that are less sensitive to changes in consumer confidence, or that might even benefit from declines in sentiment (ones that have negative confidence elasticity). They need to find the pool supplies and Christmas decorations for their business that enable them to more effectively navigate different *sentiment* seasons.

When those products aren't available or practical, then leaders need to consider what the confidence elasticity of their business requires in terms of their capital structure and the appropriate mix of debt and equity. Companies that are highly sensitive to changes in sentiment—both for cyclical reasons and because of the inherent risks of their business—need to ensure that they can withstand the potentially wild mood swings of customers, lenders, suppliers, creditors, and investors.

The same principle holds true at an individual level. If you work in an industry that has high confidence elasticity—that routinely goes through boom-and-bust cycles—you may want to consider taking on less debt and managing your personal finances more conservatively. Professional and retail investors, too, should think about confidence elasticity when constructing their portfolios, especially now.

Here's why.

Underlying the multi-slice pies of most investment portfolios today is the belief that by allocating capital carefully across various markets, financial instruments, industries, and other categories, asset managers can reduce risk. This is the principle behind simple "balanced" portfolios, wherein typically 60 percent is invested in stocks and 40 percent is invested in bonds. In some economic environments, stocks do well and bonds don't, while in other environments, the reverse is true. Over time, this balanced approach generates a higher return than investing in either stocks or bonds alone. When asset managers create investment portfolios, they do so in the belief that historical return correlations between different financial assets can be relied on and extrapolated into the future.

In many ways, you would think this kind of portfolio construction would be a great fit with the concept of confidence elasticity I've outlined. Stocks typically do well when economic confidence is rising, while bonds don't. Meanwhile, bonds typically do well when economic confidence is falling, while stocks don't. On the surface, the confidence elasticity of stocks and bonds would appear to be complementary.

In 2021, though, I began to have my doubts about that. As global equity markets were approaching their peak amid a speculative investing mania, behind the scenes, bond prices were also reaching historic highs. At the time, there were more than $18 trillion of negative-yielding bonds, a situation where investors were effectively paying issuers interest for the privilege of owning them. (Bond prices and bond yields move in opposite directions.) And the extreme confidence didn't end there: there was a tidal wave of record-high prices in real estate, private equity, and most of the other asset classes making up "diversified" investment portfolios.[14] Rather than some assets doing well while others languished, all ships had risen together atop an enormous wave of soaring investor sentiment. It was, as my friend Jesse Felder labeled it, "The Everything Bubble."[15]

While I will leave it to others to debate how we arrived at that point, what was clear was that most portfolios were composed almost entirely of assets with extremely high investor sentiment, and devoid of assets where there was low sentiment, let alone hopelessness. Stocks and bonds weren't behaving as they had in the past. The complementary confidence elasticity of the two assets, implied by historical correlations, was gone. Put simply, when it came to mood, every piece of investors' multi-sliced pie was piping hot. Framed in terms of confidence, portfolios that investors believed were well diversified weren't. They were highly concentrated in one mood: euphoria.[16]

To be fair, that was a highly unusual situation. It is very rare to see the kind of extreme confidence we saw in 2021 in so many financial assets at once.

As highly rewarding as the synchronous surge in asset prices had been on the way up for those balanced portfolios, though, it quickly turned punitive. During the first half of 2022, stocks, bonds, and most other asset classes were beaten down as interest rates rose and fears of stagflation weighed heavily on investor sentiment. Balanced investors experienced their worst losses in the past hundred years.[17] Given the across-the-board price declines, media headlines suggested that there was no place to hide for investors.[18]

While plenty of exogenous events could easily explain the broad market sell-off, the simultaneous dramatic run-up and drop-off in so many financial assets at once made me wonder whether there was a potentially significant shortcoming to today's standard portfolio construction practices. To obtain the real benefits of diversification, investors should consider more than just historical asset correlations. For an investment portfolio to be balanced, there needs to be confidence diversification. A well-diversified portfolio needs to hold a mix of assets where there is simultaneously rising investor confidence, falling investor confidence, investor euphoria, and investor hopelessness. Without that, changes in investment sentiment lead to lockstep movements in price. When constructing portfolios, investment managers should consider the investor sentiment in what they are buying and avoid buying too much of any one mood.

Confidence diversification may seem like an especially arcane application of the concepts of confidence elasticity, but it speaks to the new insights we can gain by looking at decision-making through the lens of confidence. Whether for corporations or asset managers, the objective of diversification is to better navigate not only different economic environments but different mood environments. Ultimately the goal isn't diversification per se but resilience—and that requires the ability to not only withstand the pressures of the Stress Center but have the resources and staying power to successfully navigate your way back out of it.

With respect to the specific need for confidence diversification in investment portfolios, there is a second and more urgent reason I raise the issue.

Over the past forty years, we have seen a rise in bond and stock prices, accompanied by a broad, synchronous increase in fixed-income and equity investor confidence. In financial markets, investor demand, asset prices, and confidence move as one. Since the early 1980s, interest rates have fallen steadily, while stock prices have soared.[19] While there have been short periods of divergence, confidence and the prices of financial assets broadly have risen steadily. As a result, investors have been handsomely rewarded by the parallel increases in the valuation of the many assets they now hold in their portfolios.

What will drive investment returns ahead, and whether balanced portfolios behave the way investors hope, will be a function of what happens to the synchronous sentiment moves in what were once confidence-uncorrelated markets. Given the collective extreme in investor confidence we saw in 2021, if the synchronous drop in sentiment continues, all asset prices will fall sharply in unison. "Balanced" investors won't reap the benefits of the diversification they believe they have in their portfolios; they will be punished by it.

To be clear, I don't wish for that, but if I have learned anything from almost forty years in financial services, it is that when widely assumed correlations break down in the markets, there are unexpected and far-reaching consequences. Based on what I see, "balanced" investment portfolios now run the risk of providing such a moment.

•

Confidence-elasticity studies provide a useful framework for organizations to think through and to visualize the ways rising and falling sentiment may impact consumer demand for their goods and services. With this information, businesses can not only better align their offerings with current consumer preferences but also see around the corner, to anticipate and prepare for changes in demand ahead.

Nowhere is this anticipation more important than for organizations that naturally operate in the Passenger Seat. When certainty is vital, it is critical that organizations understand not only what the customer must be certain of to begin with but what the consequences are when that certainty is in doubt.

CHAPTER 12

Better Practices in the Passenger Seat

MANY ORGANIZATIONS NATURALLY operate in the Passenger Seat. Airlines, prisons, high-end restaurants, and hospital emergency rooms can't easily turn control over to others. Nor, to be fair, can organizations where workers may require significant oversight and training before being granted control of a process all by themselves.

In the hospital, where the consequences of failure are high, we take comfort in knowing that new doctors have spent a considerable amount of time in that lower right box of the Quadrant before treating us. Medical schools provide a rigorous, structured process to migrate anxiously arriving students from the Stress Center to the Passenger Seat—years of classroom time, mentorship, and residency—before they move on to the Launch Pad and/or Comfort Zone and are given responsibility to care for patients. Many corporate internships and training and apprenticeship programs, as well as the military, operate with a similar "boot camp" model in which new recruits gain critical knowledge and skills in the Passenger Seat before they can act on their own.

Other organizations, or more specifically their leaders, create an unnecessary Passenger Seat environment by choosing not to operate with empowering migration plans. Domineering founders, micromanagers, and other authoritarian-leader types frequently create environments that, while highly certain, foster feelings of powerlessness in others. Employees remain stuck in the Passenger Seat. Decision-making, risk-taking, and authority more broadly remain highly concentrated.

To be fair, some of this authoritarianism is born of necessity. For a struggling start-up to survive, it may need a decisive, in-the-trenches, take-charge leader. Early on in a business's existence, founders may have little choice but to do or direct everything themselves.

In other cases, the situation may arise when a crisis manager comes into a troubled organization, bringing many of the same behavioral traits as a business founder, and continues to hold an overly tight rein on things even after the storm has passed. Like a dominant founder, the crisis manager is incapable of letting go. Moreover, once a dominant leader establishes the cultural norms that allow complete control, these norms can be difficult to change—especially when they have been shown to generate success.

This is also true of many "star-centered" organizations. For those supporting the star, every day feels like one: team members remain on high alert, prepared to scramble in response to the demands of an overbearing, demeaning leader. High-end restaurants, law firms, Hollywood studios, professional sports teams, and Wall Street are notorious for these command-and-control, celebrity-centric Passenger Seat environments. Interestingly, in many cases, boards of directors, owners, and financial partners end up feeling as powerless as lower-level employees in these organizations. Those in a position of oversight are hesitant to impose constraints on star performers for fear of losing them.

In all these cases, the result is an uncomfortable Passenger Seat workplace.

As you can imagine, the challenges these environments create are several.

First, left unchecked, they can easily fall into a cycle of greater and greater authoritarianism, wherein power becomes absolute, and worse, corrosively so. Just consider, for example, the career of Hollywood producer Harvey Weinstein.

Weinstein is hardly alone. The longer an organization remains in the lower right box of the Quadrant, and especially as it moves farther toward the lower right corner, the more likely it will become a workplace filled with manipulation and deceit. Prolonged, widespread powerlessness is the perfect soil for corruption. Enron, WorldCom, and Tyco shareholders learned this firsthand as the troubling inner workings of these companies were exposed to sunlight following the fall of their authoritarian CEOs. More recently, the collapses of Wirecard and FTX have revealed disconcerting parallels in behavior.

Second, Passenger Seat workplaces also tend to be devoid of leadership talent. Individuals in the organization with the capacity and ambition for greater control—who somehow threaten the authority of the leader—are either exiled or take control of their situation and exit themselves. As I shared earlier, Passenger Seat environments require compliance. The result is often a single star in the spotlight, surrounded by far less capable and less threatening backup singers and yes-men. The ones who stay are those who accept their subservience.

Ironically, this often sets up a situation where boards of directors feel like they, too, have little choice but to comply with a domineering leader. With no one inside the organization capable of running the show other than the named leader, boards feel damned if they do, damned if they don't. Out of perceived necessity, an overly authoritarian figure who continues to generate strong results remains in place rather than being ushered out. And we routinely see the same behavior in the sports world, in the entertainment industry, and on Wall Street. Richly rewarded, idolized stardom and the Passenger Seat are an all-too-familiar pair.

These kinds of environments can exist for long periods of time. Moreover, they can exist in plain sight. Bad behavior was Harvey Weinstein's signature.[1] So long as compliance can be sustained, and others are willing to accept powerlessness in exchange for paychecks and perks, little will change. Once again, the behavior and confidence of the crowd determines the fate of the leader.

That said, despite an outward appearance suggesting enormous strength, these organizations share the same inherent fragility of all Passenger Seat environments. When an authoritarian leader stumbles, the fate of the organization will be the same—like what we recently witnessed in Afghanistan. With no competent leader to step in, certainty quickly turns to chaos when the control provider exits or is exited.

Thousands of small businesses fail every year when their founder is incapacitated or dies, for this exact reason. With too much control concentrated in one individual, the organization has little resilience. And it isn't just small firms where this is the case. Five months after *The New York Times* reported that more than eighty women had accused Harvey Weinstein of sexual harassment, sexual assault, or rape, the Weinstein Company filed for bankruptcy.[2]

Whenever I hear a company referred to as an "empire" or a business executive referred to as a "cultish" leader, it warns me that no matter the success and the length of the reign, the aftermath of the leader's departure, whether through choice or circumstance, will inevitably be tragic. Over-belief in the dominance of an extremely controlling leader always leaves problems underappreciated and underexposed. And when these issues finally surface, the ship is typically rudderless and filled with rats and explosives. There is no one capable of quickly stepping in to grab the wheel, while the environment is highly corrupt and rife with problems.

And therein lie the telltale signs of authoritarian, Passenger Seat–workplace leaders.

First, there is never a clear and adequate succession plan. No one—not those above nor those below, let alone the leader himself—can imagine his unexpected departure. Implicit to the environment is the perception of its permanence.

Second, the environment is one not of an empowered team but of henchmen. Loyalty and obedience, rather than competence and initiative, are cultural norms.

Finally, troubles are silenced. Not only are big problems never discussed, even minor concerns go unmentioned. Those in the Passenger Seat must comply not only with the dominance of the leader but also with what that leader wants to believe is true.

Businesses spend millions of dollars on employee satisfaction surveys, yet few surveys openly invite feedback on the level of empowerment workers feel in their job. Just as organizations should consider seeking feedback on customer confidence, they should do the same with employee confidence. Businesses, like sports teams, do best when they are in the Comfort Zone—when employees are relaxed, capable of complex thought, collaborative, and innovative. Surveys that show large numbers of employees in the Passenger Seat or, worse, the Stress Center can warn of organizational fragility and the need for a change in leadership. Surveys asking employees to evaluate managers on empowerment, mentorship, and other leadership behaviors that encourage the advancement of others may provide valuable insight into the organization's leadership team and board of directors—assuming they are willing to act on it. So, too, would simply asking employees to mark on the Confidence Quadrant where they see themselves in their role every day.

Leaving the Passenger Seat

For many who find themselves trapped (whether in their job or elsewhere) in a Passenger Seat environment, where they feel powerless, the question quickly becomes, "How do I get out?"

The path out of the Passenger Seat, much like the path in, can take several forms.

Some routes out simply retrace the path in—as when the roller coaster returns to its starting point, or the plane lands and arrives safely at the gate. In these cases, we're happy to be back at our starting point in the Comfort Zone.

This may seem like an obvious outcome, but Passenger Seat experiences can feel like a prison, and it is useful to remember that the experience has a clear end point ahead—moreover, likely one with a positive outcome. A turbulent plane is all but certain to land safely at its destination, and the same is true for the most terrifying roller coaster. Successfully enduring the powerlessness of these experiences requires us to ignore our intense feelings of anxiety and to focus instead on the true odds of fate—to stop paying attention to the dire consequences of a highly unlikely possibility.

In other cases, though, we are right to be alarmed, such as when our exit from the Passenger Seat reflects a return to the Stress Center from which we just came—like when the plumber leaves our house and the leaky pipe still hasn't been fixed. With the pool of water in the basement growing, we feel we're right back where we started, if not worse off.

In these cases, our exit from the Passenger Seat is in the hands of others. We are the beneficiary or victim of circumstance; for good or ill, we don't exit the Passenger Seat as much as we are ejected from it. If our problem is solved, we land in the Comfort Zone. When it remains, or worse, grows, we're back in the Stress Center.

To handle these situations better, we need to remember this possible outcome as we select those we empower and follow when we are in the Stress Center. Rather than acting impulsively and emotionally, we need to slow down and be more deliberative. Not only is this likely to provide a better outcome, transitioning us successfully to the Comfort Zone, it mitigates the blame and shame that naturally accompany a return to the Stress Center. We won't beat up on ourselves for having made the wrong knee-jerk choice. (The same practice applies any time we're considering a new job. By gaining as clear an understanding as possible of an organization's "control culture" before joining it, we may avoid Passenger Seat opportunities altogether.)

Finally, there are the times when we leave the Passenger Seat because we cease to be compliant and choose to leave on our own—when we've had enough of that overbearing manager and say, "Take this job and shove it!"

In these cases, something important happens: We swap powerlessness for control and certainty for uncertainty. We exit the Passenger Seat and jump into the Launch Pad.

In the wake of the pandemic, many companies saw employees jump from the Passenger Seat to the Launch Pad. Couched as the "Great Resignation," the "Great Relocation," or the "Great Reassessment," this was a mass migration of workers seeking to take greater control of their lives. Working from home provided certainty, but that wasn't enough. Employees needed to feel a sense of control, too. While the outcome of the decision was unclear when they made it, many office workers wanted to pick where, with whom, and for whom they worked. And with the trend of "Quiet Quitting," they picked how much effort they wanted to put into their jobs, too.

I will share much more about the upper left box of the Quadrant in the next chapter, but it is important to recognize that the choice to leave the Passenger Seat for the Launch Pad isn't as easy as it might appear.

What often holds us back from jumping into the Launch Pad is our fear we may not ultimately end up in the Comfort Zone but instead may fail and fall into the lower left corner of the Stress Center, and that we will end up far worse off and regret our choice. We picture the outcome to be binary, as in Figure 12.1, but with high odds of failure. We fear we will quit our job and won't find a replacement. Home Depot won't have the part or tool we need, or we won't understand the YouTube plumbing video after all.

This fear is understandable.

First, taking control is not a skill set most of us think we possess when we're in the Passenger Seat. We often see ourselves as followers, looking to others to take the lead. Sadly, this is a notion many predatory leaders of Passenger Seat environments reinforce. Rather than building others up, they belittle. They aggressively signal that we can't and won't succeed without them.

Second, taking control may mean having specific expertise and abilities that in the Passenger Seat we think we lack. After all, this is why we

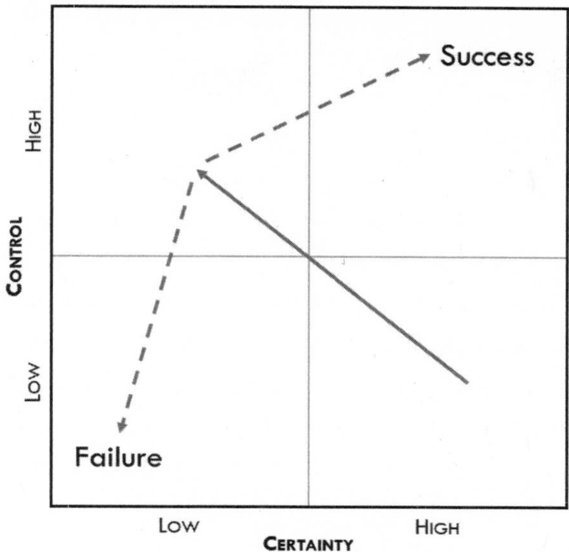

FIGURE 12.1: Imagining our exit from the Passenger Seat

wound up in the Passenger Seat in the first place: we deliberately hired someone to tackle a problem we didn't feel equipped to handle on our own. The idea that we could suddenly do so seems laughable.

Third, the Passenger Seat is an environment that often discourages risk-taking to begin with. Having ceded control to others or, worse, had it taken away from us, we have little opportunity to demonstrate our success in taking risks on our own. The Launch Pad represents unfamiliar territory. Moreover, taking initiative means taking full accountability for the consequences. Should we fail as we jump for the Launch Pad, we will have no one to blame but ourselves.

Finally, because our starting point is outside of the Comfort Zone, we see failure and its consequences more tangibly than we see the potential for success. We already feel vulnerable and anxious. Because of that, we are likely to be more pessimistic about the outcome.

With all these factors taken together, we believe the chances of success are dim, and so we remain.

All these feelings are magnified when we have experienced the Stress Center before and the Passenger Seat represents an improvement on that condition, even if a minimal one. Deliberately choosing to exit the Passenger Seat and risk returning to the Stress Center can feel overwhelming—a potential increase in vulnerability to be avoided at all costs. We are afraid of a relapse. We can't face the idea of going back, let alone going back of our own volition.

Ruminating over all the troubling possible outcomes, then, holds us captive in the Passenger Seat. We suffer from analysis paralysis as we overthink our situation and, in many cases, remain until conditions deteriorate so much that we feel like we are in the Stress Center. It is only once things have deteriorated to that point that our flight response kicks in and triggers a move to the Launch Pad.

If you listen to the stories of victims of sexual assault, especially when the abuser has some form of ongoing power or control over them, you will repeatedly hear narratives that capture the "damned if you do, damned if you don't" thinking that individuals in Passenger Seat environments wrestle with before ultimately coming forward. It is why victims so often wait until there are others who will make the jump with them—by banding together and telling their story as one, they believe they can increase their chances of being taken seriously and ultimately making it to the Comfort Zone. "Maybe now we will be believed," they say.

The same holds true more broadly with workers who have overly controlling managers. Typically, there is silence until there is a massive outcry. Groups of individuals leave en masse or stay and demand radical change that reveals a long, troubling pattern of behavior by leadership or colleagues.

Sadly, some Passenger Seat workplace environments take a true disaster to be revealed. While reading the many news reports that surfaced in the wake of the Boeing MAX series crashes, I was struck by the plane manufacturer's clear lack of appreciation for the basics of confidence-driven decision-making. Boeing not only failed to recognize the fundamental risks that go along with operating a business in the

Passenger Seat, it compounded those risks by fostering a Passenger Seat workplace environment. With naysayers silenced, the company culture all but set up the tragedy that occurred.[3]

The Nothing-to-Lose Response

As you can imagine, when we are in the Passenger Seat and our pleas for intervention are ignored, the impact on us can be debilitating. Our feelings of powerlessness soar. Voiceless, we fall to the bottom of the Passenger Seat. When there is retribution, as is often the case when calls for help go unheard and those in control feel even more empowered by the lack of response, it feels like our worst nightmare has been realized. We slide into the lower left corner of the Stress Center, awash in feelings of powerlessness and uncertainty. We feel hopeless.

Many succumb to this blow. The trauma from the experience leaves us unwilling and unable to move forward. Since we failed in our attempt to move out of the Passenger Seat, we can't see our way out of the Stress Center.

For others, though, this is the ash from which we rise. With nothing left to lose, our fuck-it and fight responses kick in.

That was the case with Tarana Burke. As she puts it, "The 'me too' Movement™ started in the deepest, darkest place in my soul."[4]

Darkness is the birthplace of many social and political movements. After long periods in the Passenger Seat, with pleas for help going unanswered and repeated retribution being visited upon us, shared hopelessness fosters a nothing-to-lose response.

It is easy to ascribe the success of social movements to the courage of those early members who took action in the face of hopelessness, but there are other important takeaways from their example for those struggling in Passenger Seat environments.

The first is to recognize that doing nothing is itself a deliberate choice. While we can blame others for forcibly moving us into the Passenger Seat, short of physical confinement, we make the choice to stay there.

This view may feel uncomfortable and/or naive to some readers, given the intense physical, economic, and social pressures frequently confronting those in the lower right box of the Quadrant. Those constraints are real, and I don't want to diminish their weight. Nor am I implying that those who remain in the Passenger Seat choose to be victimized. There are substantial structural inequalities that make it far harder for some to move out of the Passenger Seat than for others. Privileges and resources are not evenly divided. My point is simply this: reframing the Passenger Seat, from an environment in which we're imprisoned to one in which we choose to remain, forces us to consider alternatives—and, moreover, to consider how we might best prepare for those alternatives. "I am stuck here" is a very different mindset than "I am choosing to stay here until I can safely leave." Regaining control is actionable. We can take specific, deliberate steps.

For some, preparing to leave the Passenger Seat means forcing themselves to take control and to acquire new skills. Sometimes, these skills may be technical in nature, especially if we are considering a new job or profession. We need to know what will be expected of us ahead. In other cases, it may mean developing soft skills. Especially when we are in the Passenger Seat, this may mean learning how to do a better job of speaking up for ourselves and taking initiative.

Not only do we need to learn these skills, we must practice them as well. Preparing to leave the Passenger Seat requires us to expose ourselves to the other boxes of the Quadrant—to fail and fall into the Stress Center as we struggle with new skills before gaining proficiency. As we consider how we will leave the Passenger Seat, we need to think about how we will train and prepare for those challenging moments ahead.

We may also need different tools and resources. Just as we think about what to pack in our suitcase as we plan for a trip abroad, we have to develop a checklist of the things we will need as we consider our new environment.

In addition, we need to develop new routines, regimens, and habits that turn awkward, tentative steps into regular, recurring action. We forget that the enemy of control is inaction. What routines provide is the demonstration of not just control but control accompanied by System 1 thinking. When we don't have to think about what we are doing, we are in the Comfort Zone. Establishing habits unknowingly provides a critical path for us out of the Passenger Seat and into the upper right box of the Quadrant.

Needless to say, having coaches and mentors to help us and to hold us accountable, while also encouraging us, can be vital. Loneliness and futility are common feelings in the Passenger Seat. Moreover, one of the biggest obstacles to leaving the Passenger Seat is that we simply don't know how to do it. Success requires us to ask for help. What many in the Passenger Seat underappreciate is that asking for help isn't showing weakness; it is demonstrating control. Asking for help moves us to the Launch Pad.

Finally, as we commit to leaving the Passenger Seat, we must find others with experience whom we trust to help guide us. Finding "kindred spirits" at similar points along a comparable path can also be especially helpful.

As you may sense already, leaving the Passenger Seat on our own is especially challenging. There is a lot that goes into it. Moreover, it is rarely a straight-line journey from the Passenger Seat into the Comfort Zone. It is a process of self-empowerment and regaining control in our lives where it feels as though for every two steps forward we take one step back.

Here it is worth highlighting that not all Passenger Seat environments arise at the hands of others. Those struggling with addiction often associate the experience with powerlessness. For many, their lives seem to be an endless loop, back and forth between the lower two boxes of the Quadrant. The Launch Pad and the Comfort Zone seem out of reach. Sobriety requires alcoholics to take control, something that can feel all but impossible against the overwhelming pull of their addiction.

Then there are those critical voices in our head that we unknowingly empower. They, too, can leave us feeling imprisoned in the Passenger Seat. We blame and shame ourselves for poor decisions from the past and hold on to the harsh words of others long after an experience has passed. Without realizing it, we can subject ourselves to life sentences in the Passenger Seat, unwilling to throw ourselves back out there for fear of further embarrassment and failure.

Leaving the Passenger Seat often requires us to look inward—to confront the harsh, disempowering stories we cling to, to overcome the oppression we feel, both real and imagined. Here again, mentors, support groups, and counselors can play an invaluable role, helping us move forward.

Which brings me to my final better practice for the Passenger Seat: don't wait to act. No matter the reason for our entry into the Passenger Seat, if we are to have any hope of reaching the Comfort Zone, we must take control. Control will not come to us; there is no army en route to rescue us from our captivity. Control will come only from within. Moreover, without our own initiative, the vulnerability we experience will continue. In fact, without our intervention, it is likely to get worse.

That, then, leaves us three options: succumb to the powerlessness of the Passenger Seat; wait until the condition becomes so intolerable that one of our highly emotional and impulsive Five F responses kicks in; or take the deliberate steps necessary now to prepare to leave.

•

When the Passenger Seat represents a means to an end back to the Comfort Zone, we will tolerate the lack of control we experience. But even then, we aren't confident—we are compliant, a beneficiary or victim of circumstance.

Gaining confidence in the Passenger Seat, then, requires that we regain control. In the best-case scenario, control will be given to us—our plane will land safely at our destination, and we will gleefully walk up the Jetway into the terminal. The service provider we hired will have satisfied our needs.

More often, though, we will need to take control on our own. As this process typically involves exchanging powerlessness for control and uncertainty for certainty, our next stop will be the Launch Pad.

SECTION V

The Launch Pad

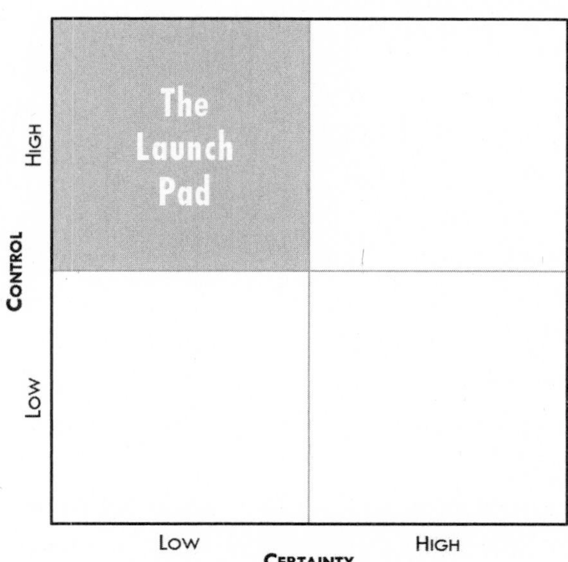

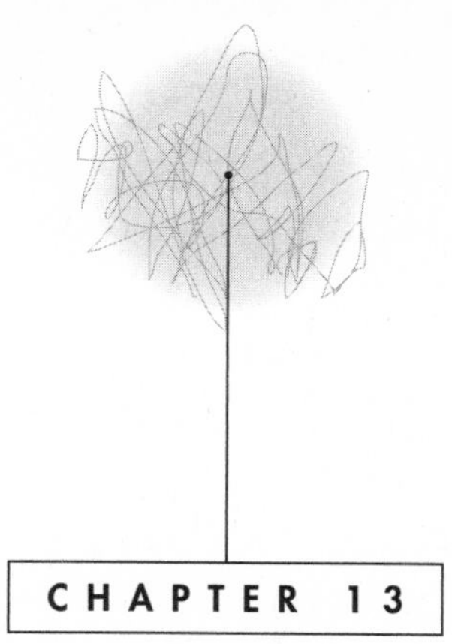

CHAPTER 13

The Launch Pad and Environments of High Control and Low Certainty

SARA BLAKELY WAS getting ready for a party when she realized she didn't have the right undergarment to provide a smooth look under her white pants. Armed with scissors and "inspired genius," she cut the feet off her control-top pantyhose. In that moment, Spanx was born.[1]

In the next two years—and while still working a full-time job—Ms. Blakely found a textile mill to produce her product, filed the necessary patents and trademarks for her business, secured a major order from Neiman Marcus, and ended up on television. Spanx Footless, Body-Shaping Pantyhose was featured on Oprah's "Favorite Things" list in 2000. Seemingly overnight, Ms. Blakely went from fax-machine saleswoman to celebrated entrepreneur, ultimately landing on the cover of *Forbes* magazine as the youngest self-made female billionaire in the world.[2]

Today, Spanx is to shapewear what FedEx is to overnight shipping—an industry-defining and ubiquitous brand. And like FedEx's Fred Smith before her, Sara Blakely found the answer to a problem in plain sight. With it, she jumped into the Launch Pad, succeeded, and landed in the upper right reaches of the Comfort Zone. Her Confidence Quadrant journey is every entrepreneur's dream.

WHEN I SPEAK with entrepreneurs, the Confidence Quadrant conversation quickly centers on the Launch Pad. They describe the upper left box—environments of high control and low certainty—as their natural habitat. They tell me the Comfort Zone, where most business leaders feel most relaxed, is too boring. Entrepreneurs find too much certainty dull. They are excited by possibility; it inspires and motivates them. What others see as troubling uncertainty, they see as potential—the chance to build a business that solves a problem and creates something new. Moreover, they want to drive it. Entrepreneurs crave the chance to be behind the wheel.

That is the nature of born risk-takers, whether they are rolling the dice in a Las Vegas casino, scaling the side of a steep cliff, or exploring the western United States for the first time like Lewis and Clark: when

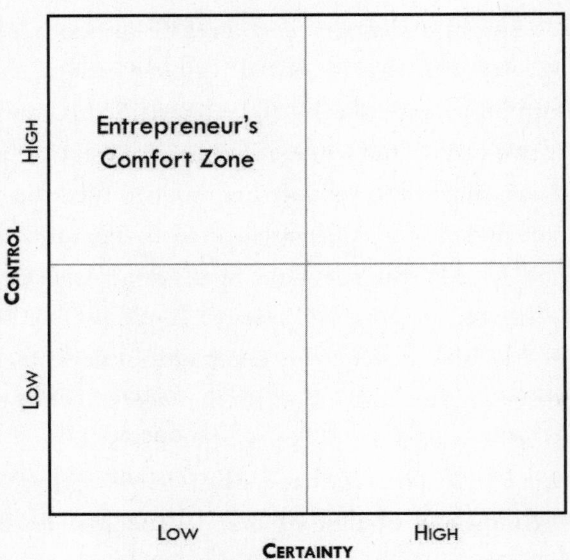

FIGURE 13.1: The Launch Pad, entrepreneurs' Comfort Zone

they have control, they are confident. The Launch Pad *is* their Comfort Zone, and at its very top is their sweet spot: extreme control (Figure 13.1).

For most of us, though, the Launch Pad lacks sufficient certainty to put us at ease. The to-be-determined nature of the upper left box—all that possibility—leaves things unfinished and far too much up in the air. If we choose to jump, as the Launch Pad requires us to do, we want to know we will land safely back on our feet in the Comfort Zone and that we won't fail and end up in the Stress Center.

Organizations in the Launch Pad

When we talk about "established" and "mature" businesses, we typically refer to successful businesses that have moved on from the Launch Pad into the Comfort Zone—organizations with scale, a long list of well-defined products, a clear customer base, and stable earnings and cash flow. Whether growing quickly, in periods of high consumer and business confidence, or facing challenges during a recession, there is a sense of certainty to their long-term future—one that is attractive to shareholders, lenders, and employees alike. We can't imagine a world without companies like Coca-Cola, Home Depot, and Microsoft. They are intensely familiar to us. They epitomize the cognitive ease and System 1 thinking that comes with being in the Comfort Zone.

Organizations in the Launch Pad don't experience that benefit. They don't have that perceived safety net of certainty. We need to use System 2 thinking in examining them, as we see more unknowns. Not surprisingly, then, we describe most entrepreneurial environments as "risky." Success is unassured and the outcome unknowable.

To compensate, Launch Pad leaders try to temper the downside consequences through greater control. When operating in the Launch Pad, leaders look to quick decision-making, constant reassessment, and frequent changes in tactics to succeed. Like drivers on an unfamiliar, twisting road, entrepreneurial leaders know they must be prepared to shift gears quickly, turn sharply, and even slam on the brakes, back up, and reverse course if necessary. Successful entrepreneurs know they must be nimble. Strategic thinking and long-term planning—classic indicators of an organization in the Comfort Zone—are out of the question; immediacy is the name of the game as leaders learn and adjust course, repeatedly. Entrepreneurs operate in Me-Here-Now mode. There's a problem to be solved and an opportunity to be seized before others catch on. When they are successful, entrepreneurs end up in the Comfort Zone and there is a clear sense of accomplishment—a "look at what I did" moment of satisfaction.

But those moments typically don't last long. Where others are content to remain in the Comfort Zone, natural risk-takers quickly want to try again—to return to the Launch Pad to see what they can do next. Like players who have successfully tackled a new video game, they want to move on to something new and more challenging. When business leaders describe themselves as "serial entrepreneurs," they reveal their calling: one Launch Pad experience after another.

Working in Launch Pad Environments

For those not behind the wheel, entrepreneurial Launch Pad environments can be especially challenging. Far from the C-suite and in an environment of high uncertainty and low control, rank-and-file employees can feel that they are in the Stress Center—on a violent roller coaster ride as a business suddenly twists and turns, driven by impulsive decision-making at the top. Even when workers are empowered, these environments are challenging. Much as the employees in Passenger Seat organizations must cope with perennial powerlessness, workers in the Launch Pad must endure endless uncertainty. Constant change is a given.

Finding employees for whom that environment is a good fit is vital. Launch Pad businesses require teams who see change as opportunity rather than loss, and who are comfortable taking control amid an environment of uncertainty.

That makes large-scale entrepreneurial environments hard to sustain. Without predictability, many employees burn out. The prolonged uncertainty exhausts them. Paradoxically, to grow and become sustainable, Launch Pad enterprises *must* eventually move into the Comfort Zone. Feelings of control and certainty must broaden both within the organization and with customers; a Me-Here-Now mindset must evolve into an Us-Everywhere-Forever business for the organization to stabilize and continue to grow.

For entrepreneurial leaders, this means ceding control to others—a behavior that rarely comes naturally. In the case of Sara Blakely and Spanx, that meant turning over the CEO position to Laurie Ann Goldman, who had initially worked with the firm as a consultant. As Blakely later told *Forbes*, "[Goldman] brought much more formality, more structure. We had formal business planning, which we'd never had before. We had one-year and three-year targets."[3] For the business to evolve—to move from the Launch Pad into the Comfort Zone—Spanx required a change in leadership (a pattern we'll see repeated later).

Another paradox develops for successful businesses in the Launch Pad: they often become very attractive as acquisition candidates to established businesses in the Comfort Zone. Offering high growth, innovation, and a "refreshing" entrepreneurial spirit, they look like the perfect solution for larger, slower-growing organizations.

What acquirers miss is that when it comes to mergers and acquisitions, most happy-with-uncertainty Launch Pad organizations are a poor cultural fit with most businesses in the Comfort Zone, where maintaining certainty and control—staying *in* the Comfort Zone—dominates the decision-making process. Entrepreneurial Launch Pad leaders who are comfortable saying, "Let's try it and see what happens," struggle with a slower, more deliberative, consensus-building, vulnerability-avoiding decision-making process.

Around the merger negotiating table, while staring at compelling pro forma earnings projections of their two combined organizations, buyers and sellers routinely think they can overcome their contrasting styles. But the two environments are in opposition to one another—one organization thrives with high certainty and the other relishes all the possibilities that accompany high uncertainty. What looks like a struggle for control after the deal closes is more likely a tug-of-war over which of the upper boxes of the Quadrant will prevail in terms of corporate culture. In almost all cases, the Comfort Zone "body" rejects the Launch Pad "transplant" culture, with the entrepreneurs quickly fleeing the scene.

And here is what routinely surprises buyers: since the entrepreneurial leaders never needed or wanted the certainty of the Comfort Zone in the first place, they don't need many reasons or much encouragement to leave. Once an acquisition has occurred, and especially as the buyer begins to impose more structure, most entrepreneurial leaders are eager to leave and try their hand at building a new business again. It is their calling.

Businesses in the Comfort Zone spend billions of dollars every year acquiring rapidly growing Launch Pad companies only to see their money go to waste. Not only do Comfort Zone acquirers typically wait until far too late in the innovation cycle to make a bold move—as with the AOL–Time Warner merger, a poster child for ill-timed Launch Pad–Comfort Zone unions—but the buyers then impose tight controls, stifling the innovation and growth they sought in the first place. In many cases, a vicious spiral ensues as slowing growth paired with an especially high acquisition premium leads buyers to double down on the controls, further inhibiting growth. Buyers all but slaughter the golden goose they just bought.

Rather than acquiring Launch Pad companies outright late in the cycle, most Comfort Zone companies would be far better off taking an equity stake in them earlier and leaving them alone when it comes to management and corporate culture.

Ford took this approach with Rivian when it formed a strategic partnership with the EV truck company in April 2019 and made a substantial investment in it. While the partnership was ultimately dissolved as

Ford's own in-house EV development efforts flourished, the company reaped an enormous financial reward, recording an $8.2 billion gain on its investment when Rivian went public in November 2021.[4] While that gain fell sharply after Rivian shares subsequently sold off, the financial return was still substantial.

By taking the approach it did, Ford was able to invest early and capitalize on the potential benefits of a fast-growing Launch Pad start-up while at the same time allowing its in-house capabilities to grow at their own pace, consistent with the company's existing Comfort Zone culture and business practices. Rather than frustrating both tortoise and hare, Ford leadership enabled each to run its own race.

Our Paths into the Launch Pad

While entrepreneurship, like the kind Sara Blakely demonstrated when she launched Spanx, draws many leaders into the Launch Pad, others arrive under different circumstances and from different locations on the Quadrant, accompanied by different feelings.

ARRIVAL FROM THE STRESS CENTER

As I shared earlier, the Launch Pad is often a required stop on our journey out of the Stress Center—as when a pipe bursts (Stress Center) and we race to Home Depot to pick up the required parts (Launch Pad) to successfully fix it (returning us to the Comfort Zone). In these moments, our feelings in the Launch Pad are typically a function of how prepared we feel. When we feel well prepared, we view our stay in the Launch Pad as temporary—a necessary means to an end on a journey that we know will safely conclude in the Comfort Zone.

When we are under- or even unprepared, we struggle. Like a new skier who took the wrong lift and suddenly finds herself at the top of a steep, black diamond slope, we feel panic set in as we drop back into the Stress Center. We don't see a clear path to the bottom of the hill.

In the Launch Pad, the amount of control we believe we have and the perceived certainty of the outcome drive our responses. Ill-prepared individuals look the same as organizations struggling in the Launch Pad—like cats on glass, clawing at whatever they can to regain control before they lose it for good.

This inherent fragility is what makes the Launch Pad and Passenger Seat so similar. Depending on our actions, the outcome is binary: calm or chaos. Either we keep making progress toward the Comfort Zone or we lose our footing and collapse into the Stress Center. The Launch Pad and the Passenger Seat are also similar because of their disproportionate reliance on one feeling—either certainty *or* control—to maintain stability. Whereas in the Passenger Seat we must have extreme certainty of the outcome, in the Launch Pad our need is to have extreme control.

This emphasis on control in the Launch Pad helps explain the extreme actions that business leaders and policymakers took in the early days of the pandemic. With everyone deep in the Stress Center, leaders weren't taking any chances as they sought to lead a mass exodus. Amid the extreme uncertainty, they did everything they possibly could to execute a successful return by way of the Launch Pad back to the Comfort Zone.

When Ellen Kullman, chief executive of 3-D printing company Carbon, Inc. and former CEO of DuPont, was asked to explain why, amid a global pandemic, businesses were simultaneously buying their suppliers, bringing contract work in-house, moving workers and production facilities closer to home, and relocating plants closer to suppliers, she spoke for far more leaders than just herself when she said, "It's about control. I want to have more control in an uncertain world."[5]

As her company was awash in the chaos of the Stress Center, her goal, like those of other business leaders, was to bring it to the very top of the Launch Pad, creating as great a perception of control as possible. With the clear ability to guide what happened next, she felt she could then create greater feelings of certainty for all her stakeholders (Figure 13.2).

Retaking control—and moving as high up into the Launch Pad as

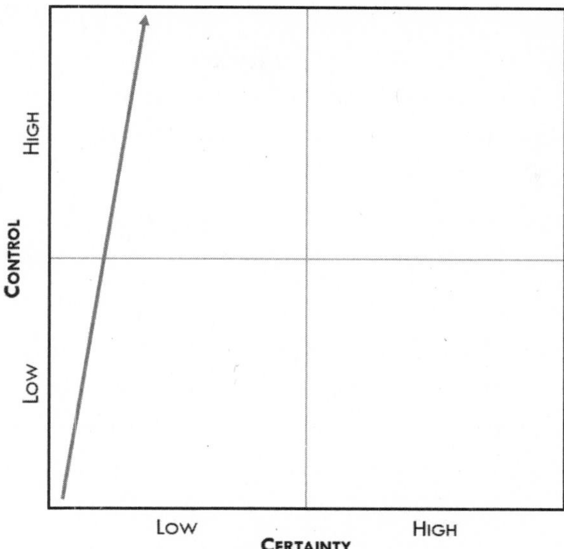

FIGURE 13.2: Taking extreme control to exit the Stress Center

possible—is "Step 1" for most crisis managers. You hear it in the language they use: Firefighters work to "control the outbreak" of a wildfire. Doctors do the same with an infection, working to "contain it" before it gets worse. During the pandemic, we heard very similar language from public policymakers with respect to controlling the pandemic and its impact as they used slogans like "flatten the curve" and "stop the spread." Messages, metaphors, and symbols of control were everywhere.

Retaking control was also front and center in the employee movements that occurred as a result of the pandemic—again, the "Great Reassessment," the "Great Migration," the "Great Resignation," and even "Quiet Quitting." At their core, these behavior patterns were all about seizing control. As the pandemic wore on and the prospect of a rapid return to normal waned, individuals redefined how, where, with whom, and for whom they wanted to spend their time. With the world crumbling around them, they took charge of what they could.

We see this natural response in the face of traumatic events. As we envision an uncertain future ahead, we take deliberate steps to ensure that we won't re-experience our powerlessness. We keep a "go bag" because we've previously been caught by surprise by a wildfire. We keep a spare key hidden outside our home or with a neighbor after being locked out.

The pandemic was no different. Since the outbreak, businesses have gone to extraordinary lengths to add resilience to their supply chains. "Just-in-time" has been replaced by "just-in-case" inventory management. Leaders have pivoted to systems that are smaller, simpler, less interdependent, more local, and more transparent.

The COVID pandemic is a great case study in the wide-ranging impacts that occur when large groups of individuals and businesses in the Stress Center simultaneously seek to take control. That inflation soared in the wake of the outbreak shouldn't have been a surprise; the panic-driven decision-making of March 2020 fueled consumer demand at the same time it slashed supply.

The Russian invasion of Ukraine prompted a similar moment of vulnerability-driven decision-making, with leaders focused on regaining control amid the uncertainty of war. Manufacturing security, energy security, and food security were front and center, with business and national leaders across the globe all seeking to increase their level of control at once. That the commodity markets soared in the midst of it all, again, should not have been a surprise. Buyers, sellers, speculators, and hedgers, too, were all doing the same.

When our feelings of uncertainty skyrocket, we compensate by seizing control of whatever we can—whether as individuals, business leaders, or policymakers. And when we all do it at once, the economic and financial-market consequences can be profound.

VOLUNTARY PATHS TO THE LAUNCH PAD

Endeavors in entrepreneurship and a desire/need to escape from the Stress Center represent two paths to the Launch Pad, but there are

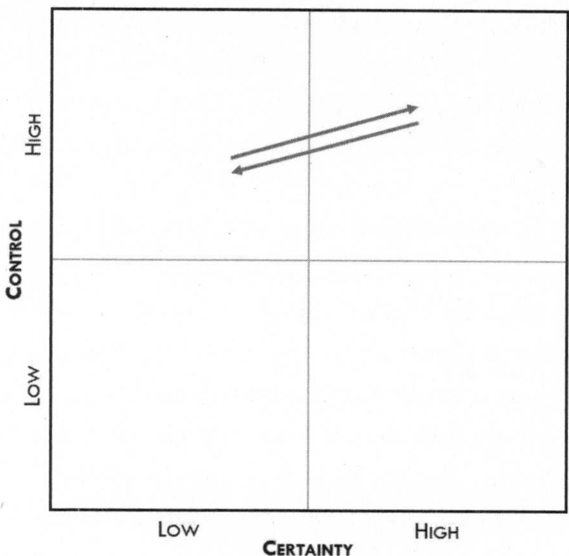

FIGURE 13.3: Leaving and returning to the Comfort Zone

others—such as when we voluntarily choose to leave the Comfort Zone to learn a new skill or take a new job. Here, we tend to take measured steps, controlling the speed with which we introduce more difficulty as we experience new feelings of uncertainty. As a new skier, we slowly snowplow our way down a gentle, wide, green (easy) trail. Then, once we have successfully navigated to the bottom enough times to feel a level of proficiency, we move on to blue (intermediate) slopes, where the trail is steeper and narrower.

When we map learning to ski on the Confidence Quadrant, our trips loop back and forth between the Comfort Zone and the Launch Pad, mimicking our journeys up and down the mountain (Figure 13.3). With each additional run and chance taken, we hope to feel more in control and to have more certainty as we race down the hill. A good day of learning to ski ends with our arriving triumphantly back in the lodge with no broken bones or sprained ankles, sitting high in the upper right reaches of the Comfort Zone, boasting of the new trails we tackled.

The Launch Pad is also the voluntary Quadrant location for when we start single-player video games, jigsaw puzzles, and crosswords—activities that bring uncertainty, a problem to solve where we must find the answer. Our success returns us to the Comfort Zone, where we began.

Some voluntary experiences in the Launch Pad have minor consequences if we fail; the puzzle and the crossword remain unfinished as we go on with our lives. Others, though, come with real consequences—consider rock climbing. Our willingness to voluntarily experience the Launch Pad has a lot to do with how we view the consequences of the actions we take there and our level of preparedness. We make our choice based on the outcome we imagine: After we've had a close call on a blue ski run, we tell our friend that we'll pass on the black diamond she suggests. We imagine we're going to lose control on our skis and don't want to end up in the lower left corner of the Quadrant, wrapped like a burrito on a toboggan as we're taken down the hill by the ski patrol.

Then there are those voluntary moments in the Launch Pad prompted by the prospect of success—of financial windfall, social status, or other gain. The Launch Pad is where we play the Powerball lottery, speculate in Bitcoin, or choose to join our friends in a round of tequila shots at the bar. In these cases, we focus on the benefits we imagine. Our actions will make us rich, let us quit our job, or make us more popular with our friends.

Not surprisingly, many entrepreneurial organizations operating in the Launch Pad emphasize to investors and employees the potential financial and status gains they will amass when their company achieves its inevitable success. They promise a big payoff for enduring often intense uncertainty. So long as those involved continue to believe in the likelihood of that rosy outcome, there is usually harmony in the ranks. The challenge comes when the outlook shifts—when certainty in the future benefit evaporates. If employees and investors in the Launch Pad enterprise sense a change in the trajectory from the Comfort Zone to the Stress Center, they are more likely to panic, get angry, and jump ship.

During the tech crash of 2021–22, we saw this reversal in attitude in real time. Earlier, as the share prices of many high-flying companies soared, employees couldn't imagine anything but the upper right corner of the Comfort Zone as the outcome of their efforts. Then, as those same share prices collapsed, and these employees imagined the Stress Center ahead, they felt betrayed. The allure of working for a fast-growing start-up with an uncertain future faded.

And therein lies the biggest rub of the Launch Pad: the way we feel there drives the way we imagine the outcome of our actions. When we are highly optimistic, we easily envision future success. We assign a high probability to an outcome in which we ultimately arrive in the Comfort Zone. On the other hand, when we are pessimistic, we can't imagine that result. Rather than the Comfort Zone, we see an inevitable end in the Stress Center. Our level of confidence drives how we feel in the Launch Pad, which in turn drives the outcome we predict, which in turn drives how we choose to act. We make decisions in the Launch Pad based on the outcome we imagine because of how we feel.

In Chapter 1, when I shared my experience flying to Los Angeles, I highlighted a similar issue with the Passenger Seat (the lower right box of the Quadrant). On a plane, our view of the environment is driven by our feelings, and the outcome that we imagine goes along with that. As a highly optimistic, experienced flyer, I unknowingly felt as though I was in the Comfort Zone even though I was actually in the Passenger Seat. I had no doubt the flight would conclude safely at the gate in Los Angeles. The nervous flyer next to me, though, spent all five hours of the flight in the Stress Center. She wasn't sure we would make it. It was the same flight, but it was experienced by passengers with disparate feelings that reflected their imagined outcomes to the flight. I overestimated my level of control of the outcome, while she underestimated the certainty of the outcome. In both cases, the way we imagined our flying experience ending came down to confidence.

You can see these same confidence-driven distortions in the Launch Pad when standing in line for a roller coaster. It doesn't take long to distinguish those in the line who feel they are in the Comfort Zone from those who are in the Stress Center: the former are strategizing about how best to get to the front car, where they will throw their hands high in the air as they descend, while the latter are frantically looking for any excuse to make an exit. But regardless of where they place themselves on the Quadrant, they will all hop on the same ride, which will return them to where they started less than one minute later. Then you can easily guess who felt as though the ride was five seconds long and who felt as though it lasted twelve years.

•

Like the Passenger Seat, the Launch Pad comes with a wide range of feelings driven by where we arrived from on the Quadrant. Our path to the Launch Pad matters. But so, too, do our comfort with uncertainty and our appetite for risk.

Before talking about risk-taking more specifically, I want to discuss one last dimension to confidence: the stories we tell. Given how important our stories are to the choices we make in the Launch Pad, and to the feelings we experience there, we need to gain a better appreciation of them and their impact.

CHAPTER 14

Confidence and the Stories We Tell

EARLY IN THIS BOOK, I made the point that there is a natural and consistent connection between our actions and our feelings of certainty and control: we act as we feel. Then I layered on Horizon Preference, suggesting that there, too, is a clear association with our level of confidence. From Me-Here-Now preferences when our confidence is low to Us-Everywhere-Forever when it is high, our Horizon Preference serves as the variable transmission mechanism linking our feelings and actions across the Confidence Spectrum. Finally, I drew in our cognitive processing and how it, too, adjusts and aligns with our level of confidence. With confidence, we lazily use System 1 thinking; without it, we intensely demand System 2.

Taken all together, our level of confidence and our preferences, our cognitive processing, and our actions find a natural equilibrium. As a result, if we know where we currently stand on one of these variables, we can reasonably deduce the others. Moreover, as one element changes, we can anticipate how the others will adjust accordingly.

Now, I want to add in one final, crucial dimension of our decision-making: our stories. They, too, have a natural association with our level of confidence, and when we act in the Launch Pad, they play a pivotal role. When we're faced with uncertainty, our stories frame the choices we make. They fill in the blanks when things feel unpredictable.

Not only is there reflexivity and equilibrium to our stories, there is utility, too. They provide useful clues revealing how we feel and, therefore, what we are likely to do next. Moreover, if we want our messages to others to be effective, they, like all stories, must mirror the confidence level—and the specific location on the Quadrant—of those we are trying to reach.

Stories: The News Reports of Our Lives

You will recall that I opened this book detailing how, every weekday afternoon, the financial media generates stories to explain what happened in the markets that day and why. But that phenomenon is not limited to the financial media. We do the same in our own lives, 24-7, with the stories we tell ourselves and others. So, too, do businesses and other organizations, with everything from their quarterly earnings releases to their management presentations. Then, of course, there is the news media more broadly. Media outlets not only report what happens and why, they also share the stories of others, often experts (and wannabe experts). And if that's not enough, we find similar storytelling every time we scroll through Twitter, LinkedIn, Facebook, Instagram, and other social media platforms. More than ever, we are awash in stories.

When it comes to all our stories, there are two elements that matter most: their relevance and their resonance. Is the message somehow useful and worth paying attention to—because it either provides us with important information or increases our connection with others? And does it feel right to us—does it validate and support what we believe to be true? As you might expect, the stories that travel the fastest and farthest among us are those that most satisfy these two criteria.

Notice that I never mentioned *accuracy*. Truthfulness matters far less to us than whether something *feels* true; it is the latter that enables us to use System 1 thinking. As a result, our most widely accepted and widely shared stories are also our least scrutinized.

The early days of the COVID pandemic provided a vivid case study of that phenomenon. As I offered in Chapter 3, in early 2020, ahead of the domestic outbreak and feeling very confident, we didn't challenge the story that the disease was "contained" within China. Then, when the news reports about Tom Hanks and Rudy Gobert upended our confidence, that "contained" story no longer mirrored our mood. Even using intense System 2 thinking, we couldn't make it fit. As we panicked, we threw "contained" overboard. We needed a new story that was relevant and resonant.

The Google Trends chart in Figure 14.1 suggests that we found both elements in the word "unprecedented." We grabbed hold of the word as if it were a life preserver in a hurricane.

Amid our surging fear, and unable to make sense of the swirling storm unfolding around us, we quickly exhausted our library of usual adjectives. We needed a word that fully captured our intense feelings

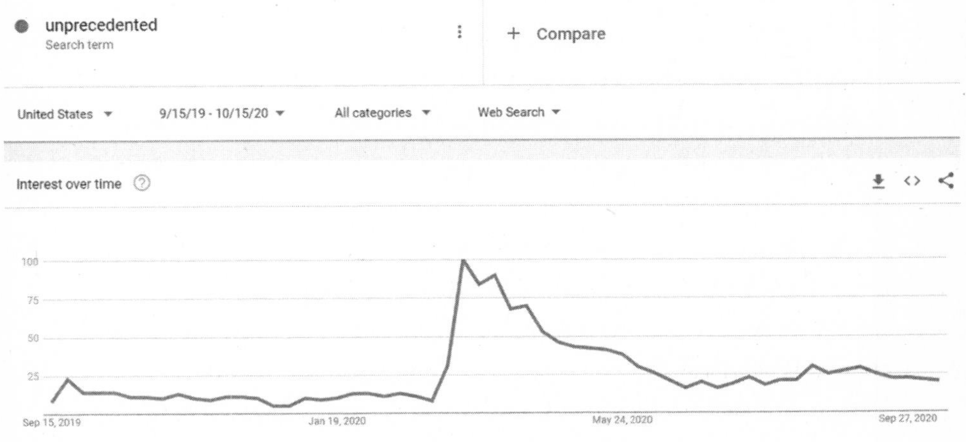

FIGURE 14.1: Google Trends chart for "unprecedented," spring 2020.
Source: Google

FIGURE 14.2: Corporate mentions of "unprecedented," 2016–2022.
Source: AlphaSense

about the rapidly unfolding COVID pandemic. This time, it truly *was* different. The moment *was* unprecedented. We were lost in uncharted waters.

At the same time, we reached for the word "unprecedented" for more than just its "never before" dictionary-definition usefulness. When we said "unprecedented," we also meant enormous and extraordinary. We were catastrophizing. As news outlets reported new daily caseloads in small increments, we were already anticipating hundreds of thousands, if not millions of cases ahead. In real time, we were translating our intense fear into mind-staggering extrapolations of the current caseload trends. Psychologically, we were bracing for an alien invasion out of a horror movie. When we said the outbreak was "unprecedented," we were signaling that we might easily be overwhelmed—physically and emotionally.

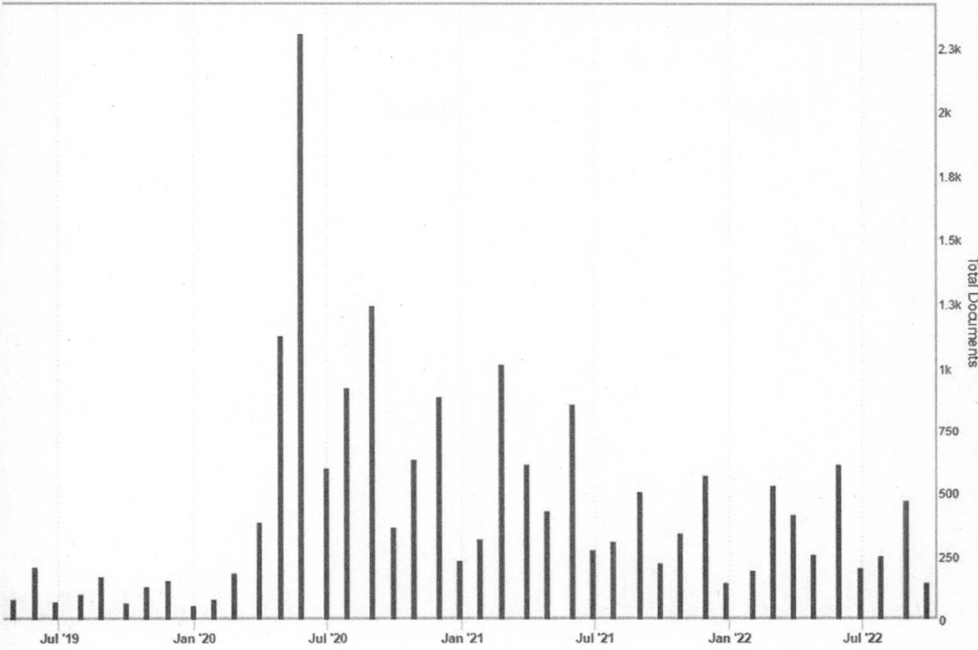

Note that there was also immediate utility to the term. "Unprecedented" implied that it was reasonable, if not perfectly normal, that the outbreak caught us off guard and unprepared. If the pandemic was unprecedented, then how could we have known to be on the lookout, let alone be braced for its impact?

Not surprisingly, blindsided business leaders dove on the word, eager to use the pandemic's "unprecedented" nature as a quick and easy explanation for their lack of preparedness. As data from AlphaSense—a software company that tracks specific word usage in corporate earnings reports and company presentations—show in Figure 14.2, when the pandemic hit, "unprecedented" became many executives' go-to adjective.[1]

As wounded investors sympathetically nodded along on dour quarterly earnings calls, "unprecedented" became a ubiquitous "Get Out of Jail Free" card. Stunned CEOs freely threw around the word as they

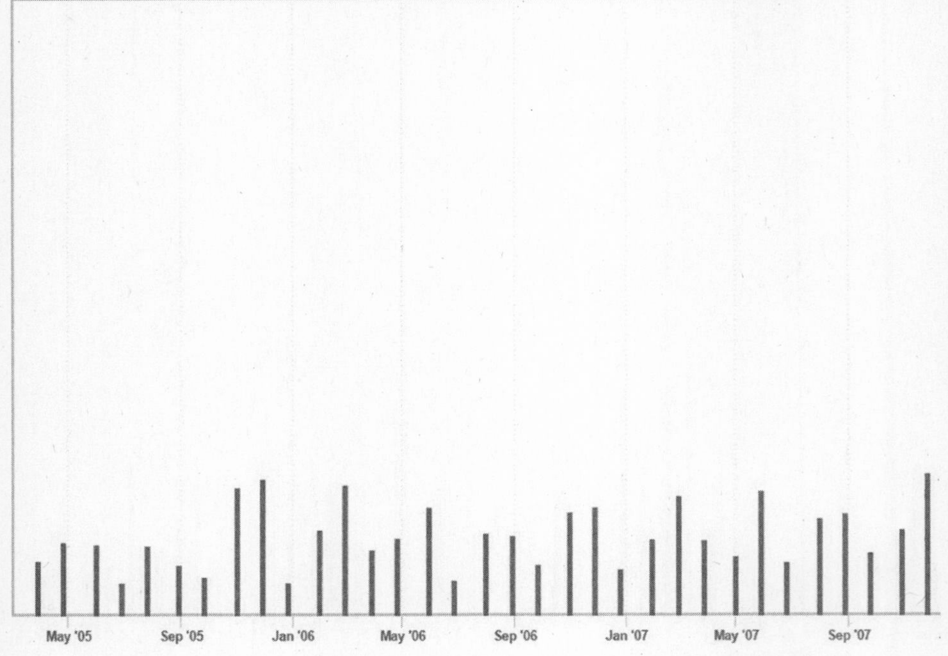

FIGURE 14.3: Corporate mentions of "unprecedented," 2005–2010.
Source: AlphaSense

blamed the pandemic for their companies' misfortune. So did asset managers and financial advisors when speaking to their clients about their investment portfolios.

And no one pushed back.[2]

Investors readily accepted the narrative of an unprecedented pandemic. Yes, the word perfectly expressed how they felt about the outbreak, but it also served as useful shorthand for Americans' much larger story: none of us had seen the pandemic coming, we'd never experienced a pandemic before, and so, of course, we were all unprepared.

And because *all* of us had been blindsided, the pandemic *had* to be unprecedented. The implied causal relationship was clear. We didn't need to spend any more time dwelling on how we could have been better prepared or how we might have responded more effectively. Amid the storm, at least one thing appeared certain: the pandemic was unprece-

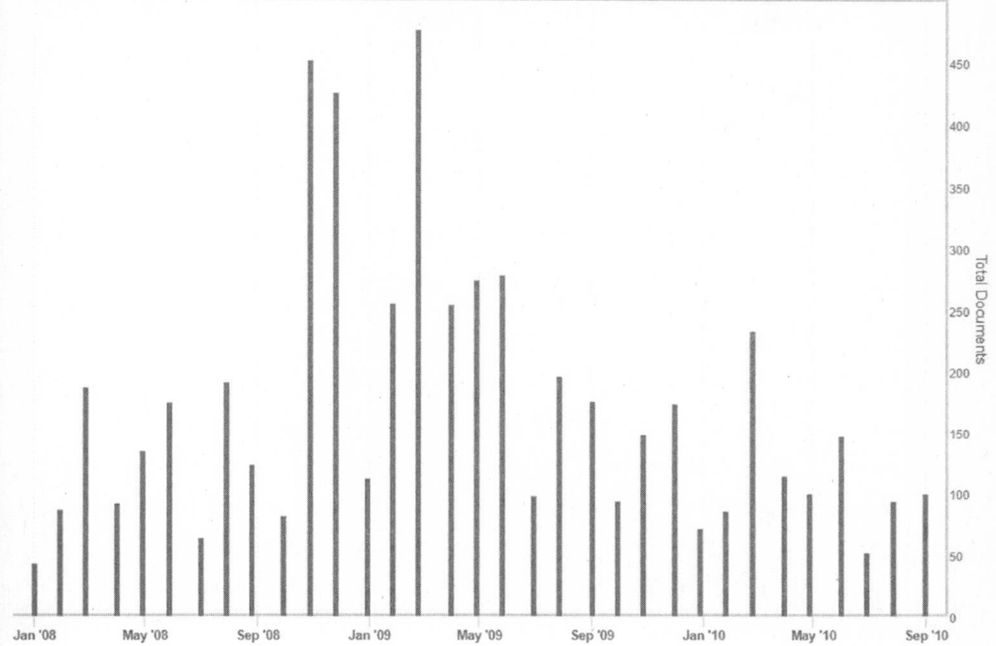

dented, and that meant those we might otherwise have held accountable would be off the hook.

Ironically, we had precedence for our sudden, widespread use of the adjective "unprecedented." Blindsided executives had reached for the word in similar circumstances before. As Figure 14.3 shows, during the 2008 financial crisis, bank CEOs and other business leaders joined upended mortgage borrowers in adopting the word as the explanation for the crisis they, too, had been unprepared for.

Yet again, a "contained" threat quickly turned into an "unprecedented" crisis as the unforeseen consequences exploded in size and scope.

And if there was one word in which we all sought solace on 9/11, it was "unprecedented."

When major crises hit and we find ourselves at our most vulnerable, our vocabulary naturally pivots to reflect the extreme uncertainty and powerlessness we feel, and we routinely reach for the word "unprecedented."

Put simply, the words we use and the stories we tell to describe the world around us mirror how we feel about it.

Reading Sentiment Through Popular Narratives

Our word choices matter, especially those in our widely shared narratives. The topics we choose to talk about and the words we use to describe them provide a powerful lens through which to gauge our confidence level. Adjectives like "contained" and "unprecedented" not only describe what we think, they also accurately capture our feelings, our explanations, even our facial expressions. They're all but emojis.

Moreover, when adjectives are widely shared, as those two words were in early 2020, they reveal the stories we feel most confident about. As mentioned earlier, single words in popular narratives tell powerful and often complex stories in an easy-to-understand social shorthand. They paint broad, universally understood, simple images, the way a bold yellow sign by the side of the road with a leaping stag on it warns us to keep our eyes peeled for deer. The descriptors in our popular narratives are streets signs, stereotypes, and social cues rolled into one.

Narratives also serve as social currency, in that the more accurately they reflect our collective sentiment, the more widely they will be accepted and shared. The external validation that comes from the quick acceptance of our stories by others not only boosts our feelings of certainty and control but lets us know we fit in. Shared beliefs provide security and reassurance. If others think the same thing I do, then I am part of the crowd and, therefore, my thoughts must be valid. Even as adults—decades away from the peer pressure of middle school—we desperately crave the approval and affirmation of others. Often unknowingly, our shared storytelling satisfies that craving. When others readily agree with our thoughts, we feel powerful, and when those thoughts are dismissed by others, we quickly feel like outsiders. Our shared stories reinforce social norms; they reflect confidence.

When we rushed for a word to explain the pandemic in mid-March 2020, we chose "unprecedented" the way we choose all adjectives. We picked the term not for its precision or accuracy as much as for its immediate, easy fit with how we felt and how it would quickly communicate a longer and more elaborate story: the pandemic was extraordinary, literally without precedent, and because it was beyond our control, we should be forgiven for being blindsided. Like a unanimous "Guilty!" verdict at the end of a trial, this one word summed up our evaluation of the evidence and our judgment on it.

Ultimately, it didn't matter whether the inferences and implications of "unprecedented" were true or not. What mattered was that those inferences and implications *felt* true. Our popular stories are always just that—impulsive, immediate, System 1–processed reflections.

Remarkably, when it comes to the question of how we feel broadly, the best answers often lie in our laziest, most impulsive, most widely shared narratives. Visit a big sporting event and you can see this in real time. The loud chants about quarterbacks, receivers, and referees tell you all you need to know about fan sentiment. When the ball is dropped, crowds don't wait for nuance or explanation, let alone the video replay; they provide a quick summation—words that easily capture the essence of what we mean and feel, often ripe with colorful expletives to drive home the point. Crowds yell front-page *New York Post* headlines, not *New Yorker* columns.

While we may be able to hide our feelings when we interact one-on-one, we leave obvious narrative clues in plain sight when we act as a crowd. Spend a few hours watching CNBC, Fox Business, or Bloomberg TV and you will quickly gain a feel for the current zeitgeist and investor confidence in the financial markets. Financial television is in the business of presenting the current state of the hive mind at work.

Then there is social media. Our popular narratives are on full display 24-7 as they get shared via likes and retweets filled with hashtags. Like our Google search terms, the trending topics on social media also reflect how the crowd feels. Formed around simplicity and impulsiveness, Twitter is a real-time barometer of mood—so much so that many quantitative investors use it as a tool to track investor sentiment.[3] As our confidence changes, so, too, do the tweets and stories we share expressing, affirming, and justifying our feelings of certainty and control.

Visualizing Our Most Popular Stories

Today, we have easily accessible analytical tools and resources that enable us to spot and follow our most resonant stories. With Google Trends, for example, we can type a specific word or phrase into its search engine, and it quickly provides a normalized measure of the search volume for the term over a selected time period.

But Google Trends provides more than just a visualization of what we are interested in. Our web searches reflect how we feel, too. As shown earlier in Figure 5.1 and again in Figure 14.4 below, the terms "seasonal depression" and "comfort food" illustrate that not only do we suffer from the former (searches for "seasonal depression" increase in the fall and bottom out in the early summer) but, as our mood drops, we naturally crave comfort foods, too.

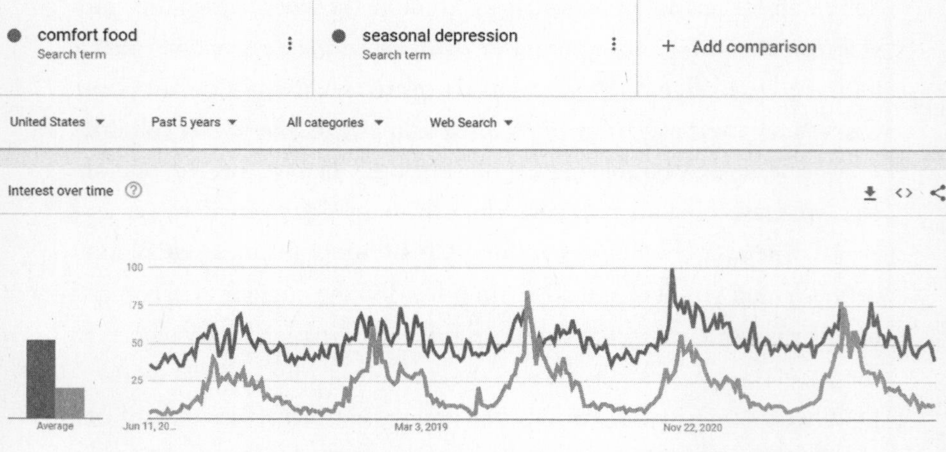

FIGURE 14.4: Google Trends chart for "seasonal depression" and "comfort food." *Source: Google*

Google Trends also tracks the ebb and flow of our most popular narratives. As our stories change, so do the words we use in our searches.

I use Google Trends data a lot, especially during times of stress. As the early September 2022 chart of "European energy crisis" in Figure 14.5 shows, search data enables us to watch as emotional intensity rises.

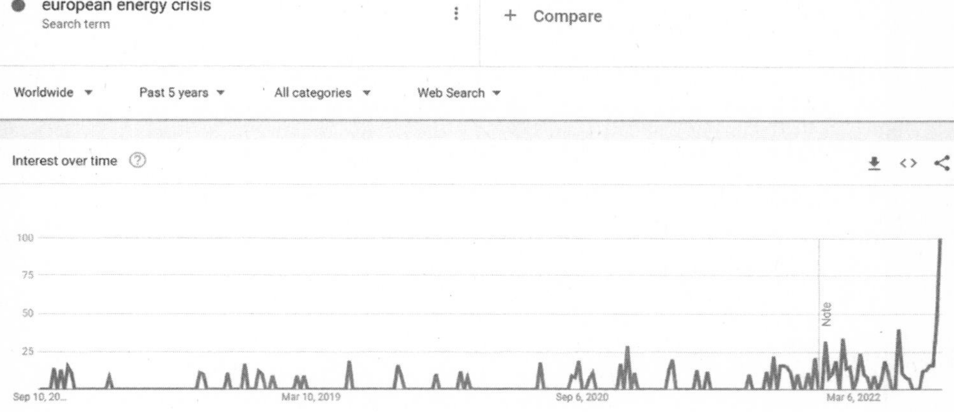

FIGURE 14.5: Google Trends chart for "European energy crisis."
Source: Google

Problems can fester for long periods of time before they become crises. But once that transition occurs, highly emotional and impulsive behavior takes hold. Google Trends data enable us to visualize changes in mood and prepare for what is coming next—like, in the figure above, how consumers and policymakers will respond to higher fuel prices and the potential of shortages ahead.

Advertising and Business and Political Messaging

I also pay close attention to popular advertisements. They say as much about the audience and its location on the Confidence Quadrant as they do about the products and services onstage.

When advertisers use lines like "in these uncertain times"—as they do a lot these days—they are parroting back to us how they think we feel. They know the phrase will resonate with us; we won't blink when we read their well-sculpted copy. Effective advertising validates our feelings. When we lack confidence, advertisers know words like "uncertain" will affirm the story we already have swirling in our heads.

Successful advertisers also mirror consumers' Horizon Preference. They use simple language focused on tangible benefits when confidence is low and abstract messaging alluding to possibility when it is high.

And it isn't just advertisers who approach their storytelling this way.

When CEOs feel good, their revenue forecasts become "robust," "all but certain," and "propelled by strong tailwinds." Investor-relations teams are masters at signaling leadership sentiment. When C-suite confidence is high, corporate messaging is rich with language about opportunity and leadership certainty and control so that you, as an investor, can relax and feel comfortable.

On the other hand, during difficult times, you will hear business leaders talk about the "lack of visibility" to future sales and earnings. With those three words, they unknowingly admit they are in Me-Here-Now mode. The same is true when "challenges" and "hurdles" and other barriers to success are liberally on offer. When confidence is low, CEO messages pivot to defense and what leaders are doing to prevent things from getting worse. Moreover, low-confidence business narratives are filled with the same "blame and shame"–assigning narratives that we all turn to when we are in the Stress Center.

Political campaigns work the same way. During election season, you can watch talking points and slogans evolve as candidates alter their messages, trying to best mirror changing voter mood. When mood is high, messages reinforce how candidates will not just preserve voters' confidence but also enhance it. In his 2012 reelection campaign, President Barack Obama chose the slogan "Forward"[4]—quite the contrast to the "Change" and "Hope" used when he was first seeking the office amid the 2008 banking crisis. When voter mood is low, political ads emphasize how a candidate can and will restore confidence.

The resonance of Donald Trump's "Make America Great Again" campaign slogan during the 2016 presidential campaign said all you needed to know about Republican voters' sour mood heading into that election. His message was all about restoring the lost confidence of his supporters. It's hardly surprising, then, that Hillary Clinton's high-confidence slogan, "Stronger Together," didn't resonate with Trump voters.

Confidence, Narratives, and the Media

Then there are the media outlets: newspapers, magazines, and television shows. Front-page headlines, cover-story images, and nightly "top news stories" are all specifically chosen to resonate and mirror current mood. The media is in the business of selling stories. Savvy editors and producers know that the stories that will sell best—that will draw in readers, listeners, and viewers—are those that are the easiest for us to accept and to circulate and the ones that best mirror how we feel.

While dramatic news stories may *alter* how we feel, most headlines simply *reflect* how we feel. They don't change us as much as they align with our changed mood. During the 2008 housing crisis, you could watch how, as the mood darkened, so did the tone of the news coverage of the housing market. At the bottom, when Lehman Brothers collapsed, there was saturated pessimism across media and Main Street. Conversely, ahead of the crisis, news stories were universally positive, emphasizing the successes of builders, home buyers, and lenders alike. *Time* magazine even ran a cover headlined "Home $weet Home."[5]

And the media's mirroring of mood didn't stop there. There were entire television series tied to the real estate boom. Shows like *Cribs* took viewers into the lavish homes of the rich and famous, while *Flip This House* accompanied home speculators as they bought, renovated, and resold homes at a profit. When the housing market turned down, these extreme-confidence series disappeared. A new line-up of "fixer-upper" shows took their place, showing hosts making the most of a less-than-desirable home—better aligning with our somber mood.

Many like to blame the media for our collective behavior, suggesting that certain television channels or radio announcers are causing our confidence to change—that *they* lead us to believe certain things or to act in a certain way. While that narrative may feel comfortable, consider that how we feel also drives who and what we trust for information in the first place. Popular television and radio are no different from popular music: we wouldn't be listening or watching if it didn't somehow feel right to us.

And don't think the major media don't know this. In response to a question about why Fox News wasn't airing live coverage of the first January 6 investigation hearing, prime-time host Laura Ingraham told viewers, "We actually do something called, ya know, cater to our audience."[6]

Confidence and Narratives: Chicken or Egg?

This gets to the core challenge with the media and our confidence-related narratives more broadly: we can't easily distinguish those that are cause from those that are effect. Other than when there is a clear disruption or intervention—when a major event occurs—our actions and reactions are indistinguishable. We aren't lab mice whose variables, save one, can be easily controlled for. Our lives are in constant motion, moving seamlessly from one event to the next. As we finish one experience, we rarely pause to specifically assess how our feelings may have changed and the ways our new feelings might impact what we do next. We simply keep going, ignoring whether what we did was an independent action or a specific reaction to what occurred immediately prior.

After more than a decade of watching narratives come and go, I've stopped worrying altogether about the issue of causation. One big reason is that I am never quite sure where I may be jumping into the "Action-Reaction Cycle" at any given moment (Figure 14.6).

FIGURE 14.6: The narrative-action-confidence cycle

We are a constant swirl of stories, feelings, and actions. Moreover, we often have multiple, overlapping spirals of all three taking place at once in our roles as a parent, a spouse, a child, a coworker, a boss . . . As conversations around the dinner table reveal, we wear many hats at once, each with its own associated feelings, stories, and actions. This sets up the real likelihood that the orderly circular flow I presented in Figure 14.6 looks more like a knotted string of Christmas lights.

This is not to say that narratives aren't important or that they should be ignored. But given the complexity and constant motion of our lives, I find it far more valuable to simply freeze things—to create a snapshot, as it were, of our coincidental behaviors (Figure 14.7).

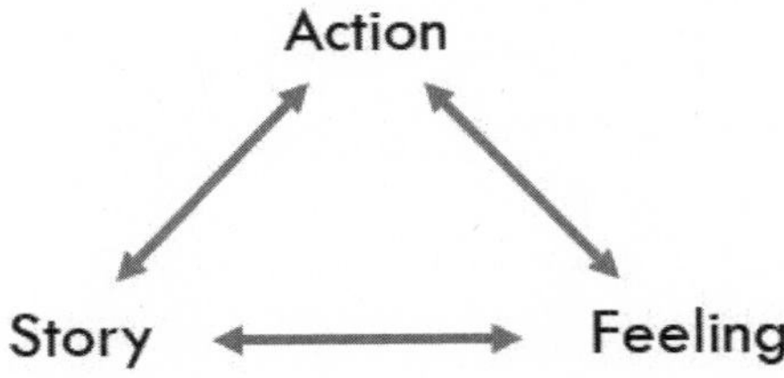

FIGURE 14.7: Narrative-action-confidence equilibrium

By looking at just one snapshot, we can see that at any given moment, there is clear reflexivity—that our actions, our stories, and our level of confidence mirror one another. Captured at once, they exist in equilibrium.

My approach may seem like a cop-out to some—who may think that, as a social scientist, I should care deeply about getting the question of causation right. But my focus is utility, and through that lens, my rather simplistic approach is extremely helpful. If our feelings, stories, and actions all comfortably coexist in equilibrium, then all I need to see is one element of the snapshot to reasonably deduce the other two.

This is especially clear when we are in the Launch Pad. Say, for example, we're getting ready to plan our next summer vacation. If we are confident, we'll be sharing fun, exotic locations we want to explore. We will book our flights and hotels quickly for fear of missing out. If we are not confident, we'll raise concerns about potential social unrest abroad. We'll hold off on booking our trip.

Just as when we are in the Passenger Seat, our Launch Pad stories reveal our true feelings. And in both environments, our stories and feelings can change in a flash. With unexpected turbulence, a planeload of passengers can go from feeling confident and exchanging comments about how smooth the flight is to feeling panicked and joining together in prayer.

Whether we start with action, confidence level, or story, because there is equilibrium, if we know one element, we can anticipate the other two.

Virtuous and Vicious Narrative Cycles

This same principle holds true at work and in groups, with broader implications. Say a CEO describes the economic environment as "improving." It is reasonable to believe that so, too, is her confidence level. Moreover, if that CEO feels better and sees an improving economy, then it is very reasonable to anticipate she will be considering hiring more employees and making capital investments ahead (Figure 14.8).

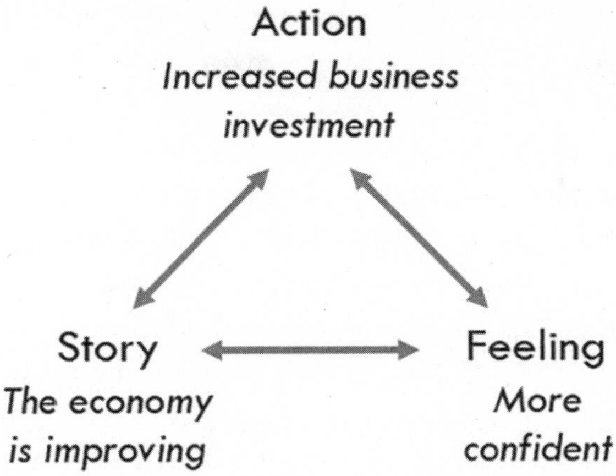

FIGURE 14.8: Equilibrium during an economic recovery

Again, there is equilibrium.

With this specific equilibrium, though, it is not hard to see how a virtuous cycle might then develop. Much as an "improving economy" narrative generates a certain response from the CEO, her actions will likely become the input and basis for even more positive and widely shared stories and even stronger confidence ahead. Newly hired workers will gain confidence and tell their friends and families that their new employer must be doing well as the business ramps up to support the incremental investments of the optimistic CEO. The actions and stories validate and support an "improving economy" narrative. Unless something intervenes, our collective positive responses—in our level of confidence, in our stories, and in our actions—become the fuel that fosters broader and even more positive actions by others. With that, the breadth and depth in sentiment expands. We then have a virtuous cycle in which positive narratives fuel positive actions, leading to further positive narratives, and on and on . . .

Still, it is worth pausing to consider just how poorly received a lone CEO's voice expressing optimism might be near a low in confidence.

"Improving" narratives don't resonate with others when the broader audience lacks certainty and control—the music doesn't fit the mood, as it were. Collective doubt can easily silence the optimistic in the same way high confidence does the naysayer. You can easily imagine the "You want to do what?!" reaction an eager CEO might have received from her board had she suggested a major expansion shortly after the 2008 banking crisis. The proposed action wouldn't fit the widespread narrative or the mood. With that response, it is highly unlikely that the CEO would move forward. She would have to wait until confidence improved more broadly before approaching her board again.

As we will see in the next chapter, it's not just popular narratives that provide clues about mood. So, too, do those narratives where opposition and resistance are high.

Spotting Narrative Tipping Points

In virtuous cycles, as confidence rises and "improving" narratives become more readily accepted, there appears to be a tipping point where not only does resistance abate but it suddenly feels as though everyone then wants to rush in to grab hold of the evolving story. As reluctance and disbelief turn to eagerness and trust, it's as if the wind has shifted 180 degrees, from a strong headwind to a blistering tailwind. Suddenly, we need to share the belief to fit in, whereas earlier adoption would have turned us into outsiders.[7] (The same tipping-point concept applies to vicious cycles as well—where our reluctance to accept a pessimistic narrative suddenly falls away.)

We saw a vicious-cycle tipping point in real time when the news about Tom Hanks and Rudy Gobert hit. Before then, suggesting that the outbreak was not contained would have been seen as overly dramatic and far too dour. Had you talked about a global crisis ahead, you likely would have been compared to a man on the street corner with one of those "The World Is Coming to an End" signs. But after that point, calling the outbreak "contained" would have been laughable.

Big Truths and the Oversimplicity of Widely Shared Narratives

It is worth highlighting that as new economic/confidence cycles begin, optimistic narratives take far longer to develop than the negative narratives that arise when confidence is falling. Trust is like a tall Lego tower: it takes a long time to build, but just one wrong move can send it crumbling to the ground. As narratives mirror confidence, they move at the same pace.

In my class, I analogize the evolution of our confidence-related narratives to the smoothing process of sea glass. When new narratives first appear, they are like fragments of a broken bottle: there are too many sharp edges, and no one wants to touch them. Our early narratives are complicated, confusing, and uncomfortable in our hands. They are filled with conflicts and challenges and lack utility. There are too many what-ifs still to be thought through. Like writers with a first draft of a book, with our fledgling narratives we are formulating our thoughts.

But over time, as with broken bottle glass in the ocean, the edges of these narratives are worn away. As our confidence rises, our accompanying stories become simpler, more resonant, and easier to share. We edit and refine them. As the cycle progresses, and our stories are shared and affirmed by others, they become even smoother; they become clearer and more simplistic. This makes them easier both to understand and to share. That simplification process is a critical component to the contagious effect of widely shared narratives.

I witnessed this firsthand with my own narrative about the economic inequality arising from COVID. "The K-shaped recovery" was simpler, resonated far more, and was easier to share than my clumsy initial coinage: "the work-from-home confidence divide."[8]

As we approach extremes in sentiment (both high and low), not only are our stories highly simplistic, they are often prefaced by a spoken or implied "of course." There is all but universal agreement on what the story is and what it suggests is ahead. There is a very simple "Big Truth."

"Contained" and "unprecedented" are two examples of recent widely shared, intensely believed, highly simplistic Big Truths. So, too, were the Big Truths that "home prices only go up" and "your house is your best investment" just before the 2008 financial crisis. In their moment, all four of these stories could have been preceded by the words "of course" and understood by a middle schooler. Big Truths are so attractive—and so smooth—that everyone can and wants to hold them.[9]

Evaluating Narratives

In assessing the relative confidence of a team or a group (and gauging where within a virtuous or vicious cycle the group may be), it is helpful to look at narratives in their four dimensions:

How widely held is the shared view?
How optimistic/pessimistic is the shared view?
How complex/simple is the shared view?
How strident are those who share and oppose the view?

The weekend Lehman Brothers collapsed, the pessimistic sentiment was intense and saturating. Investors and the media were all but shouting that things were going to get worse. At the opposite end of the Confidence Spectrum, in early 2021, not only was Elon Musk "invincible," journalists routinely described his fervent following as "cultish."[10] In both cases, the crowd passionately shared simple and extreme narratives.

Taken together, the breadth, depth, simplicity, and intensity of our stories reveal as much about how we feel as they do about what we believe to be true. As our confidence and our narratives become more extreme (in either direction), our story becomes more simplistic, the crowd that shares our story grows, and the crowd believes it more firmly and seeks to impose it on others. You're an outsider, or even an enemy, if you don't agree.

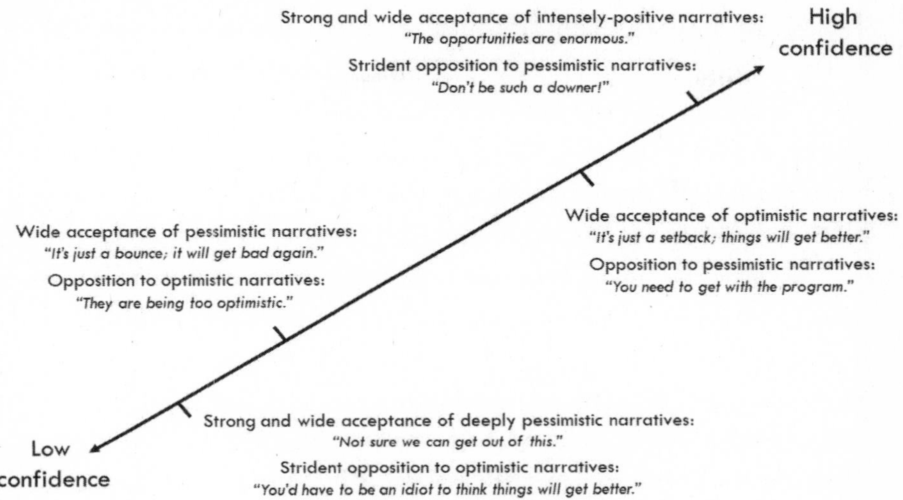

FIGURE 14.9: Popular narratives along the Confidence Spectrum

Narratives and Confidence Turning Points

The tendency of virtuous and vicious cycles to foster more simplistic narratives that are more fervently believed and shared raises the question of why those cycles don't continue into perpetuity.

There are two reasons. One is that something significant eventually comes along that runs counter to our story, either raising sufficient doubt about our current story or upending it altogether. There is an intervention, as it were, to our narrative—such as when we get in a car accident and then tell ourselves we aren't the "good driver" we thought we were. The equilibrium that previously existed is disrupted, and in the wake of the event, a new equilibrium must be established. If the event is meaningful enough to us, our well-formed virtuous cycle can quickly send us back to square one. This is exactly what happened when many heard the news about Tom Hanks. In a flash, they found themselves back in the lower left corner of the Stress Center.

The second reason a cycle is broken is saturation. To use a contagion analogy, there comes a point when everyone who is going to be infected by the narrative already is, such as in 2006, when demand for housing peaked as the last willing and able home buyers entered the market.

This then begs the question: What draws even the most reluctant believer to accept a story? Why do we capitulate to extreme narratives like "housing prices only go up" and "COVID is contained" at precisely the wrong moment, over and over?

Well, by the time a virtuous or vicious cycle reaches its terminal point, the underlying story has been repeatedly proven to be true. It is far easier to believe that home prices only go up when there are charts, stories, and other "evidence" showing that to be just the case. I often joke that there is underappreciated omnipotence to business charts with long, upwardly sloping lines for metrics like profit and revenue. The same is true with vertical stock- and commodity-price charts. To suggest a violent decline is laughable. There is no hope for a counterargument. At the top of the cycle, sources of validation and support are everywhere.[11]

Moreover, those sources of affirmation include the actions of others. Again, equilibrium exists across confidence, stories, and actions. In 2006, house flipping was on broad display, and stories of how much money others had made buying and selling homes were everywhere. If you weren't talking about how you were making money in real estate, you were an outsider.

Finally, there is something subtle that takes place as we approach the terminal point in the cycle. It's something that exists within the stories themselves: they contain extreme feelings related to power and trend extrapolation, often to a ridiculous degree.

At the top of the housing market, we believed not only that housing prices had always gone up but that those upward price movements were unstoppable—that they would continue to go up forever. In that moment, we were eagerly extrapolating the current trend and its related shared narrative far, far out into the future. Home prices, we were certain, would rise as far as the eye could see. And at the bottom of the housing crisis, in 2009, we said the same thing about home prices, only heading in the opposite direction. Even after a dramatic decline, we believed that nothing could stop home values from going lower.

At the top and bottom of virtuous cycles, there is the same extreme narrative trend extrapolation.

As you might imagine, when taken together, the seemingly unlimited supply of affirming "evidence" combined with an enormous, fervent crowd of narrative believers all but forces us to take action. *Of course* we buy at the top and sell at the bottom. We can't resist. The gains (or losses) we envision ahead are obvious and immense. The extreme alignment of confidence and story draws us to act—to establish equilibrium.

Earlier, I listed four questions we need to ask when analyzing popular narratives. But there is a fifth, and it may be the most important:

How *extreme* is the trend extrapolation of the narrative?

Popular stories have a consistent evolution. They begin with resistant roots filled with words like "couldn't possibly" and then evolve to "might," to "will," to ultimately "must forever." We heard this in housing and more recently with electric vehicles. At both extremes in sentiment, we collectively over-believe and oversimplify a story that we believe will continue forever.

And note that I said "story." I didn't say "product," "stock," "company," or any other specific business item that is headline worthy. Great products without great stories don't succeed. We don't have confidence in *things*; we have confidence that is reflected in the stories we tell about the things that matter to us. Consider Tesla—it was never about the car as much as it was what the car symbolized and what the future held. Love him or hate him, Elon Musk is a master storyteller, offering "coming attractions" that rival the best from Hollywood.

Leaders need to appreciate the importance of narratives: their fate depends on it. They should pay as much attention to story cycles as they do to product cycles, especially because extremes in stories are powerful contrarian indicators, cautioning dramatic change may be ahead. Awash in record profits and performance bonuses, the executive teams at Lehman Brothers, Bear Stearns, and other Wall Street banks missed the many red flags on full display in the housing- and mortgage-market narratives, not to mention their own earnings reports. Not only did everyone believe the Big Truth that home prices only go up, they were acting on that story, too.

I pay especially close attention to popular narrative adjectives when they begin to reflect mounting intensity and extrapolation. When positive trends have gone on for a long period of time and the crowd is extremely confident the trend will only continue, words like "unstoppable" and "unassailable" frequently make headlines, and "relentless" is overrun by "incessant." These words always make my ears perk up, particularly when they appear on magazine covers or newspapers' front pages in big, bold type. They caution that the crowd may have become far too confident in a trend.

For example, *Time* magazine's January 27, 2014, cover caption, "Can Anyone Stop Hillary?" occurred just as Secretary Clinton's popularity was cresting.[12] Similarly, the headline "Can Anyone Catch the Cell Phone King?" preceded a stark reversal in fate for Nokia when it appeared on the cover of *Forbes* in November 2007.[13] At the other end of the Confidence Spectrum, on October 1, 2011, *The Economist* ran an especially bleak story illustrated on the cover by an image of a large vortex with the words "BE AFRAID" in big red letters in the middle of it. The subtitle of the story was "Unless politicians act more boldly, the world economy will keep heading towards a black hole."[14]

Just the reverse then happened. The global economy rebounded shortly thereafter.

When obvious, widely shared, extreme trend extrapolations are expressed across the media and no one even blinks, they caution that the end of a cycle may be near. Savvy C-suite executives and policymakers should pay attention. Whether on the cover of *Time*, *Forbes*, or *The Economist*, expressions of invincibility and hopelessness have a funny way of being contrarian indicators and surprising people.

And here, one last time, I want to return to March 2020.

As much as the word "unprecedented" captured everything about how we felt, our broad reach for the word itself cautioned that we were rapidly nearing an extreme low in confidence. We *all* believed the conditions were likely to remain unprecedented. We were catastrophizing, extrapolating an extremely pessimistic story, as we always do near lows in confidence.

On March 22, 2020, when *Wall Street Journal* subscribers read the headline "The Worst of the Global Selloff Isn't Here Yet, Banks and Investors Warn," it is safe to say few subscribers blinked.[15] Accompanied by a chart detailing how much lower firms like Credit Suisse, Goldman Sachs, and Bank of America still expected the markets to drop, readers had all the validation and support they needed. Things could and would only get worse.

Hours later, the stock market bottomed. As quickly as it began, a vicious spiral had suddenly exhausted itself. At that moment, everyone who could and would believe that things would only get worse believed it. Moreover, they had acted on their feelings. Everyone who was going to sell had done so.

As had been the case after 9/11 and the collapse of Lehman Brothers, "unprecedented" didn't mark the beginning of the end but rather indicated that the worst was already behind us.

•

Every day, we are surrounded by popular stories. If we take a moment to listen, they will tell us not only how we feel and where we are on the Quadrant but what we are likely to do next. And when our stories are extreme and over-believed, they routinely warn that a dramatic reversal in sentiment and our behavior is at hand. They are invaluable clues in plain sight.

PS: Individual Narratives and Confidence

Most of what I have covered in this chapter dealt with the widely shared stories we tell others. Before returning to the Launch Pad, I want to offer a few thoughts on the stories we tell ourselves.

Like popular narratives, these stories, too, exist in equilibrium with our own feelings and actions. Moreover, they fuel the same kind of virtuous and vicious cycles leading to simple, powerful, overextrapolated narratives that exist at both extremes in confidence. We tell ourselves we are invincible at our peaks in confidence and that we are worthless at our lows.

Like crowds and business leaders at extremes in sentiment, we, too, need to be especially careful not to confuse the ease and resonant forcefulness of our narratives with their accuracy. There is inherent peril to exaggerated self-aggrandizement and to self-defeat paired with catastrophizing—especially the latter. As I tell my students, when we are stressed, our mean voice naturally comes out to play.

Thanks to Google Trends data, we can see this, too.

As shown earlier in Figure 2.4 and again in Figure 14.10 below, every night between 1:00 and 2:00 a.m., the search interest for the word "anxiety" peaks. There is a natural, daily cycle to our stress level. You aren't the only one waking up in the middle of the night worried.

While I haven't included the related charts, shortly after every one of the peaks noted above, you will find comparable peaks for searches for

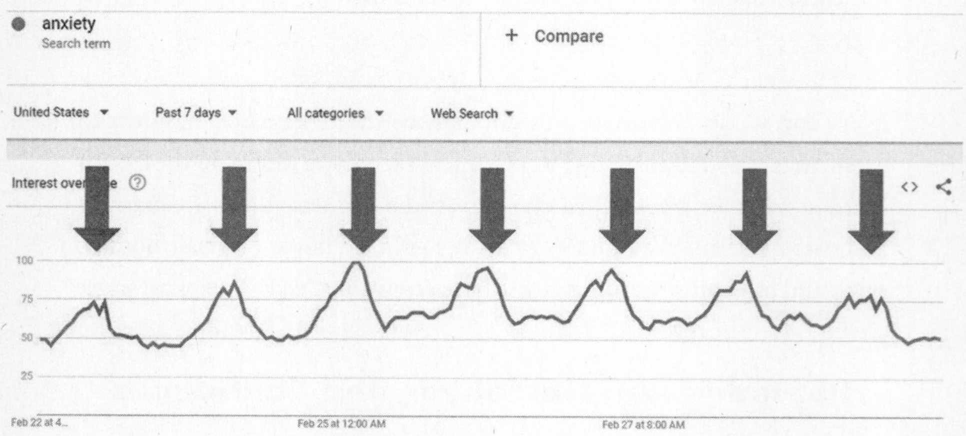

FIGURE 14.10: One week Google Trends chart for "anxiety."
Source: Google

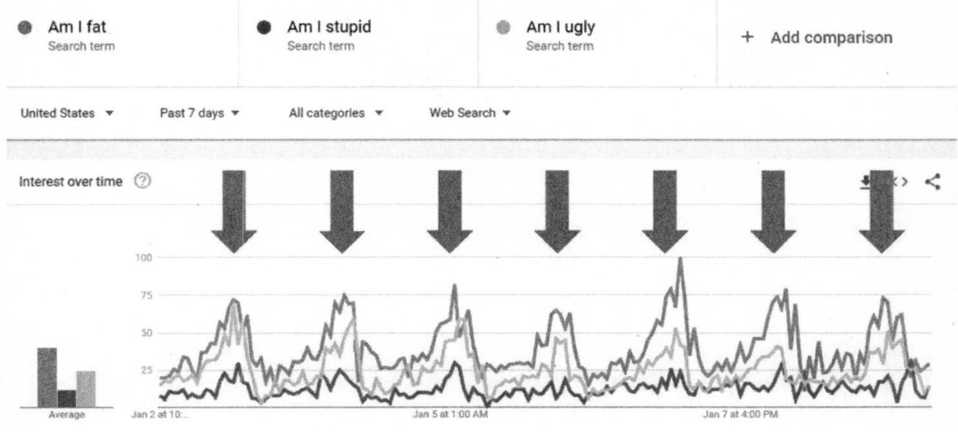

FIGURE 14.11: One week Google Trends chart of self-criticisms.
Source: Google

things like "how to roll a joint," "bars open near me," "how to meditate," and "pornography." Yet again, how we feel drives what we do. And when we are out of our Comfort Zone, we look for ways to eliminate stress.

What's more troubling, though, is that right as searches for "anxiety" peak, so do searches for "am I fat," "am I stupid" and "am I ugly."

We become our own worst enemy as our confidence drops.

I realize this is tangential to the topic at hand, but charts like Figure 14.11 are valuable reminders not only to be nicer to ourselves when we feel vulnerable but also of why employee confidence, not employee satisfaction, matters so much. In the workplace, self-doubt can quickly become collective doubt when the source of it is shared. It's not hard to imagine that in the middle of the night, stressed-out employees are wondering whether their boss thinks they are doing a good job and whether they should find a new one.

Then again, we don't need to imagine. While the chart is not as clear or as compelling as Figure 14.11, every major search peak for "will I be fired" occurs—yes—in the middle of the night.

CHAPTER 15

Better Practices in the Launch Pad

DECISION-MAKING IN the Comfort Zone is remarkably easy. There, we feel we have certainty and control. For good and ill, we all but *know* what will happen even before we act. The Stress Center creates a near-opposite experience, where we all but act before we think. There, we're highly emotional and impulsive. Our extreme vulnerability and the intense urgency to do something about it that arises from those feelings drives us to a reaction rather than a thoughtful response. Deliberation isn't on the table.

The Launch Pad rests in between. While we don't tend to notice it, this is where all our deliberate decision-making takes place. With control, yet no certainty, we must consider and weigh potential outcomes. We must settle on a single future that we imagine.[1] We need a story. And as our discussion of narratives has shown, we are most likely to pick the one that mirrors our mood.

Financial Decision-Making in the Launch Pad

When we are in the Launch Pad, nowhere does the impact of relative confidence on our stories and imagined outcomes come into play more than in our financial choices. As I remind my students at the beginning of each semester, *all* financial decisions take place in the upper left box of the Confidence Quadrant. Our choices to invest or borrow money all involve decision-making amid uncertainty. We won't know whether the decision we make today will result in the outcome we imagine until sometime in the future.

As a result, our investment decisions look something like this: Feeling confident, we imagine the stock market going up in the future and, as a result, we buy stocks now so that we will profit from the positive future we imagine. The same process works in reverse, too: feeling vulnerable, we imagine the stock market going down and, as a result, we sell stocks now so that we will avoid the losses we imagine ahead.

Or, put even more simplistically, the way we feel in the Launch Pad determines the percentages we assign to our outcomes in the Comfort Zone and Stress Center (Figure 15.1).

When we feel highly confident and see a very bright future ahead, we imagine an end in the upper right corner of the Comfort Zone. Similarly, when we lack confidence and see only uncertainty and powerlessness ahead, landing deep in the Stress Center feels inevitable. In both cases, we then act accordingly.[2] When it comes to the choices we make amid uncertainty, we are always driven by imagined outcomes.

This behavior extends far beyond the world of investments. Consider the many decisions business leaders make every day. Everything from hiring new employees to launching new products to acquiring new businesses requires a positive imagined outcome. Without it, things would never move forward. Risks wouldn't be taken.

The same applies to the choices we make in our own lives. Whether we are headed down a ski slope or walking down the aisle, our decisions reflect the confidence-driven future we imagine. As much as we may try

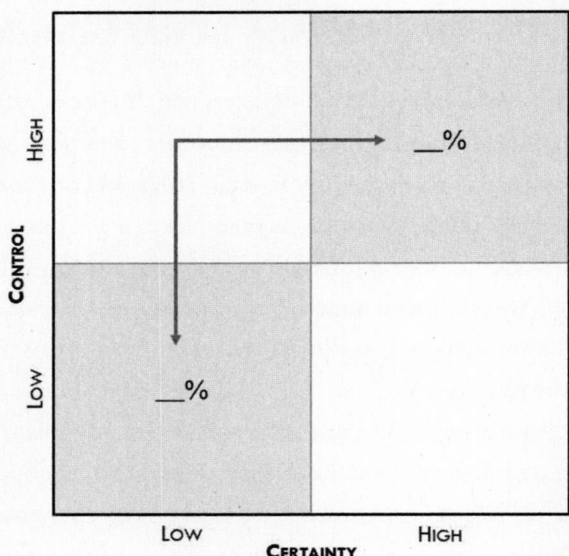

FIGURE 15.1: Launch Pad decision outcome probabilities template

to live in the present, our decision-making now reflects what we imagine for our future outcome.

When it comes to decision-making, few of us bother to stop to objectively calculate the precise percentages required in Figure 15.1. We don't, as decision-making expert and former professional poker player Annie Duke recommends, think in bets—rigorously and unemotionally assessing and, more important, reassessing the probabilities of the two outcomes and their relative payoffs to our actions as conditions change.[3] Instead, we go with the future we imagine that reflects our feelings of certainty and control. If we think the future for Company XYZ looks bright, we buy its shares. When we don't, we sell them. Our stories drive our decision-making.

We have plenty of excuses for not taking a more rigorous, deliberative, and objective approach: Assigning expected values is slow. We don't have the skills. We don't have the time. Invariably, we avoid using System 2 thinking if we don't have to.

We also have plenty of preexisting beliefs and biases, such as that the stock market only goes up, the game is rigged against us, or strange things happen during Mercury retrograde. We have a vast library of heuristics (rules of thumb) that cut our deliberative decision-making process short. Especially when it comes to choices that are inherently complex, like most financial decisions, we boil them down to things that we believe have worked or have not worked for us and others in the past.

Finally, we have priming—all those glamorous investment-management ads featuring happy, good-looking, successful people and their dogs sitting on luxurious sailboats, all because they put money in the markets long ago and are now reaping the rewards. And if we aren't staring at these ads, we are listening to our friends at a bar, scrolling FinTwit, or watching FinTok videos. All this input gets in the way of making unemotional, highly deliberate, objective choices.

So do our highly emotional prior experiences, like coping with a pandemic or losing our home to foreclosure during the 2008 banking crisis. Whenever we are looking ahead, we can't help but look at the future we imagine through the lens of our past experiences.

When we journey into the Launch Pad, we bring a lot of baggage.

As much as I wish everyone would follow the advice of Annie Duke, superforecasting pioneers like Philip Tetlock, and other decision-making experts, I don't think that is realistic.[4] Changing how we make decisions—undoing our bad habits and replacing them with better ones—requires us not only to change how we think but also to do so in ways that run counter to our natural instincts. In other words, it requires us to be deliberately deliberative: to use more slow, effortful System 2 thinking when we would much prefer our quick, lazy System 1 alternative.

That is hard enough as an individual, but when it comes to group decision-making and, moreover, crowd decision-making, that switch to System 2 thinking is all but impossible. Shared behavior requires and reflects System 1 thinking. As I discussed earlier, widespread acceptance requires that something feel familiar, true, good, and effortless.

Like it or not, crowds invariably resort to impulsive, System 1 decision-making. It's not something we can change, but we can certainly identify and appreciate it and, in so doing, learn how the same decision-making processes of the crowd apply to our own choices.

By increasing our awareness of our feelings of certainty and control (and where we are on the Confidence Quadrant), we can better appreciate how the outcomes we imagine may be distorted and, as a result, how our choices may be flawed.

To illustrate what I mean by this, consider how home buyers in 2006 likely assigned the relative outcome probabilities to their purchases (Figure 15.2).

Given the long upward trend in home prices, the media's attention to the financial success of house flippers, and high consumer confidence, buyers were especially optimistic that they would make money. Ending up in the Stress Center seemed all but impossible. Home buyers were making financial decisions based on the outcomes they imagined, which perfectly mirrored their ebullient mood.

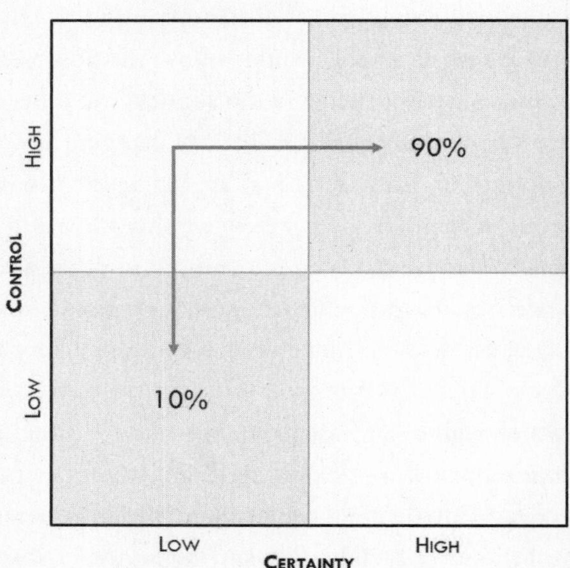

FIGURE 15.2: High probability of a positive outcome scenario

The same was true in late 2008, just in reverse. At the bottom of the housing crisis, buyers were convinced home values would only drop farther. Even with home prices substantially lower than at the peak of the housing market, there were few interested buyers. Pessimistic potential homebuyers assigned a high probability to an outcome in the Stress Center and then acted on it. They *avoided* buying homes at a time when home prices made purchasing far more affordable. Buyers were unwilling to take the risk.

You would think experienced business leaders would act differently, but the same pattern of behavior exists in C-suites and boardrooms. From key hiring decisions to major acquisitions, executives make choices driven by the outcomes they imagine, not appreciating the role their own self-confidence plays in the pictures they paint in their mind. They fail to appreciate that when their confidence is high, they will naturally take too much risk because they envision far too positive an outcome, and when it is low, they will take too little.

As I tell business leaders and investors, the higher the odds you assign to an outcome in the Comfort Zone or the Stress Center, the more likely it is that you will be wrong. We routinely overestimate the certainty of the outcomes we imagine, good and bad. As a result, we take too much *and* too little risk at precisely the wrong moments.

Using Feelings of Certainty as an Objective Measure of Sentiment

Anytime we feel certain about what lies ahead, we need to appreciate that this feeling of certainty reflects our own confidence level far more than it does the accuracy of our forecast of the future. As a result, it would be prudent for us to reconsider our conviction in these moments and be open to not just the possibility but the clear likelihood that the outcome will be far different from the one we imagine. When we can't even picture that alternative outcome, our own lack of imagination should itself be a warning signal.

The same is true at the other extreme in confidence. When we are convinced the future is uncertain, we are revealing more about how we feel than we are about what the future will bring. The future is inherently unknown; it always was and always will be uncertain. What changes is our own conviction—and that tells us everything we need to know about our relative confidence level.

And here's where it gets challenging: if we are going to rely on our gut feelings for direction, we should strive to do the opposite of what our feelings suggest is logical. When it comes to financial risk-taking, for example, we should take far more risk when we imagine the future to be terrifying and far less when we are absolutely certain of unicorns and rainbows ahead.

For some, that is impossible. They simply can't look at their own feelings objectively. An alternative, and potentially more effective, approach is to take ourselves out of the picture altogether—to simply assess the feelings of certainty being expressed by others.[5]

In my work with investors, I do this every day. When I see indiscriminate selling, for example, I know that those involved are absolutely certain prices are only going to fall. And when selling becomes widespread and newsworthy and saturated on social media sites, like Twitter, I know we are rapidly approaching a low in sentiment. Where others may feel compelled to join in and dump their stocks, I advise just the opposite behavior. Well-advertised sell-offs and "markets in turmoil" news specials offer a huge relative advantage to buyers. As uncomfortable as it may feel, these moments are the ideal ones in which to take more risk.

Perception Distortion and the Confidence Quadrant

Up until now, I have shown the Confidence Quadrant with four equally sized boxes. While this is useful in introducing the framework, few of us actually see the world that way. How much certainty and control we feel we have—how big our Comfort Zone feels relative to the size of the other boxes of the Quadrant—itself reflects our current level of confidence. Just as our level of confidence distorts our perception of the physical world around us, it also distorts our "view" of our imagined world. In the same way a batter sees a bigger ball when he is confident, we all see a bigger Comfort Zone when we are confident.

At the risk of oversimplification, in terms of relative certainty and control, here is how we likely view the world around us and envision the relative sizes of the boxes of the Quadrant when we feel confident.

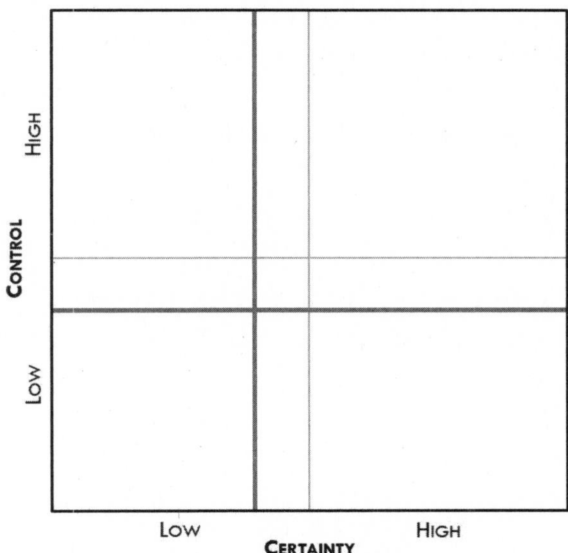

FIGURE 15.3: Confident person's view of the Quadrant

When we are confident, our imagined worldview reflects our own feelings of more certainty and control than may factually exist. Our optimism reflects our belief that whatever may come, we will figure it out.

There are tangible benefits to this worldview. Having confidence enables us to use more System 1 thinking, providing emotional and mental bandwidth and saving precious energy and time for other needs. It helps us be more relaxed, which then leads us to take risks—to build, to grow, and to expand. This has huge implications for human survival.

A confident worldview enables and encourages us to reproduce and to have children.

Researchers, like neuroendocrinology expert Robert Sapolsky, have identified a long list of physical and mental well-being benefits that come when we feel certain and in control in our lives.[6] Humankind ultimately depends on a worldview like the one in Figure 15.3—that we believe the cup of life is, and will continue to be, more than half full.

But consider what this means in terms of our decision-making. If you look closely at Figure 15.3, you will notice that the shifted axes cause our optimism-driven Comfort Zone to annex parts of what previously had been the Launch Pad, the Passenger Seat, and even the Stress Center. In those areas of the Quadrant, we now feel more certainty and/or control than really exists. As a result, we will unknowingly take more risk.

Now, let's apply the same approach to someone who is overconfident, who sees far greater certainty and control in their life than exists.

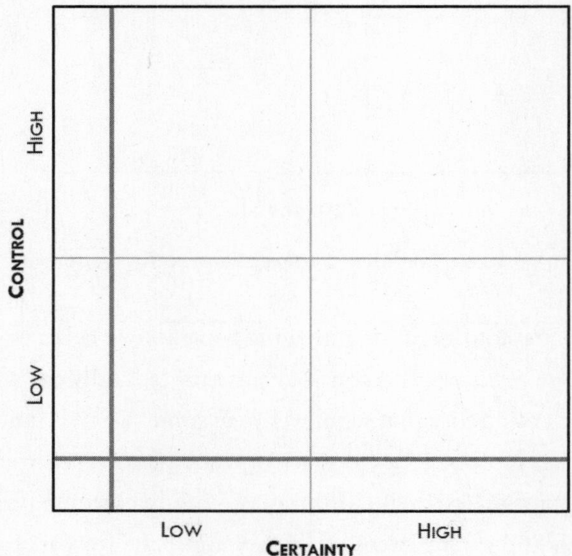

FIGURE 15.4: Overconfident person's view of the Quadrant

With the Launch Pad all but consumed by the Comfort Zone, someone with this worldview would make most decisions based on the false belief that things can only get better. And look at the relative size of the Stress Center: it's tiny. With the worldview in Figure 15.4, we can't imagine failing. We are "king of the world!" Every lottery ticket feels like a Powerball winner.

Looking at the behavior of home buyers and mortgage lenders in 2006, Figure 15.4 was likely the widely shared worldview. When I suggested earlier that these participants saw little chance of a residential housing crisis, this image helps explain why.

But at the bottom of the crisis, in early 2009, the same participants had a completely inverted worldview.

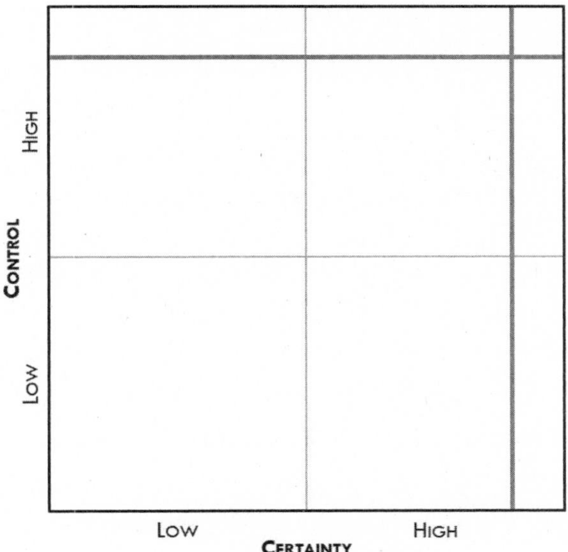

FIGURE 15.5: Underconfident person's view of the Quadrant

The odds of success and failure felt reversed. No one was taking any chances. And why would they, judging from the minuscule size of the imagined Comfort Zone in Figure 15.5?

That same no-risk-taking mindset ultimately resulted in the failure of Lehman Brothers. When given an ultimatum, no one—not lenders, not counterparties, not existing shareholders, not the government—would step up to save the brokerage firm. Everyone thought things were only going to get worse.

Bankruptcies are always accompanied by a "things are only going to get worse" mindset. Our Quadrants are overrun by gigantic Stress Centers that we can't imagine exiting. We typically overlook this phenomenon when it comes to feelings of hopelessness more broadly. It isn't just that we feel extremely uncertain and powerless; we also perceive the distance between where we are, in the lower left corner of the Stress Center, and where we want to be, in the Comfort Zone, to be so vast as to be unbridgeable.

The same principle holds in reverse when we feel invulnerable. Powerlessness and uncertainty are so psychologically distant from how we feel, we can't imagine them as even a remote possibility.

How to Assess Confidence Quadrant Distortion

Whether I am looking at an industry, the markets, or just morning news headlines, I often begin with a blank Confidence Quadrant (Figure 15.6).

I ask myself a series of questions: Where does the crowd imagine the axes of the Quadrant today? What do the behaviors I see suggest as far as participants' worldview and how they imagine the future? Where were the axes a month or a year ago? How have behaviors changed since then? Has confidence improved or deteriorated for those involved?

Appreciating the current worldview gives me insight into how participants likely view the outcomes of their decisions and, in turn, what risks they are willing to take. With that information, I can better anticipate what they might do next, particularly by gauging what a growing or shrinking Comfort Zone or Stress Center ahead might mean for the choices people make. Moving the crosslines around enables me to create multiple scenarios. Not only am I then not surprised when the

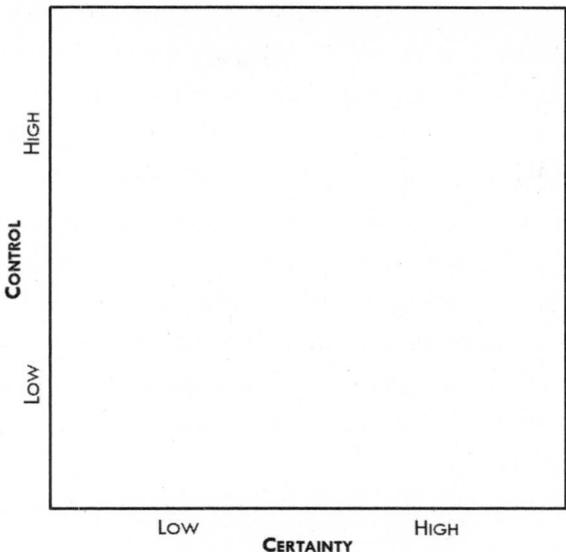

FIGURE 15.6: Blank Quadrant template

"unexpected" happens, I can also consider whether or not to prepare for its implications. In March 2020, this approach led my students and me to pack up for the semester when we left for spring break. We anticipated that if confidence fell farther because the outbreak had expanded, the university would close. We wouldn't be returning to campus anytime soon. We took a relatively small action—loading up our cars—with very limited downside that positioned us well in case conditions deteriorated.

Often, I will also drill down on the very upper right and lower left corners of the Quadrant and try to come up with the specific actions and behaviors I should expect to see there. I try to define what the two ends of the Confidence Spectrum—the best- and worst-case scenarios—might look like. What might extreme overconfidence and intense Us-Everywhere-Forever thinking lead to, versus extreme underconfidence and Me-Here-Now thinking? What might participants do when they feel invulnerable on the one hand, or defeated on the other?

For example, in the spring of 2022, as commodity prices soared in the wake of Russia's invasion of Ukraine, I thought through the implications of extreme food prices and widespread food scarcity. What could/should businesses do to prepare, given the likely behavior of customers, suppliers, and employees as the Stress Center suddenly grew?

Most scenario planning undertaken by businesses focuses on financial implications and what might happen to sales, earnings, or capital. The analysis doesn't typically consider the behavioral impacts and how the preferences, decisions, and actions of everyone involved are likely to change, whether driven by rising or falling confidence. Outcomes are presented without an understanding of their true causes and those causes' real-world significance.

As I shared earlier, while our feelings of confidence are highly subjective, we can objectively identify specific behaviors that might accompany them at different intensity levels. For example, widespread bidding wars for homes and businesses happen only in times of especially high confidence. The action demonstrates confidence elasticity at its best. Bidding wars suggest participants believe that prices will only go up; they reflect extreme trend extrapolation that buyers urgently want to beat. Bidding wars are the jumbo jets of finance; they occur only near extreme peaks in sentiment—and often in sizes comparable to jumbo jets, since everyone expects the trend not only to continue but to accelerate.

When Royal Bank of Scotland and Barclays began a bidding war for Dutch banking giant ABN AMRO in the summer of 2007, they unknowingly signaled that confidence among European bank CEOs was extremely high.[7] While executives saw unlimited possibility ahead, the supersized nature of the target and the aggressiveness of the bidders cautioned me that participants were rapidly approaching the upper right corner of the Quadrant. All they saw was an enormous Comfort Zone ahead. The landscape was all unicorns and rainbows.

Watching the behaviors of those involved and knowing what they suggested as far as placement on the Quadrant, it was difficult to see how any merger would be successful. Given the extreme confidence setup, the ultimate buyer would woefully overpay and then pay a high cost for it. As in other bidding wars, the runner-up would likely end up far ahead of the winner in the end.

Ultimately, that is what happened. Royal Bank of Scotland, the winning bidder, collapsed during the 2008 financial crisis and required the government to step in to save it; it became the "Bank That Almost Broke Britain."[8] Meanwhile, Barclays, the second-place bidder, was able to purchase the remains of Lehman Brothers for pennies on the dollar.

Similar patterns of behavior occur at the opposite end of the Confidence Spectrum. In the depths of the pandemic, in March 2020, I used a chart identical to Figure 15.5, along with the same long list of impulsive decisions being made by individuals, business leaders, and policymakers that I shared in Chapter 4, to suggest that we had reasons to be optimistic. By considering the situation and the sentiment of others objectively, and having already thought through and identified what behaviors at an extreme low would probably look like, I could strip out the extreme emotion. Where others saw enormous downside risk and limited upside, I saw the reverse. Crises occur only at lows in confidence. I was optimistic about the rebound in confidence I saw ahead and encouraged others to be as well.[9]

Panic, more broadly, offers similar clues as an objective sentiment measure. It tells us that the crosslines of the Quadrant are moving violently toward the upper right corner, creating a rapidly growing Stress Center that all but engulfs everyone's Comfort Zone. When I see market panic, I tell my clients that while I don't know at what level the markets will bottom out, I expect the moment to come very soon. Not only is collective panic difficult to sustain, the crosslines of the Quadrant can shift only so far before they hit the very edge.

Underconfidence

Previously, when I shared Figure 15.4, with its supersized Comfort Zone, I suggested that it captures how an overconfident person likely sees the world. I doubt you blinked at my interpretation. Most of us have paid the price for being too confident in something and taking too much risk, having felt too certain and too in control of something we imagined that didn't come to pass. We didn't get the promotion we were sure we'd get. With hindsight, we realize we misled ourselves: The enormous Comfort Zone we imagined didn't exist after all. Instead, the Stress Center we couldn't imagine was where we landed, and it was far larger than we believed possible.

As much as we accept overconfidence as reality, we struggle with the notion that there could be a mirroring condition. The idea that Figure 15.5, with its enormous Stress Center, could reflect *underconfidence* feels far less comfortable. That we could, and would consistently, underestimate the certainty and control in our lives—in the same way as we overestimate them—doesn't make intuitive sense to us. Faced with a pandemic or a collapsing housing market, we find the idea that we overestimated our uncertainty and powerlessness ridiculous. We get our back up. We think, "*Of course* what we felt was warranted. How were we to have known that house prices would rebound or that effective vaccines would be around the corner?"

We couldn't know. But due to our underconfidence, we were so focused on things getting worse that we weren't open to the possibility that things might get better—in that moment, we couldn't believe there could even *be* a Comfort Zone. We catastrophized; we fell victim to the closed-mindedness I've mentioned. Since we already felt so low and were so certain of the dire outcome we imagined, we failed to appreciate that the worst was actually behind us. To think otherwise contradicted the stories we were hearing from others and telling ourselves.

We need to be more open to the idea that we overreact at *both* ends of the Confidence Spectrum—that we are as likely to be underconfident as overconfident; that we can be as resistant to calls for optimism at lows in confidence as we can be to calls for pessimism at peaks. Moreover, we need to better appreciate that in both instances, our behavior is equally self-defeating. Where overconfidence leads us to take too much risk, underconfidence causes us to take too little. We imagine worst-case scenarios ahead that won't come to pass, and as a result, we fail to act on opportunities.

Underconfidence happens routinely and predictably, too. We always experience it in the wake of a crisis. Amid our extreme feelings of uncertainty and powerlessness, we are naturally hesitant to take risks again, and that tentativeness gets exacerbated when the crisis arises from our own overconfidence that preceded it. Then, our stories include blame and shame.

Underconfidence can accompany many first-time experiences, too. We overestimate the potential perils when we travel to new places, meet new people, or try new activities. With nothing yet to compare a new experience against, we allow our imaginations to run wild with what-if scenarios.

Knowing when our underconfidence is likely to naturally arise can help us overcome it. In the same way that our own wild success should caution us to reduce risk because we are prone to overconfidence, crises/failures and first-time situations should encourage us to increase our risk-taking.

There are other steps we can take to counter our tendency to fall victim to over- and underconfidence. One is to recognize that outside of controlled environments and games of chance, certainty isn't possible. The future is inherently unknown. Everything we think we see ahead is imagination. We've made it up—always. We shouldn't ever lose sight of that. Moreover, we shouldn't forget that, whether dire or rosy, the clarity of the outcomes we imagine mirrors our level of confidence. Our forecasts are far more feeling- than fact-driven. When we see no other outcome than the one we imagine, we are inherently admitting our over- or underconfidence.

Before we make major decisions, we need to revisit Figure 15.7.

Anytime we fill the blanks with an especially high or low percentage, we need to appreciate the message: we're likely kidding ourselves. With respect to the real-world decisions we make in the Launch Pad, it

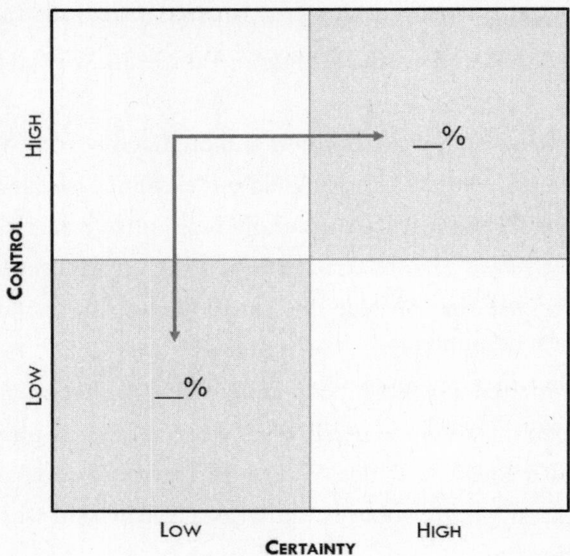

FIGURE 15.7: Launch Pad decision outcome probabilities template

is helpful to remind ourselves that the farther away we get from the expectation of a 50/50 outcome, the more over- or underconfident we are likely to be.

This may feel like an overly simplistic way to approach decision-making, but we make our most self-punishing decisions at our extremes in confidence. We commit too aggressively to do the wrong thing at precisely the wrong time, when our stories are loudest and most strident. We succumb to our extreme imagination. We overbuy at the top, and we sell out at the bottom. We buy the biggest house we can possibly afford at the top of a housing bubble, while taking our entire investment portfolio to cash at the bottom of a financial crisis. And that's not unique to individuals; C-suites follow the same pattern.

We underappreciate that given the supersized scale and especially poor timing of our extreme sentiment choices, they have an oversized impact on long-term performance. Our decisions at the top debilitate us, while those at the bottom hold us back. Simply by avoiding these impulsive and highly emotional choices, we can dramatically reduce the volatility of outcomes while improving our long-term results.

•

The Launch Pad is the environment of the Confidence Quadrant where we make deliberate choices whose outcome is unknown. As we need to fill in the blanks when it comes to the future, our stories there play an outsized role in the decisions we make.

To make better choices, we must remember just how reflexive our stories are—that they say more about how we feel than they do about the future ahead. When we are taking risks in the Launch Pad, stories laden with extreme certainty must be handled with care.

CONCLUSION

OVER THE COURSE of this book, we've covered a lot of ground. We've examined the many ways our changing feelings of certainty and control impact the choices we make in our lives, as well as in the businesses where we lead, work, and shop. Using case studies and real-world examples, we've explored a new framework for understanding our behaviors and even predicting our responses in different environments.

In real estate, they say, it all boils down to location, location, location. In the same way relative proximity to great schools and public transportation drives property values and the effort necessary to buy or sell a home, our location on the Confidence Quadrant determines what we value most and how hard or easy things feel to us. That location also drives how we think, as well as our perception of the world around us, our actions, and our stories. And when we move as a crowd, the change in our Quadrant location impacts what happens in business, financial markets, politics, and society. Like the countries my father pointed to in the atlas on our kitchen table decades ago, specific locations on the Quadrant have unique cultures and norms.

Sometimes we get to choose our next destination. We willingly move into the Launch Pad or the Passenger Seat as we deliberately take risks or follow the lead of others. Far more often, though, we don't get that choice. Instead, we are moved involuntarily.

Most of the time, our positive involuntary shifts go unnoticed. They occur in tiny increments, as a virtuous cycle propels us toward the upper right corner of the Quadrant. Our confidence subtly rises from a small achievement, such as when week-on-week sales results improve marginally, or when we spend a few more minutes on the field than on the bench with our soccer team. We feel better, more confident, but we don't pause to consider why.

At other times, unexpected events shove us violently out of our Comfort Zone. We're T-boned at an intersection, we receive a cancer diagnosis, or we lose our job. We're thrust into the Stress Center, and we must find our way back.

Like it or not, real life moves us around the Quadrant.

Knowing our location on the Quadrant, even when it's not where we want to be, gives us a head start and a competitive advantage. As unfamiliar or uncomfortable as a given moment may feel, there's certainty that comes from knowing we are in a specific square, especially when it's not the Comfort Zone. That knowledge prepares us and helps us be on alert for the pitfalls and challenges ahead. Just like a commercial airline pilot or an ER doctor, we can be ready for the aborted landings and emergencies in our lives. We can notice feelings, identify patterns, create plans, and practice procedures to regain certainty and control.

Rather than putting all our energy into avoiding crises—seeking to be perfect or flawless in our execution—we are better served knowing we *will* make mistakes and there *will* be crises ahead. Moments in the lower left corner of the Quadrant are a natural part of life. We can and must expect them.

With this in mind, we should strive not to always be confident but to be resilient—able to persevere and make our way back to the Comfort Zone, no matter where we land on the Quadrant. That may seem easier said than done, but through my research and by watching others successfully apply the Confidence Quadrant in their own lives, I have gathered a few tips for navigating the many twists and turns that life brings.

First, keep track of your location on the Quadrant as you go about your day-to-day life, complete a specific task, or tackle a new challenge. Over time, you will come to appreciate not only just how much we all move around the Quadrant but also what kinds of events and experiences boost and deplete the levels of certainty and control you feel. Don't be afraid to challenge yourself and consider that you may be overconfident or underconfident in your assessment—that where you think you are on the Quadrant may not in fact be your true location, nor where you will remain indefinitely. Remember to give yourself more scrutiny in your highs in confidence and be kinder to yourself in your lows.

Second, it's important to recognize that the stories we tell ourselves aren't facts as much as they are mirrors of our own sentiment. Try to step back and look at them objectively. Watch as your stories change with your movement around the Quadrant.

Be especially careful not to fall victim to stories at extremes in mood. Resilience requires us to fight against our most intense instincts, to display caution and pessimism at peaks in confidence and to engage in risk-taking and optimism at lows.

Third, remember that certainty and control are actionable. While at times it's very difficult, we *can* take steps to regain each of them when either or both are lost. Moreover, eliminating vulnerability requires we be proactive. Even to follow others, we must take the initiative.

Fourth, focus on the present. Until we restore our confidence, there is little to be gained by revisiting how or why we arrived in the Stress Center or in catastrophizing about what may be ahead. Both waste time and energy that could be used to move forward. Progress requires us to know and to focus on where we want to go next and how to get there.

Finally, in those moments of extreme despair and hopelessness, remind yourself that you have been in the Stress Center before and have found your way back to the Comfort Zone. You've already successfully handled and survived every previous worst day of your life. In that process, you have developed valuable skills and gained experience that enabled you to return to the Comfort Zone. Those skills can be applied now. Don't lose sight of them. Too often what we remember from a past crisis is the awful thing that happened rather than all that we learned from the experience, the many ways we grew from it, and how we moved forward despite it.

These tips don't just apply to how we handle our own lives. I've watched *Fortune* 500 business leaders, small-business managers, entrepreneurs, coaches, parents, nurses, teachers, guidance counselors, doctors, and even marketers use them to help others regain feelings of certainty and control. At the end of the day, those who are most successful in their role, whatever it may be, are those who can most effectively eliminate feelings of vulnerability in others and help them become more resilient—who recognize and appreciate where others are on the Quadrant and know how to inspire and motivate them on their journey back to the Comfort Zone. They know that success doesn't come from confidence but, rather, from how we act and what we accomplish when we are without it.

So now it's your turn. I have provided a map and a guidebook that describes the different confidence environments you will encounter in life as well as their potential pitfalls, challenges, and opportunities. I hope these tools help you better navigate your own journey, as well as the journeys of those around you, no matter where you land on the Quadrant.

ACKNOWLEDGMENTS

IF THERE IS one experience that reliably shoves you out of the Comfort Zone and brings out the Five Fs in a person, it is the process of writing a book. Thankfully, I encountered many people who generously shared their time, talents, wisdom, and kindness along my journey through every box of the Quadrant.

To begin, I want to thank the many experts whose research helped frame my thinking and shape this book, especially Daniel Kahneman, Nira Liberman, Robert Prechter, Tim Wilson, Roy Baumeister, Keith Stanovich, Denny Proffitt, Tracy and Colin Cross, Nassir Ghaemi, Annie Duke, Philip Tetlock, Robert Sapolsky, Sendhil Mullainathan, Eldar Shafir, and Alan Hall. Many took time out of their schedules to speak with me and respond to my question-filled emails. Their books and research papers are well worth your time.

Then there are the individuals whose real-world experiences and personal Quadrant maps enriched my understanding of the connections between confidence and decision-making, especially Sonny Leo, Caroline Bobrick, Peter Sim, Rob Rosenbaum, Jen and Gregg Goldstein, Terry Gillis, Jim Nelson, Leigh Morgan, Lindsay Greenberg, Michael Fairbanks, Samantha Lowe, Julia Moch, Courtney Curtiss, Jonathan Wood, Sophie Willis, Jennifer Gallagher, Peter Robison, and Kara Pelster. Thank you for sharing your stories from the emergency room, the cockpit, the plant floor, and the many places in between.

There are also those whose challenging questions over the years forced me to think more deeply, especially John Authers, Heather Long, Spencer Jakab, Stephanie Pomboy, Todd Harrison, Kevin Depew, Jesse Felder, Jonathan Taplin, Grant Williams, Terry Shaw, Paul Rathbun, Rob Roy, Ken Muench, and Greg Dzurik.

I am also thankful to the members of the New America World Economic Roundtable who welcomed me and my ideas while keeping me on my toes, especially Sherle Schwenninger, Cam Cowan, Dan Alpert, Michele Wucker, Constance Hunter, Jay Pelosky, Steven Blitz, Robert Hockett, Peter Tchir, Eric Best, Jonathan Carmel, and Lincoln Ellis.

It was through a New America roundtable presentation that I met Rana Foroohar. Not only is she an exceptional journalist and author, she also generously introduced me to extraordinary editors: Claire Howorth, Miranda Green, Brooke Masters, Tony Tassell, Jonathan Derbyshire, and Cordelia Jenkins. All kindly welcomed my ideas and improved them at every turn.

At William & Mary, Sarah Stafford, Berhanu Abegaz, Kathy O'Brien, and my colleagues in the economics department made me feel at home. Michael Arnold, Michael Chajes, and Ray Peters did the same at the University of Delaware. And an additional thank you goes to Peter and Anna Sim and Steve and Mava Miles for providing wonderful spots in Williamsburg to stay and write.

Which brings me to my students: Wherever you took my class, know how much I enjoyed having you in it. I learned far more from you than you did from me.

To Patty and Dave Sweeney, Mike and Kathleen Clem, and Bob Smith, thank you for reading my wandering early drafts and for your always kind feedback.

To Simon Rogers, at Google; Nick Mazing, at AlphaSense; Jon Clifton, Lydia Saad, and Scott Wright, at Gallup; and Chris Hickman, at BuzzFeed: thank you for generously sharing the charts and images that helped tell this story.

To my writing coach and agent, Wendy Goldman Rohm, thank you for helping me find not only my voice but also the perfect home in which to craft this book. To Adrian Zackheim and Niki Papadopoulos at Portfolio, thank you for seeing possibility and for your encouragement along the journey. Thank you, too, to Veronica Velasco, Kimberly Meilun, Ryan Boyle, and Molly Pisani for helping to shape the book in your hands.

To my editor and now dear friend, Noah Schwartzberg, the words "thank you" don't feel like enough. While my name may be on the cover, your extraordinary fingerprints are on every page of this book. I could not have asked for a better partner on this journey.

To my friends who are family—Tom Taylor, Julie James, Bob Newman, Bill Carver, Dave DiGiacoma, Ed Schmidt, Lois Tilton, Sandy Nickerson, and the Millers and McCrackens—thank you for your support and friendship. And I feel equally blessed by the love of my exceptional son- and daughter-in-law, Thomas and Abby, and my extended family of Rollinses, Dermodys, Iacones, Guldners, Horgans, Wilsons, and Pulisics.

To my brother, John, and sister, Meg, thank you for loving me when I wasn't always lovable and for providing me with wonderful memories of our times together—even when there was nothing "bon" about it.

I began this book sharing my experience with my father and his atlas. It seems only fitting that I close with a story about my mother. You see, there was a second book on our kitchen table: the dictionary. That was Mom's book. If you stumbled over the meaning of an unfamiliar word, she made you look it up. Mom believed that there was always a way to find the answer and to learn something new. She still does—now in her eighties, she's recently taken up painting.

So, to my mom, thank you for being an extraordinary role model for lifelong learning to all of us.

To my daughter, Molly, and son, Bennett, know how much fun it has been to go on this book-writing journey with you. Whether it was the perfect word or a much-needed laugh, you provided just what I needed. I am humbled by your resilience and perseverance, not to mention your awesome musical abilities (especially in the car on the way to school). I couldn't be prouder of you. I love you to the moon and back, back, back.

Finally, to my wife, Janet: Thank you for pushing me out of my Comfort Zone and helping me find my way back out of the Stress Center, not only with this book but in life over our more than forty years of friendship and marriage. I am blessed to be your husband. Whether we're sitting on the floor and talking till dawn or taking in dinner and a show, it's been an extraordinary journey. We will always belong together.

NOTES

INTRODUCTION

1. Robert Sapolsky, *Behave: The Biology of Humans at Our Best and Worst* (New York: Penguin Press, 2017), 127.
2. Meryl P. Gardner, Brian Wansink, Junyong Kim, and Se-Bum Park, "Better Moods for Better Eating? How Mood Influences Food Choice," *Journal of Consumer Psychology* 24, no. 3 (July 2014): 320–35.
3. "2016 General Election: Trump vs. Clinton," *HuffPost*, accessed October 26, 2016, https://elections.huffingtonpost.com/pollster/2016-general-election-trump-vs-clinton [inactive]; Andrew Dugan, "U.S. Economic Confidence Index Stays at -12," Gallup, October 25, 2016, https://news.gallup.com/poll/196655/economic-confidence-index-stays.aspx.
4. Robert Prechter has written extensively on the connection between music and social mood, including in *The Wave Principle of Human Social Behavior and the New Science of Socionomics* (Gainesville, GA: New Classics Library, 1999), 245–48, and more recently in *Socionomic Studies of Society and Culture: How Social Mood Shapes Trends from Film to Fashion* (Gainesville, GA: Socionomics Institute Press, 2017), which contains more than a hundred pages of socionomic studies on pop music stars, including the Beatles and Frank Sinatra. Other researchers have looked at the connection between music sentiment and the stock market; see, for example, Alex Edmans, Adrian Fernandez-Perez, Alexandre Garel, and Ivan Indriawan, "Music Sentiment and Stock Returns Around the World," *Journal of Financial Economics* 145, no. 2, part A (August 2022): 234–54, available at SSRN: https://dx.doi.org/10.2139/ssrn.3776071.

CHAPTER 1: VISUALIZING CONFIDENCE

1. National Geographic Society, *Atlas of the World*, 5th ed. (Washington, DC: National Geographic Society, 1981).

2. "Shared Solution," National Geodetic Survey, OPUS: Online Positioning User Service website, accessed August 14, 2022, www.ngs.noaa.gov/OPUS/getDatasheet.jsp?PID=BBCD57&style=modern.
3. Paul Hannon and Saabira Chaudhuri, "Why the Economic Recovery Will Be More of a 'Swoosh' Than V-Shaped," *Wall Street Journal*, updated May 11, 2020, www.wsj.com/articles/why-the-economic-recovery-will-be-more-of-a-swoosh-than-v-shaped-11589203608.
4. Peter Atwater, "The WFH Confidence Divide," LinkedIn, March 30, 2020, www.linkedin.com/pulse/wfh-confidence-divide-peter-atwater. I want to give a shout-out here to social media finance pundit @IvanTheK, who, for obvious reasons, first coined the term and generously let me run with it.

CHAPTER 2: THE CONFIDENCE QUADRANT AT WORK

1. The New England Complex Systems Institute has done extensive research looking at the connections between food scarcity and social unrest that can be found here: "Food Crisis," New England Complex Systems Institute, accessed February 2, 2022, https://necsi.edu/food-crisis. With respect to the Arab Spring uprisings more specifically, I recommend this paper by Marco Lagi, Karla Z. Bertrand, and Yaneer Bar-Yam: "The Food Crises and Political Instability in North Africa and the Middle East," NECSI (August 15, 2011), available at SSRN: http://dx.doi.org/10.2139/ssrn.1910031.
2. Justin McCarthy, "U.S. Economic Confidence at Highest Point Since 2000," Gallup, January 23, 2020, https://news.gallup.com/poll/283940/economic-confidence-highest-point-2000.aspx.
3. McCarthy, "U.S. Economic Confidence."
4. Bernie DeGroat, "Confident Consumers Confront Coronavirus," Michigan News press release, University of Michigan, February 28, 2020, https://news.umich.edu/confident-consumers-confront-coronavirus.
5. Peter Atwater, "Confidence and the Coronavirus," LinkedIn, March 8, 2020, www.linkedin.com/pulse/confidence-coronavirus-peter-atwater. This article became the first in a series that I wrote as the outbreak was unfolding, in which I explored the connection between the pandemic and how we felt using the Confidence Quadrant.
6. Jeffrey M. Jones, "U.S. Economic Confidence Shows Record Drop," Gallup, April 17, 2020, https://news.gallup.com/poll/308828/economic-confidence-shows-record-drop.aspx.

CHAPTER 3: THE CONFIDENCE SPECTRUM: INVINCIBLE TO DEFEATED

1. Kevin Fallon, "Tom Hanks Getting the Coronavirus Finally Broke Us," *Daily Beast*, March 13, 2020, www.thedailybeast.com/tom-hanks-getting-the-coronavirus-finally-broke-us.
2. Royce Young, "Sources: Jazz Center Rudy Gobert Tests Positive for Coronavirus," *ESPN.com*, March 11, 2020, www.espn.com/nba/story/_/id/28887057/jazz-center-rudy-gobert-tests-positive-coronavirus.

3. Chris Stanford, "Coronavirus, N.B.A., Tom Hanks: Your Thursday Briefing," *New York Times*, March 12, 2020, www.nytimes.com/2020/03/12/briefing/coronavirus-nba-tom-hanks.html; Brooks Barnes, "Disney Parks and Cruise Line Will Close in Response to Coronavirus," *New York Times*, March 21, 2020, www.nytimes.com/2020/03/12/business/disneyland-coronavirus.html.
4. Avie Schneider, "Dow Plunges 2,300 Points: Stocks In Meltdown As Panic Selling Continues" NPR, March 12, 2020, www.npr.org/2020/03/12/814853898/stocks-in-meltdown-over-trumps-coronavirus-plan; Conor Sen (@conorsen), "Yeah, you should probably just shut the markets here," Twitter, March 12, 2020, 9:52 a.m., https://twitter.com/conorsen/status/1238100465897832448.
5. Fallon, "Tom Hanks Getting the Coronavirus Finally Broke Us."
6. Jenni Carlson, "Opinion: How NBA's Thunder-Jazz Game Made Coronavirus Real for the Rest of Us," *Oklahoman*, March 13, 2020, www.oklahoman.com/story/sports/nba/2020/03/13/coronavirus-nba-rudy-gobert-made-virus-real-for-rest-us/5039965002.
7. Myah Ward, "15 Times Trump Praised China as Coronavirus Was Spreading Across the Globe," *Politico*, April 15, 2020, www.politico.com/news/2020/04/15/trump-china-coronavirus-188736.
8. Chris Stanford, "Coronavirus, Stock Markets, Primary Elections: Your Tuesday Briefing," *New York Times*, March 17, 2020, www.nytimes.com/2020/03/17/briefing/coronavirus-stock-markets-primary-elections.html.
9. Reuters Staff, "Factbox: Tesla, Apple, Starbucks Warn of Virus Hit; Firms Restrict Travel, Flights Cancelled," *Reuters*, January 28, 2020, https://jp.reuters.com/article/uk-china-health-business-impact-factbox-idUKKBN1ZR2NI.
10. Johnny Fulfer, "Panic of 1857," *Economic Historian*, January 6, 2022, https://economic-historian.com/2020/07/panic-of-1857.
11. *The Economic Outlook: Hearing Before the Joint Economic Committee*, 110th Cong. (March 28, 2007) (testimony of Ben S. Bernanke, chairman of the Federal Reserve of the United States), www.federalreserve.gov/newsevents/testimony/bernanke20070328a.htm.
12. Andy Marker, "The Most Useful Crisis Management Examples: The Good, Bad, and Ugly," *Smartsheet*, August 19, 2020, www.smartsheet.com/content/crisis-management-examples.
13. 9/11 Commission, *The 9/11 Commission Report: Final Report of the National Commission on Terrorist Attacks Upon the United States* (Washington, DC: U.S. Government Printing Office, 2004), available at www.govinfo.gov/content/pkg/GPO-911REPORT/pdf/GPO-911REPORT.pdf.
14. Amanda Kelly, "James Burke: The Johnson & Johnson CEO Who Earned a Presidential Medal of Freedom," Johnson & Johnson, December 12, 2017, www.jnj.com/our-heritage/james-burke-johnson-johnson-ceo-who-earned-presidential-medal-of-freedom.

CHAPTER 4: THE STRESS CENTER AND ENVIRONMENTS OF LOW CONFIDENCE

1. Office of Mary Barra, "Coronavirus Update," General Motors Corporation, March 13, 2020, https://news.gm.com/newsroom.detail.html/Pages/news/us/en/2020/mar/0312-coronavirus.html.
2. "McDonald's Provides Update on COVID-19 Impact to the Business and Reports First Quarter 2020 Comparable Sales," McDonald's, press release, April 8, 2020, https://corporate.mcdonalds.com/corpmcd/our-stories/article/covid19-business.html.
3. American Airlines Newsroom, "American Airlines Announces Additional Schedule Changes in Response to Customer Demand Related to COVID-19," American Airlines, press release, March 14, 2020, https://news.aa.com/news/news-details/2020/American-Airlines-Announces-Additional-Schedule-Changes-in-Response-to-Customer-Demand-Related-to-COVID-19-031420-OPS-DIS-03/default.aspx.
4. "General Motors Fortifies Balance Sheet in Response to COVID-19," General Motors, press release, March 24, 2020, https://investor.gm.com/news-releases/news-release-details/general-motors-fortifies-balance-sheet-response-covid-19.
5. "General Motors Fortifies Balance Sheet in Response to COVID-19," General Motors, press release.
6. Chris Stanford, "Coronavirus, Stock Markets, Democratic Debate: Your Monday Briefing," *New York Times*, March 16, 2020, www.nytimes.com/2020/03/16/briefing/coronavirus-markets-democratic-debate.html.
7. Adam Tooze, *Shutdown: How Covid Shook the World's Economy* (New York: Viking Press, 2021), 111–30.
8. "What Happens to Your Body during the Fight or Flight Response?" *Health Essentials* (blog), Cleveland Clinic, December 9, 2019, https://health.clevelandclinic.org/what-happens-to-your-body-during-the-fight-or-flight-response.
9. Kriti Gupta, "Bubble Expert Grantham Addresses 'Epic' Stock Euphoria," *Bloomberg*, June 22, 2021, www.bloomberg.com/news/articles/2021-06-22/bubble-expert-jeremy-grantham-addresses-epic-equities-euphoria.

CHAPTER 5: INTRODUCING HORIZON PREFERENCE

1. The nascent field of socionomics is filled with fascinating and important connections between investor mood and political, social, and cultural behavior. More information about the Socionomics Institute's books and research can be found here: https://socionomics.net.
2. Akane Otani, "Staying In Worked during the Stock-Market Rout. Dining Out Didn't," *Wall Street Journal*, February 27, 2020, www.wsj.com/articles/staying-in-worked-during-the-stock-market-rout-dining-out-didnt-11582799400.

3. Miguel Bustillo and David Kesmodel, "'Local' Grows on Wal-Mart," *Wall Street Journal*, August 1, 2011, www.wsj.com/articles/SB10001424052702304223804576448491782467316.
4. The book was published amid the U.S. real-estate mania of the early 2000s: Thomas L. Friedman, *The World Is Flat: A Brief History of the Twenty-First Century* (New York: Farrar, Straus and Giroux, 2005).
5. In May 2014, I gave a TEDx talk at William & Mary on "America's Chronic Case of Underconfidence," in which I shared the basic Me-Here-Now principles of Horizon Preference. Following my talk, Michael Luchs, a professor of marketing in the Mason School of Business, told me it reminded him of construal level theory (CLT), a concept developed by Yaacov Trope and Nira Liberman that describes the connection between psychological distance and the extent to which people's thinking is abstract or concrete. I wasn't familiar with CLT, but in looking at it, I not only saw the connection but realized I had overlooked an important dimension: hypotheticality. Horizon Preference not only affirms the principles of CLT but then suggests there is confidence-related variability to it.
6. Jung-Yi Yoo and Jang-Han Lee, "The Effects of Valence and Arousal on Time Perception in Individuals with Social Anxiety," *Frontiers in Psychology* 6, art. 1208 (August 17, 2015), https://doi.org/10.3389/fpsyg.2015.01208.
7. Just as I was finishing up my book, this article came out highlighting the many ways our experience with COVID disrupted our sense of time: Josh Zumbrun, "Why Dates and Times Seem to Lose Their Meaning," *Wall Street Journal*, October 7, 2022, www.wsj.com/articles/why-dates-and-times-seem-to-lose-their-meaning-11665135002.
8. Dennis Proffitt and Drake Baer, *Perception: How Our Bodies Shape Our Minds* (New York: St. Martin's Press, 2020), 41.
9. An excellent resource on the many ways that scarcity impacts our decision-making is Sendhil Mullainathan and Eldar Shafir's *Scarcity: Why Having Too Little Means So Much* (New York: Times Books, 2013).
10. Rana Foroohar, "From 'Just in Time' to 'Just in Case,'" *Financial Times* (London), May 4, 2020, www.ft.com/content/f4fa76d9-aa11-4ced-8329-6fc8c250bc45.
11. Amy Gamerman, "The Walk-In Kitchen Pantry Is the New Designer Shoe Closet," *Wall Street Journal*, December 2, 2020, www.wsj.com/articles/the-walk-in-kitchen-pantry-is-the-new-designer-shoe-closet-11606940431.
12. Joe Minihane, "Destination Trouble: Can Overtourism Be Stopped in Its Tracks?" *CNN*, July 2, 2019, www.cnn.com/travel/article/how-to-stop-overtourism/index.html.
13. David Koenig, "American Airlines CEO: We'll Never Lose Money Again," September 28, 2017, www.usatoday.com/story/travel/flights/todayinthesky/2017/09/28/american-airlines-ceo-well-never-lose-money-again/715467001.

14. "American Airlines Reports Fourth-Quarter and Full-Year 2020 Financial Results," American Airlines Newsroom, press release, January 28, 2021, https://news.aa.com/news/news-details/2021/American-Airlines-Reports-Fourth-Quarter-and-Full-Year-2020-Financial-Results-CORP-FI-01/default.aspx.
15. Joe Weisenthal, "New Mattress Has Built-In Safe!" *Business Insider*, February 18, 2009, www.businessinsider.com/get-a-mattress-with-a-built-in-safe-2009-2.

CHAPTER 6: BETTER PRACTICES IN THE STRESS CENTER

1. The words are the author's but the essential experience was confirmed by Peter Robison, author of *Flying Blind: The 737 MAX Tragedy and the Fall of Boeing* (New York: Doubleday, 2021), in an interview with the author, July 11, 2022.
2. Olga Rudenko, "The Comedian-Turned-President Is Seriously in Over His Head," *New York Times*, February 21, 2022, www.nytimes.com/2022/02/21/opinion/ukraine-russia-zelensky-putin.html.
3. Lily Kuo, "Meet the Former Comedian Who Just Turned Italian Politics Upside Down," *Quartz*, February 26, 2013, https://qz.com/56844/beppe-grillo-the-former-comedian-who-just-turned-italian-politics-upside-down.
4. Nassir Ghaemi, *A First-Rate Madness: Uncovering the Links between Leadership and Mental Illness* (New York: Penguin Books, 2012).
5. Nassir Ghaemi, "Volodymr Zelenskyy: Can Comedians Be Great Crisis Leaders?" *Psychology Today*, March 14, 2022, www.psychologytoday.com/us/blog/mood-swings/202203/volodymr-zelenskyy-can-comedians-be-great-crisis-leaders.

CHAPTER 7: THE COMFORT ZONE AND ENVIRONMENTS OF HIGH CONFIDENCE

1. "FedEx History," FedEx Corporation, accessed June 10, 2022, www.fedex.com/en-us/about/history.html.
2. "FedEx Corporation 1995 Annual Report," FedEx Corporation, accessed June 10, 2022, https://s21.q4cdn.com/665674268/files/doc_financials/annual/1995/1995annualreport.pdf.
3. *Good to Great: Why Some Companies Make the Leap and Others Don't* was first published in October 2001. Like so many books targeted to business leaders, it tends to deify those whose fates were about to dramatically reverse.
4. Reid Hoffman and Chris Yeh, *Blitzscaling: The Lightning-Fast Path to Building Massively Valuable Companies* (New York: Currency Press, 2018).
5. Dennis Proffitt and Drake Baer, *Perception: How Our Bodies Shape Our Minds* (New York: St. Martin's Press, 2020), 6–7.
6. Georges Ugeux, "The FTX Collapse: Why Did Due Diligence, Regulation, and Governance Evaporate?" *CLS Blue Sky Blog*, November 30, 2022, https://clsbluesky.law.columbia.edu/2022/11/30/the-ftx-collapse-why-did-due-diligence-regulation-and-governance-evaporate.
7. "The King of Con-men," *The Economist*, December 22, 2012, www.economist.com/christmas-specials/2012/12/22/the-king-of-con-men.

8. Jane Frankenfeld, "Shitcoin," Investopedia.com, updated June 24, 2021, www.investopedia.com/terms/s/shitcoin.asp.
9. Associated Press, "Bernanke: Subprime Mortgage Woes Won't Seriously Hurt Economy," *CNBC,* May 17, 2007, www.cnbc.com/id/18718555.

CHAPTER 8: CONFIDENCE AND COGNITIVE EASE

1. Dennis Proffitt and Drake Baer, *Perception: How Our Bodies Shape Our Minds* (New York: St. Martin's Press, 2020), 86–97.
2. Daniel Kahneman, *Thinking, Fast and Slow* (New York: Farrar, Straus and Giroux, 2011), 60.
3. Keith E. Stanovich and Richard F. West, "Individual Differences in Reasoning: Implications for the Rationality Debate," *Behavioral and Brain Sciences* 23, no. 5 (October 2000): 645–65.
4. Stephen Silver, "The Story of the Original iPhone, That Nobody Thought Was Possible," *Apple Insider*, June 29, 2018, https://appleinsider.com/articles/18/06/29/the-story-of-the-original-iphone-that-nobody-thought-was-possible.
5. Kahneman, *Thinking, Fast and Slow,* 60.
6. Erin Blakemore, "'Songs to Do CPR To' Playlist Could Be a Lifesaving Soundtrack," *Washington Post*, November 10, 2018, www.washingtonpost.com/national/health-science/songs-to-do-cpr-to-playlist-could-be-a-lifesaving-soundtrack/2018/11/09/c544aa58-e1f9-11e8-b759-3d88a5ce9e19_story.html.
7. Stef Schrader, "Think Your Car Door Sounds Nice and Solid When It Slams? It's Faked," *TheDrive*, August 19, 2020, www.thedrive.com/news/35871/think-your-car-door-sounds-nice-and-solid-when-it-slams-its-faked.
8. Marie Kondo, *Spark Joy: An Illustrated Master Class on the Art of Organizing and Tidying Up* (Berkeley, CA: Ten Speed Press, 2016).
9. Peter Atwater, "After Years of Abstraction, Things Are Getting Real for Markets," *Financial Times* (London), January 11, 2022, www.ft.com/content/8eaef215-e055-4dd2-b124-bf7e5e070fc9.

CHAPTER 9: BETTER PRACTICES IN THE COMFORT ZONE

1. "Rebuilding a Giant: Mary Barra, CEO, General Motors," *New Corner*, June 5, 2015, www.new-corner.com/rebuilding-a-giant-mary-barra-ceo-general-motors.
2. Tesla price chart, *Yahoo! Finance*, accessed May 4, 2022, https://finance.yahoo.com/chart/TSLA.
3. Robert F. Bruner, "Hugh McColl and Nationsbank: Building a National Footprint Through M&A," Darden Case No. UVA-F-1420, October 16, 2003, available at SSRN: https://dx.doi.org/10.2139/ssrn.909747.
4. Noam Scheiber, "H. Wayne Huizenga, Owner of Teams and a Business Empire, Dies at 80," *New York Times,* March 23, 2018, www.nytimes.com/2018/03/23/obituaries/h-wayne-huizenga-entrepreneur-and-team-owner-is-dead-at-80.html.

5. Rob Price, "People Are Creating Massive Lines Outside Apple Stores to Score an iPhone X (Days Before Launch)," *Inc.*, November 2, 2017, www.inc.com/business-insider/massive-lines-iphone-x-apple-store-people-queue-days-tim-cook.html.
6. "Signet Banking Corporation," Virginia Museum of History and Culture, accessed May 20, 2022, https://virginiahistory.org/research/research-resources/finding-aids/signet-banking-corporation.
7. "I Feel That I Am Making Daily Progress," Quote Investigator, accessed June 1, 2022, https://quoteinvestigator.com/2014/02/12/casals-progress.
8. Jeffrey K. Liker, *The Toyota Way: 14 Management Principles from the World's Greatest Manufacturer*, 2nd ed. (New York: McGraw Hill, 2020).
9. Matt Egan, "Wells Fargo Dumps Toxic 'Cross-selling' Metric," CNN, January 13, 2017, https://money.cnn.com/2017/01/13/investing/wells-fargo-cross-selling-fake-accounts/index.html.
10. Halah Touryalai, "The Bank That Works," *Forbes*, January 25, 2012, www.forbes.com/sites/halahtouryalai/2012/01/25/wells-fargo-the-bank-that-works/?sh=2d7f09e6718e.
11. Reuters Staff, "Lehman Demotes CFO Callan, Names New COO," Reuters, June 12, 2008, www.reuters.com/article/businessNews/idUSN0521169620080612.
12. Antony Currie, "Erin Callan Puts Nail in Lehman Coffin," Reuters, March 25, 2016, www.reuters.com/article/idUS79983182720160325.
13. "Lehman Brothers Holdings Inc. Reported Third-Quarter Profit Fell 3 Percent," *New York Times*, September 18, 2007, www.nytimes.com/2007/09/18/business/worldbusiness/18iht-18lehman.7548319.html.

CHAPTER 10: THE PASSENGER SEAT AND ENVIRONMENTS OF HIGH CERTAINTY AND LOW CONTROL

1. Dan Lamothe and Shane Harris, "Afghan Government Could Fall Within Six Months of U.S. Military Withdrawal, New Intelligence Assessment Says," *Washington Post*, June 24, 2021, www.washingtonpost.com/national-security/afghan-government-could-fall-within-six-months-of-us-military-withdrawal-new-intelligence-assessment-says/2021/06/24/42375b14-d52c-11eb-baed-4abcfa380a17_story.html.
2. Ruby Mellen, "Two Weeks of Chaos: A Timeline of the U.S. Withdrawal from Afghanistan," *Washington Post*, August 10, 2022, www.washingtonpost.com/world/2022/08/10/afghanistan-withdrawal-timeline.
3. Susannah George, Missy Ryan, Tyler Pager, Pamela Constable, John Hudson, and Griffe Witte, "Surprise, Panic and Fateful Choices: The Day America Lost Its Longest War," *Washington Post*, August 28, 2022, www.washingtonpost.com/world/2021/08/28/taliban-takeover-kabul.
4. Brooks Barnes, "Disney Brings Back Bob Iger After Ousting Chapek as CEO," *New York Times*, November 20, 2022, www.nytimes.com/2022/11/20

/business/disney-robert-iger.html; Heather Haddon, "Howard Schultz Is Back as Starbucks CEO. Here's His To-Do List," *Wall Street Journal*, April 3, 2022, www.wsj.com/articles/howard-schultz-is-back-as-starbucks-ceo-heres-his-to-do-list-11648994580.

5. Christopher Bingham, Bradley Hendricks, Travis Howell, and Kalin Kolev, "Boomerang CEOs: What Happens When the CEO Comes Back?" *MIT Sloan Management Review*, September 17, 2020, https://sloanreview.mit.edu/article/boomerang-ceos-what-happens-when-the-ceo-comes-back.
6. Dawn Kopecki, "Can Brian Moynihan Save Bank of America?" *Bloomberg*, September 8, 2011, www.bloomberg.com/news/articles/2011-09-08/can-brian-moynihan-save-bank-of-america#xj4y7vzkg.
7. Lisa Fickenscher, "Bed Bath & Beyond CEO Is Pushed Out as Sales Plummet," *New York Post*, June 29, 2022, https://nypost.com/2022/06/29/bed-bath-beyond-ceo-mark-tritton-ousted-as-sales-plummet.
8. William Langewiesche, "The Lessons of ValuJet 592," *The Atlantic*, March 1998, www.theatlantic.com/magazine/archive/1998/03/the-lessons-of-valujet-592/306534.
9. "ValuJet grounded," CNN, June 17, 1996, www.cnn.com/US/9606/17/valujet.grounded.
10. Dominic Gates, "Boeing 737 MAX Can Return to the Skies, FAA Says," *Seattle Times*, November 18, 2020, www.seattletimes.com/business/boeing-aerospace/boeing-737-max-can-return-to-the-skies-says-faa; Chris Isidore, "Boeing's 737 Max Debacle Could Be the Most Expensive Corporate Blunder Ever," CNN Business, November 17, 2020, www.cnn.com/2020/11/17/business/boeing-737-max-grounding-cost/index.html.

CHAPTER 11: CONFIDENCE ELASTICITY

1. Gas prices are also psychologically proximate—they are highly familiar to us, as a highly commoditized product whose prices are observed everywhere and every time we fill up. We are well aware when gas prices change.
2. There has been some very interesting research done that looks at the impact of changing gas prices on consumer sentiment: Carola Binder and Christos Makridis, "Gas Prices and Consumer Sentiment," Gallup, August 13, 2020, https://news.gallup.com/opinion/gallup/317282/gas-prices-consumer-sentiment.aspx; Emily Badger and Eve Washington, "Why the Price of Gas Has Such Power over Us," *New York Times*, October 25, 2022, www.nytimes.com/2022/10/25/upshot/gas-prices-biden-midterms.html.
3. Annie Gasparro, "More Shoppers Buy Store Brands, Eating Into Big Food Companies' Sales," *Wall Street Journal*, July 23, 2022, www.wsj.com/articles/more-shoppers-buy-store-brands-eating-into-big-food-companies-sales-11658581202.
4. "British Airways Retires Entire 747 Fleet After Travel Downturn," *BBC News*, July 17, 2020, www.bbc.com/news/business-53426886.

5. I am not alone: former Federal Reserve Board chairman Alan Greenspan was known to keep a close eye on men's underwear sales. He believed a decline warned of a potential economic slowdown. Nichole Goodkind, "Is a Recession Coming? Alan Greenspan Says the Answer Is in Men's Underwear," CNN, March 26, 2022, www.cnn.com/2022/03/26/economy/recession-underwear-alan-greenspan/index.html.
6. Peter Atwater, "After Years of Abstraction, Things Are Getting Real for Markets," *Financial Times* (London), January 11, 2022, www.ft.com/content/8eaef215-e055-4dd2-b124-bf7e5e070fc9.
7. @SentimenTrader, "Last week, U.S. options traders opened 94.8 million new equity and ETF contracts. The smallest of traders buying call options—pure speculation—accounted for 20.5 million of those. At 21.6% of total volume, that's a record high," Twitter, December 5, 2020, 9:05 a.m., https://twitter.com/sentimentrader/status/1335235220551962627.
8. Robert R. Prechter, Jr., *The Wave Principle of Human Social Behavior and the New Science of Socionomics* (Gainesville, GA: New Classics Library, 1999).
9. The Socionomics Institute has a vast library of research reports documenting the clear impact of changing social mood on economic, financial, political, social, and cultural decision-making, available at https://socionomics.net.
10. "Russia vs. Ukraine: See One Indicator That Predicted the Invasion a Month in Advance," Elliott Wave International, accessed July 15, 2022, www.elliottwave.com/European-Markets/Will-Russia-Invade-Ukraine-Yes-Suggests-This-Indicator.
11. Peter Atwater, *Moods and Markets: A New Way to Invest in Good Times and in Bad* (New York: FT Press, 2012), 107.
12. Brian Melley, "Chipotle Agrees to Record $25 Million Fine Over Tainted Food," AP News, April 21, 2020, https://apnews.com/article/business-ap-top-news-us-news-boston-los-angeles-3cce663eeeb0654c5334ae08a5b25b3c.
13. Brett Molina, "Family Dollar Recall: Rodent Infestation That Closed 404 Stores Cost Company $34 Million," *USA Today*, March 4, 2022, www.usatoday.com/story/money/shopping/2022/03/04/family-dollar-recall-rodent-infestation/9375195002.
14. Peter Atwater, "The Critical Importance of Confidence Diversification to Today's Investment Portfolios," LinkedIn, August 12, 2021, www.linkedin.com/pulse/critical-importance-confidence-diversification-todays-peter-atwater.
15. Jesse Felder, "Welcome to the Everything Bubble," *The Felder Report*, May 13, 2015, https://thefelderreport.com/2015/05/13/welcome-to-the-everything-bubble.
16. Peter Atwater, "Bubble Bursting Shows the Need for 'Confidence Diversification,'" *Financial Times* (London), August 23, 2022, www.ft.com/content/ad458a6c-6cd6-4452-a64f-7541588d9e51.
17. Ben Johnson (@MstarBenJohnson), "From @BankofAmerica Global Research: YTD annualized return for the 60/40 portfolio is the worst in 100 years,"

Twitter, October 14, 2022, 10:31 a.m., https://twitter.com/MstarBenJohnson/status/1580929309023563777.

18. John Authers, "There's No Hiding from the Bad News This Time," Bloomberg, June 13, 2022, www.bloomberg.com/opinion/articles/2022-06-13/markets-have-nowhere-to-hide-from-this-terrible-inflation-report.
19. As mentioned, bond prices and bond yields move in opposite directions: as interest rates rise, bond prices fall, and the reverse.

CHAPTER 12: BETTER PRACTICES IN THE PASSENGER SEAT

1. Michael Wolff, "Harvey Weinstein: Everyone Knew," *GQ* (UK), December 1, 2017, www.gq-magazine.co.uk/article/harvey-weinstein-everyone-knew.
2. Brooks Barnes, "Weinstein Company Files for Bankruptcy and Revokes Nondisclosure Agreements," *New York Times*, March 19, 2018, www.nytimes.com/2018/03/19/business/weinstein-company-bankruptcy.html.
3. Peter Robison, author of *Flying Blind: The 737 MAX Tragedy and the Fall of Boeing* (New York: Doubleday, 2021), interview with the author, July 11, 2022.
4. "History & Inception," MeToo Movement, accessed July 24, 2022, https://metoomvmt.org/get-to-know-us/history-inception.

CHAPTER 13: THE LAUNCH PAD AND ENVIRONMENTS OF HIGH CONTROL AND LOW CERTAINTY

1. "About Us," Spanx, accessed November 16, 2021, https://spanx.com/pages/about-us.
2. Clare O'Connor, "How Sara Blakely of Spanx Turned $5,000 into $1 Billion," *Forbes*, March 14, 2012, www.forbes.com/global/2012/0326/billionaires-12-feature-united-states-spanx-sara-blakely-american-booty.html.
3. Clare O'Connor, "Top Five Startup Tips from Spanx Billionaire Sara Blakely," *Forbes*, April 2, 2012, www.forbes.com/sites/clareoconnor/2012/04/02/top-five-startup-tips-from-spanx-billionaire-sara-blakely.
4. Edward Ludlow, "Ford Sees $8.2 Billion Gain on Its Investment Following Rivian's IPO," Bloomberg, January 18, 2022, www.bloomberg.com/news/articles/2022-01-18/ford-sees-8-2-billion-gain-on-investment-following-rivian-s-ipo.
5. Thomas Gryta and Chip Cutter, "Farewell Offshoring, Outsourcing. Pandemic Rewrites CEO Playbook," *Wall Street Journal*, November 1, 2021, www.wsj.com/articles/pandemic-rewrites-ceo-rulebookputting-reliability-before-efficiency-11635779679.

CHAPTER 14: CONFIDENCE AND THE STORIES WE TELL

1. Jeran Wittenstein, "'Unprecedented' Has Become Corporate America's Go-To Descriptor," *Bloomberg*, April 22, 2020, www.bloomberg.com/news/articles/2020-04-22/-unprecedented-has-become-corporate-america-s-go-to-descriptor.

2. Andrew Ross Sorkin, Jason Karaian, Sarah Kessler, Michael J. de la Merced, Lauren Hirsch, and Ephrat Livni, "Behold the Highest-Paid C.E.O.s," Dealbook, *New York Times*, June 11, 2021, www.nytimes.com/2021/06/11/business/dealbook/ceo-highest-pay.html.
3. Johan Bollen, Huina Mao, and Xiao-Jun Zeng, "Twitter mood predicts the stock market," *Journal of Computational Science 2*, no. 1 (March 2011): 1–8, https://doi.org/10.48550/arXiv.1010.3003.
4. Rachel Weiner, "Obama Unveils New Campaign Slogan: 'Forward,'" *Washington Post*, April 30, 2012, www.washingtonpost.com/blogs/the-fix/post/obama-unveils-new-campaign-slogan-forward/2012/04/30/gIQA3SrbrT_blog.html.
5. "Home Sweet Home," *Time*, June 13, 2005, http://content.time.com/time/covers/pacific/0,16641,20050613,00.html.
6. Dominick Mastrangelo, "Ingraham on Fox News, Jan. 6: We Know How to 'Cater to Our Audience,'" *The Hill*, June 8, 2022, https://thehill.com/blogs/pundits-blog/media/3516029-ingraham-on-fox-news-jan-6-we-know-how-to-cater-to-our-audience.
7. Experts often talk about narratives spreading like a contagious disease. While there are similarities, the analogy overlooks the natural resistance that exists to fledgling narratives and the eagerness with which we embrace widely shared stories. Narratives are like a virus where our immunity is intense at the beginning of the outbreak and collapses as it spreads.
8. Peter Atwater, "The WFH Confidence Divide," LinkedIn, March 30, 2020, www.linkedin.com/pulse/wfh-confidence-divide-peter-atwater.
9. Peter Atwater, *Moods and Markets: A New Way to Invest in Good Times and in Bad* (New York: FT Press, 2012), 58–59.
10. Matthew Rozsa, "The Cult of Elon Musk: Why Do Some of Us Worship Billionaires?," *Salon*, April 29, 2022, www.salon.com/2022/04/29/the-of-elon-musk-why-do-some-of-us-worship-billionaires.
11. British bond yields offer a recent real-time example: after a steady forty-year decline in yields, no one could imagine interest rates rising, let alone rising as violently as they did in 2022. Greg Ip, "As Bond Investors' Bets Blow Up, They Might Usher In Era of Higher Rates," *Wall Street Journal*, October 13, 2022, www.wsj.com/articles/as-bond-investors-bets-blow-up-they-might-usher-in-era-of-higher-rates-11665658801.
12. Popularity: "Favorability: People in the News," Gallup, accessed August 14, 2022, https://news.gallup.com/poll/1618/Favorability-People-News.aspx#3; magazine cover: "Can Anyone Stop Hillary?," *Time*, January 27, 2014, http://content.time.com/time/covers/0,16641,20140127,00.html.
13. Stipe, "*Forbes* in 2007: Can Anyone Catch Nokia?," Nokiamob.net, December 11, 2017, https://nokiamob.net/2017/11/12/forbes-in-2007-can-anyone-catch-nokia.
14. "Be Afraid," *The Economist*, October 1, 2011, www.economist.com/leaders/2011/10/01/be-afraid.

15. Anna Hirtenstein and Akane Otani, "The Worst of the Global Selloff Isn't Here Yet, Banks and Investors Warn," *Wall Street Journal*, March 22, 2020, www.wsj.com/articles/the-worst-of-the-global-selloff-isnt-here-yet-banks-and-investors-warn-11584877018.

CHAPTER 15: BETTER PRACTICES IN THE LAUNCH PAD

1. Anytime we consider the future, we imagine. This may seem fantastical, but the future is always unknown. We *must* imagine it.
2. One of the underappreciated aspects of investing is that once we have made our decision to invest, we move from the Launch Pad into the Passenger Seat. Whether it is because of the actions of company management or those of other investors, our investment return is driven by the behavior of others; until we choose to sell, we are a beneficiary or a victim of their choices. This passive phenomenon is often then compounded when we invest in index funds or give funds to money managers to invest on our behalf.
3. Annie Duke, *Thinking in Bets: Making Smarter Decisions When You Don't Have All the Facts* (New York: Portfolio Press, 2018).
4. Philip E. Tetlock and Dan Gardner, *Superforecasting: The Art and Science of Prediction* (New York: Crown Publishing, 2016).
5. This is especially relevant when investing. Market prices reflect the confidence of the crowd. The behavior of others ultimate determines whether we make or lose money on what we buy.
6. Robert Sapolsky, *Behave: The Biology of Humans at Our Best and Worst* (New York: Penguin Press, 2017).
7. Julia Werdigier, "Royal Bank of Scotland Begins Bidding War for ABN AMRO," *New York Times*, April 25, 2007, www.nytimes.com/2007/04/25/business/worldbusiness/25iht-abn.1.5433568.html.
8. Sean O'Grady, "*The Bank That Almost Broke Britain*, Review: A Timely Look at the Financial Crisis," *Independent* (UK), October 2, 2018, www.independent.co.uk/arts-entertainment/tv/reviews/the-bank-that-almost-broke-britain-review-bbc-2-two-rbs-fred-goodwin-a8564891.html.
9. Nathan Warters, "W&M's Atwater, a Decision-Making Expert, Says 'Optimism Will Return,'" William & Mary News Archive, March 13, 2020, www.wm.edu/news/stories/2020/wms-atwater,-a-decision-making-expert,-says-optimism-will-return.php.

INDEX

Page numbers in *italics* refer to figures.

ABN AMRO, 274
abstraction, 195, 196
  eliminating, 149–51
  preference, 94–98, *95*, *96*, *97*
accountability, 60, 153, 241
action-reaction cycles, 248–51, *249*, *251*
addiction, 217
advertising, 245–47
Afghanistan, 173–74, 209
AIDS, 84–85
Airbnb, 158
aircraft, 190–93
  safety and crashes of, 58, 108–9, 182, 199–200, 214–15
air travel, xvi–xvii, 13–19, *14*, *15*, *16*, *17*, *18*, *19*, 35, 37, 39, 46, 183, 206, 233, 250
  COVID and, 70, 72
alcoholism, 217
AlphaSense, *238–39*, 239, *240–41*
Amazon, 127, 148
AMC, 77
American Airlines, 70, 72, 103
Anheuser-Busch, 91
Antoncic, Madelyn, 169–70
anxiety, 37–38, *37*, 260–61, *260*
AOL–Timer Warner merger, 226
Apple, 54, 148
  iPhone, 146, 147, 160–61
Arab Spring, 31–32, 40
architecture and building, 150
athletes, 132, 141
authoritarianism, 174–76, 179, *180*, 207–9
automobiles, 147
  electric, 157–59, 226–27, 257
AutoNation, 159

banking crisis, *see* financial crisis of 2008
Bank of America, 159, 178–79, 259
bankruptcies, 65, 272
banks, 274–75
  trust in, 184–85
Barclays, 274–75
Barra, Mary, 70, 71, 157–58
Bear Stearns, 258
Bed Bath & Beyond, 179
Bernanke, Ben, 138
Best Buy, 45
beta tests, 149–50
Bezos, Jeff, 127
bidding wars, 274–75
Biden, Joe, 173
Bingo Card, Overconfidence, 166–68

Black Lives Matter, 40, 198
Blakely, Sara, 221–22, 225, 227
blame, 59–60, 62, 80, 114, 215, 246, 277
blitzscaling, 131
Blockbuster Video, 159
Bloomberg Businessweek, 178–79
Boeing, 58, 108–9, 182, 190–93, 199, 214–15
bonds, 202–3
Boots & Coots, 47
bullwhip effect, 84
Burke, James, 60, 63, 64
Burke, Tarana, 215
businesses and organizations
  accountability in, 60, 153, 241
  bankruptcies in, 65, 272
  continuous improvement culture in, 164–66
  and customer confidence versus customer satisfaction, 184–85
  defense and offense capacities in, 83
  entrepreneurial, 163–64, 168, 222–26, 230, 232
  Launch Pad, 43–45, *43*, *45*, 47, 223–27
  leaders in, *see* leaders
  mapping on the Quadrant, 40–47, *41*, *43*, *45*
  mergers and acquisitions of, 58, 154, 159–60, 162, 225–27, 274–75
  messaging by, 245–47
  panics at level of, 57–58
  Passenger Seat, 41–47, *41*, *45*, 181–84, 206–7
  S-curve growth pattern in, 145–46
  star-centered, 207–10
  zero-sum thinking in, 120

Callan, Erin, 169
Capital One, 163
Carbon, Inc., 228
Carlson, Jenni, 52
Carnival Cruise Line, 102–3
Casals, Pablo, 165
Cast Away, 11
causation, 59–60
Centers for Disease Control and Prevention (CDC), 71, 74
certainty, xvi–xvii, xxii, xxiv, 4
  confidence level and, 20
  in Confidence Quadrant, *5*, 6–12, *7*, *8*, *9*, *11*, *13*
  decision-making and, 10
  in Launch Pad, 10–11
  in Passenger Seat, 9–11
  preservation of, 12
  in Stress Center, 7
  see also Confidence Quadrant
China, 198
Chipotle, 200
Citigroup, 127
Clinton, Bill, 63
Clinton, Hillary, xx–xxi, *xxi*, 247, 258
cognitive ease, 140–55, 160, 164
  abstraction and, 149–51
  familiarity in, 145–48, 151
  as fluency, 141
  simplicity and, 148–49, 153
cognitive processing
  perils of, 153–55
  System 1 and System 2, 142–48, *143*, 151, 153–55, 158, 160, 162, 170, 177, 217, 223, 235, 237, 243, 264–66, 269
Cole, USS, 198–99
Collins, Jim, 130
Colonial Pipeline ransomware attack, 58
comedians, 116, 122
Comfort Zone, 6–9, *7*, 12, *13*, 33, 37, 38, 41–43, 65, 78, 80, 92, 94, 122, 156, 185, 210, 217, 223, 224, 281–83
  air travel and, 13, *14*, *18*, *19*
  arc from Stress Center to, 134–35, *134*
  better practices in, 156–70
  COVID and, 34–35, *35*, 37, 52, 71, 74

crisis management and, 110
decision-making in, 262
emergency room doctors and, 25–26
entrepreneurship and, 163–64, 168
environments of high confidence and, 125–39
Five Fs of extreme confidence in, 137–39
high school senior year and, 24
investors and, 40
invulnerability and mania in, 65, 134–39, 164–70
Launch Pad and, 12, 222–23, *222*, 225–27, 231–33, *231*, 263
leaders and, 114–15, 120, 121, 141, 156–58
Passenger Seat and, 12, 176–81, *180*, 211, 213, 218
perception distortion in, 132–33, *133*
playing offense in, 130–32
risk-taking in, 128, 130–33, *133*, 138, 167
success and, 31
System 1 thinking in, 143
time as perceived in, 98
unnoticed perks of, 160–62
Us-Everywhere-Forever preferences in, 93, *93*, 127–30, 158, 225, 235
communication, in Stress Center, 117–19
comparison, 121
computers, 46, 58, 147
Conference Board, 32, 189
confidence, xiv–xvi, xxii, 140
certainty in, *see* certainty
cognitive ease and, *see* cognitive ease
control in, *see* control
Horizon Preference and, 101–5
overconfidence, xvii, 83, 136, 157, 165–68, 170, 270–71, 275–78
underconfidence, 163, 273, 275–79, *278*
vulnerability and, xvii–xviii, 50–51, 93, 95
worldview distorted by, 20
confidence elasticity, 187–205
consumer sentiment and, 189–90, *190*, 201–2
customer trust and, 199–200, *199*
diversification and, 200–205
economic cycles and, 189–90, *190*
exogenous events and, 196–99, *197*
improving results using, 189–200
specific products and, 190–96, *191*, *192*, *195*
Confidence Quadrant, 3–29, *5*, *13*, 30–47, 87, 280–83
assessing confidence level of others with, 31–40, *35*
mapping confidence cycles on, *see* Confidence Spectrum
mapping experiences on, 13–23, *14*, *15*, *16*, *17*, *18*, *19*, *21*, *22*
perception distortion and, 268–75, *269*, *270*, *271*, *273*
uncovering issues using, 23–29, *24*, *26*, *27*
see also Comfort Zone; Launch Pad; Passenger Seat; Stress Center
Confidence Spectrum, 48–66, *49*, 80, 87, 235
arc in, 134–35, *134*
overreactions in, 276
sentiment cycles and, 48–55
confidence theater, xiv, 117
consumers, *see* customers
Container Store, 152–53
continuous improvement, 164–66
control, xvi–xvii, xxii, xxiv, 4
confidence level and, 20
in Confidence Quadrant, *5*, 6–12, *7*, *8*, *9*, *11*, *13*
in Launch Pad, 10–11
in Passenger Seat, 9, 10
preservation of, 12
in Stress Center, 7
see also Confidence Quadrant

COVID-19 pandemic, xv, xxii, 21–23, *21*, *22*, 34–37, *34*, 44, 48, 51–56, 61, 79, 84–85, 90, 96–97, 103, 107, 152, 198, 265, 276
  airlines and, 192
  Carnival Cruise Line and, 103
  decisions made in response to, 70–72, 83–84, 89, 228–29, 275
  employee movements following, 212, 229
  extreme vulnerability and, 54–55
  Five F responses and, 72–77
  Hanks and Gobert and, 51–54, 70, 96, 237, 252, 255
  K-shaped economic recovery from, 23, 253
  Me-Here-Now preferences and, 89, 97–98, 101
  narrative turning point in, 53–54, 70, 96, 237, 255, 256
  psychological and physical distance and, 53–54, 75, 96
  restaurants and, 44, 71, 72, 151–52
  supplies during, 100–101, 197, 230
  System 1 and System 2 thinking in, 144, 155
  as "unprecedented," 237–41, *237*, *238–39*, 243, 259
  vaccines and, 74, 101
CPR, 149
credibility, 119
credit, 161
Credit Suisse, 259
crises, 31, 59, 65, 101, 106, 275
  fast and furious responses to, 70, 72, 81, 82, 92, 108
  management of, 60–61, 63–64, 79, 106–19, *111*, 151, 229
  narrow definitions of, 63–64
  recovery from, 109–10
  see also panics
cryptocurrencies, 133, 138, 154, 158, 168, 196
Cuomo, Andrew, 74
customer confidence, 184–85, 188–89
  global, 201
  see also confidence elasticity
customers
  sentiment of, 32–36, 38–40, 189, 201–2
  satisfaction of, 184–85, 188–89
  trust of, 199–200, *199*

Daily Beast, 52
Damon, Matt, 168
decision-making, xv, xvii–xx, xxii–xxiv, 10, 94, 145, 207, 223, 230, 233, 263–64, 270, 277–79
  in Comfort Zone, 262
  financial, 263–67, *264*, *266*
  invulnerability and, 136
  in Launch Pad, 262–67, *264*, *266*, 277–79
  psychological distance distortion and, 98–101
  in Stress Center, 70, 262
  stressor accumulation and, 32
Deepwater Horizon oil rig explosion, 58
defense, playing, 83
Dell, 46
depression, seasonal, 90–91, *91*, 244, *244*
Disney, 52, 176
distance, physical, 53–54, 95, 129
distance, psychological, 53–54, 75, 95–97, 112, 114, 115, 118
  distortion of, 98–101
diversification, 200–205
Domino's Pizza, 90
dot-com bubble, 33, 34, 40, 138, 154–55
Duke, Annie, 264, 265
DuPont, 228

Economist, 258
economy and finance, xiii, xviii
  COVID economic recovery, 23, 253
  crisis of 2008 in, *see* financial crisis of 2008
  cycles in, 48–50, 189–90, *190*, 193, 201

dot-com bubble, 33, 34, 40, 138, 154–55
global economy, 258
in Greece, 103–4
Hemline Index and, 86–87
in Italy, xxii
panics of 1837 and 1857, 56
securitization in, xviii–xix, 127
surveys on feelings about the economy, xx, *xxi*, 32–33, *33*, 35, *36*
see also investors
Eilish, Billie, xxii
electric vehicles (EVs), 157–59, 226–27, 257
emergency rooms, 25–26, *26*, 38, 61–63, 84, 99, 104, 112, 151, 153, 206
emergency training, 148–49
EMTs, 149
Enron, 138, 208
entrepreneurs, 163–64, 168, 222–26, 230, 232
environmental sentiment, 36–40
Ethiopian Airlines, 108
European energy crisis, 245, *245*
exploration, 129, 162, 222

Facebook, 148
Fallon, Kevin, 52
familiarity, 145–48, 151
Family Dollar stores, 200
fantastic, in extreme confidence, 137
Fauci, Anthony, 74
fearlessness, 50
Federal Aviation Administration (FAA), 46, 61, 182, 183
FedEx, 125–27, 129, 131, 159–60, 162, 221
Felder, Jesse, 203
FEMA, 198
festive, in extreme confidence, 137
fight response, 72–73, 78, 80, 198, 215
financial crisis of 2008, xix, 33, 56–58, 87, 91, 116, 157, 163, 178, 247, 252, 254, 265, 275
housing bubble in, xxiv, 34, 40, 65, 84, 103, 107, 133, 138–39, 247–48, 254, 256–58, 267, 276
and trust in banks, 184–85
as "unprecedented," *240–41*, 241
financial decision-making, 263–67, *264*, *266*, 268
First-Rate Madness, A (Ghaemi), 116–17
first responders, 25, 38, 61, 104, 149, 151
First Union, 163
Five Fs of extreme confidence, 137–39
Five Fs of stress responses, 72–82, 87–90, 145, 218
fight, 72–73, 78, 80, 198, 215
flight, 72–74, 76, 78, 80
follow, 72, 74–76, 78, 80, 82, 175
freeze, 72, 76, 78
fuck it, 72, 76–78, 90, 113, 198, 215
flashy, in extreme confidence, 137
flight response, 72–74, 76, 78, 80
follow response, 72, 74–76, 78, 80, 82, 175
FOMO (fear of missing out), 129
food, 274
comfort, 90–91, *91*, 193, 244, *244*
see also restaurants
Food and Drug Administration (FDA), 46
Forbes, 165, 221, 225, 258
Ford Motor Co., 226–27
Fortune, 63
Fortune 500 companies, xix–xx, 283
Four Corners, 5–6
Fox News, 248
Franken, Al, 116
fraudulent, fictitious, and fake activity, 138, 166
Freeman, Robert, 163
freeze response, 72, 76, 78
frenetic, in extreme confidence, 137
Friedman, Thomas, 94
FTX, 133, 208
fuck-it response, 72, 76–78, 90, 113, 198, 215

Fuld, Dick, 169
futuristic, in extreme confidence, 137

Gallup, Inc., 32, 36, 189
  economic confidence surveys of, xx, *xxi*, 33, *33*, 35, *36*
GameStop, xxiii, 77
gasoline, 58, 100, 188
Gateway, 46
General Electric, 83, 128
General Motors, 70–72, 157–58
Ghaemi, Nassir, 116–17
goals, 165
Gobert, Rudy, 52, 54, 70, 96, 237, 252
Goldman, Laurie Ann, 225
Goldman Sachs, 259
Good to Great (Collins), 130
Google searches, 244, 245
  for "am I fat," "am I stupid," and "am I ugly," 261, *261*
  for anxiety, 37–38, *37*, 260–61, *260*
  for comfort food and seasonal depression, 90–91, *91*, 244, *244*
  for European energy crisis, 245, *245*
government regulation, 46–47, 85, 161–62
Grammy Awards, xxii
Grantham, Jeremy, 77
Greek debt crisis, 103–4
Gregory, Joseph, 169
Grillo, Beppe, 116

halo effect, 53, 115
Hanks, Tom, 11
  COVID and, 51–54, 70, 96, 237, 252, 255
Hemline Index, 86–87
hero's journey, 11
high school senior year, 24–25, *24*
Hoffman, Reid, 131
home buying, 266–67, 271, 278
  bidding wars in, 274
  bubble in, xxiv, 34, 40, 65, 84, 103, 107, 133, 138–39, 247–48, 254, 256–58, 267, 276
Home Depot, 43, 73, 198, 212, 227
Horizon Preference, 92–94, 101, 121, 126–27, 155, 235, 246
  abstraction preference and, 94–98, *95*, *96*, *97*
  confidence correlation and, 101–5
  Me-Here-Now, *see* Me-Here-Now preferences
  Us-Everywhere-Forever, 93, *93*, 127–30, 158, 191, 193, 195, 273
hospitals, 185, 198, 206
  emergency rooms, 25–26, *26*, 38, 61–63, 84, 99, 104, 112, 151, 153, 206
HuffPost, xx, *xxi*
Huizenga, Wayne, 159

Iger, Robert, 176
imprisonment, 180–81
Ingraham, Laura, 248
innovation, 146, 149, 158, 161, 195
investors, xiii, xviii, 40, 59–60, 77, 82, 86–87, 135, 154, 232, 263, 265, 268
  cryptocurrencies and, 133, 138, 154, 158, 168, 196
  manias and, 133, 135–36, 138
  portfolios of, 202–5
  risks and return levels and, 194–96, *194*, *195*
  on *Shark Tank*, 150
  Twitter and, 244
  see also stocks, stock market
invulnerability, 65, 134–39, 272, 273
  countering, 164–70
iPhone, 146, 147, 160–61
Italy, xxii, 54, 116

January 6 investigation, 248
Johnson & Johnson, 60, 63

Kahneman, Daniel, 141–42, 146
kaizen, 165
Kinko's, 127
Kondo, Marie, 152
Kroger, 189, 191
Kullman, Ellen, 228

Launch Pad, 10–12, *11*, *13*, 250, 280
  air travel and, 16, *17*, *19*
  better practices in, 262–79
  businesses operating in, 43–45, *43*, *45*, 47, 223–27
  Comfort Zone and, 12, 222–23, *222*, 225–27, 231–33, *231*, 263
  confidence-driven distortions in, 233–34
  COVID and, 71
  crisis management and, 111
  decision-making in, 262–67, *264*, *266*, 277–79
  environments of high control and low certainty and, 221–34
  exiting Passenger Seat into, 212–14, 217, 218
  Passenger Seat as similar to, 228
  paths into, 227–34, *229*, *231*
  perception distortion and, 268–75, *269*, *270*, *271*, *273*
  stories and, 236
  Stress Center and, 73, 75, 263
  underconfidence and, 275–79, *278*
  and using certainty as measure of sentiment, 267–68
leaders, 31, 78–84, 97
  Comfort Zone and, 114–15, 120, 121, 141, 156–58
  confidence and, 114, 163, 168–70
  crisis management and, 60–61, 63–64, 79, 106–19
  cultish and controlling, 207–10
  departure of, 209
  narratives and, 257
  in Passenger Seat workplaces, 208
  rethinking, 168–70
  Stress Center and, 114–15, 117–22
Lehman Brothers, 65, 83, 169–70, 247, 254, 258, 259, 272, 275
LIFO (last in, first out), 138
LinkedIn, 131
Lowe's, 43
lying, 119
MacGregor, Gregor, 138
Madoff, Bernie, 138
mania, 65, 134–38
maps, 3–4
marathon runners, 100
McColl, Hugh, Jr., 159
McDonald's, 70
McGee, Skip, 170
media, xiii, 236, 243
  confidence and, 247–48
medical experiences, 26–28, *27*
Me-Here-Now preferences, 88–93, *93*, 97–98, 101–5, 107, 112, 114, 115, 117–19, 127, 158, 235, 246, 273
  cognitive ease and, 152, 153
  entrepreneurs and, 224, 225
  investments and, 194
  time distortion and, 99–100
mental illness, 116–17
mergers and acquisitions (M & A), 58, 154, 159–60, 162, 225–27, 274–75
metrics, 121
Middle East oil crisis, 100
Moderna, 74
Mondelēz International, 91
Morning Consult, 32
Moynihan, Brian, 178
music, xxii, 196, 248
Musk, Elon, 158, 254, 257

Nabisco, 91
narratives, *see* stories
natural disasters, 197–98
NBA, 51–52
Netflix, 148, 158
news media, xiii, 236, 243
New York Times, 54, 209
NFTs, 154, 196
9/11 attacks, 46, 47, 56–58, 61, 63, 84, 107, 198–99, 241, 259
Nokia, 258
Nordstrom, 194
North Carolina National Bank, 159
nothing-to-lose response, 215–18

Obama, Barack, 246–47
Occupy Wall Street, 198
offense, playing, 83, 130–32
oil, 58, 100, 188
Oklahoman, 52
optimism, 6, 134, 137, 159, 168, 189, 233, 251–54, 266, 269, 270, 275, 276, 282
overconfidence, xvii, 83, 136, 157, 165–68, 170, 270–71, 275–78
overthinking, 153–55

panics, 57–58, 65, 275
  confidence turning points and, 64–65
  management of, 59–61
  patterns of, 55–59
  personal, 58–59
  societal, 56–57
  vulnerability-driven approach to, 61–65, 108–9
  see also crises
Parker, Douglas, 103
Passenger Seat, 9–12, *9*, *13*, 250, 280
  air travel and, 14, *15*, 18, 108, 233
  authoritarianism and, 174–76, 179, *180*, 207–9
  best practices in, 206–18
  businesses operating in, 41–47, *41*, *45*, 181–84, 206–7
  in celebrity-centric environments, 207–8
  Comfort Zone and, 12, 176–81, *180*, 211, 213, 218
  crisis management and, 110–12, *111*
  environments of high certainty and low control and, 173–86
  imprisonment and, 180–81
  Launch Pad as similar to, 228
  leaving, 210–15, *213*
  nothing-to-lose response and, 215–18
  paths to, 174–81
  Stress Center and, 10, 74–76, 175–77, 211, 212, 214–16
Pelosi, Nancy, 198
personal panics, 58–59
pessimism, 7, 189, 213, 233, 247, 252, 254, 259, 267, 276, 282
Pfizer, 74
Phillips, Matt, 54
Polaroid, 92, 104–5
political and social movements, 40, 179, 198, 215
political messaging, 245–47
Poyais, 133, 138
Prechter, Robert, 196
pre-positioning, 33–34, 38, 40
presidential elections
  of 2012, 246–47
  of 2016, xx–xxi, *xxi*, 247
  of 2020, 23
price elasticity, 187–89
product demand, 187–88
proof-of-concept processes, 149–50, 161
prototypes, 149–50, 161
Putin, Vladimir, xxiii, 115

randomness, 59–60
regulations, 46–47, 85, 161–62
resilience, xxiv, 117, 122, 204, 209, 230, 281–83
restaurants, 130, 206, 207
  COVID and, 44, 71, 72, 151–52
  food safety and, 200
risk-taking, 12, 50, 113, 128, 130–33, *133*, 138, 167, 207, 222, 234, 263, 268, 270–72, 276–77, 279, 280, 282
Rivian, 226–27
roller coasters, 87–88, 177, 180, 233–34
Royal Bank of Scotland, 274–75
runners, 100
Russian invasion of Ukraine, xxiii, 101, 115–17, 188, 197, 230, 274

safety, 183, 189
  aircraft, 58, 108–9, 182, 199–200, 214–15
  food, 200
S&P 500, 52
Sapolsky, Robert, 270
Schultz, Howard, 176
scrutiny, 118, 132–33, *133*, 136, 138
securitization, xviii–xix, 127

self-esteem, xiv, xv
sentiment
  Confidence Spectrum and, 48–55
  consumer, 32–36, 38–40, 189, 201–2
  environmental, 36–40
  situational, 38–40
September 11 attacks, *see* 9/11 attacks
Servpro, 47
sexual assault victims, 214
Shark Tank, 150
Signet Bank, 163
simplicity, 148–49, 153, 162
situational sentiment, 38–40
Sliney, Ben, 61, 64
Smith, Fred, 125–27, 129, 162, 221
social and political movements, 40, 179, 198, 215
social distance, 101
social media, xiv, 51, 52, 57, 58, 74, 82, 104, 152, 236, 243–44, 268
  Twitter, 52, 104, 236, 244, 268
social mood, 32–36
societal panics, 56–57
SPACs (special purpose acquisition companies), 154, 196
Spanx, 221–22, 225, 227
stability, 129
Stanovich, Keith, 142
Starbucks, 54, 176
stocks, stock market, 40, 57, 59–60, 77, 82, 85, 86, 90, 161, 196, 202–3, 259, 263, 265
  call options and, 196
stories (narratives), 235–61, 262, 277, 279, 282
  adjectives used in, 258
  advertising, business, and political messaging, 245–47
  Big Truths in, 253–54, 258
  confidence and, 247–50, 259–61
  confidence extremes and, 254, *255*
  confidence turning points and, 255–59
  COVID pandemic turning point, 53–54, 70, 96, 237, 255, 256
  evaluating, 254
  evolution of, 257
  individual, 259–61
  Launch Pad and, 236
  leaders' appreciation of, 257
  media and, 247–48
  reading sentiment through, 242–44
  simplistic, 253–54, 255, 257
  tipping points in, 252
  "unprecedented" in, 237–42, *237*, *238–39*, *240–41*, 243, 259
  virtuous and vicious cycles in, 250–52, 255–57
  visualizing, 244–45, *244*, *245*
Strack, Donnie, 51
Stress Center, 7–9, *8*, 12, *13*, 33, 34, 36, 39, 41–44, *41*, *43*, 47, 78–85, 105, 112, 114, 122, 126, 210, 233, 246, 281, 282
  air travel and, 14, *15*, 16–18, *17*, *18*
  arc from Comfort Zone to, 134–35, *134*
  arrival in Launch Pad from, 227–30, *229*
  better practices in, 106–22
  communication in, 117–19
  comparison and, 121
  COVID and, 21–23, *21*, *22*, 35–36, *35*, 52, 70–72, 74, 76, 77
  crises and, 31, 110, *111*
  crisis leadership abilities and, 113–17
  crisis management and, 106–12, *111*
  decision-making in, 70, 262
  emergency room doctors and, 25–26
  environments of low confidence and, 69–85
  expert advice and, 75, 175
  Five Fs responses and, *see* Five Fs of stress responses
  high school senior year and, 24–25
  Launch Pad and, 73, 75, 263
  leaders and, 114–15, 117–22
  Me-Here-Now preferences in, 88–93, *93*, 97–98, 105, 117, 118
  panics and, 59, 61
  Passenger Seat and, 10, 74–76, 175–77, 211, 212, 214–16
  social movements and, 40
  System 2 thinking in, 143

Stress Center (*cont.*)
time as perceived in, 98, 118
transparency of, 80–85
volunteering and, 121–22
zero-sum thinking and, 120
stressors, 32
Stumpf, John, 165
Sullenberger, "Sully," 11
Swift, Taylor, xxii
System 1 and System 2 thinking, 142–48, *143*, 151, 153–55, 158, 160, 162, 170, 177, 217, 223, 235, 237, 243, 264–66, 269

Taiwan, 198
Target, 179
Tea Party, 40
technology, 56–58, 73–74, 86, 87, 195
technology industry, 125, 161, 233
terrorism, 198–99
Tesla, 158, 159, 257
Tetlock, Philip, 265
Thinking, Fast and Slow (Kahneman), 141–42
Timberlake, Justin, xxii
time, 98–100, 118, 129
Time, 247, 258
Transportation Services Administration (TSA), 46, 183
travel, 94, 103, 128, 129, 147, 190, 193, 250
see also air travel
Tritton, Mark, 179
Trump, Donald, xx–xxi, *xxi*, 51, 54, 247
trust, 101, 114, 119, 128, 147, 253
in banks, 184–85
customer, changes in, 199–200, *199*
Twain, Mark, 86
Twitter, 52, 104, 236, 244, 268
Tyco, 208
Tylenol, 60, 63

Uber, 41–42, 99, 104, 158
Ukraine, xxiii, 101, 115–17, 188, 197, 230, 274
underconfidence, 163, 273, 275–79, *278*
underthinking, 154
University of Michigan, 189
"unprecedented," use of word, 237–42, *237*, *238–39*, *240–41*, 243, 259
Us-Everywhere-Forever preferences, 93, *93*, 127–30, 158, 191, 193, 195, 225, 235, 273

ValuJet, 182
volunteering, 121–22
vulnerability, 12, 37, 41, 58, 60, 69, 70, 76, 80–83, 97, 100, 105, 107, 113, 143, 147, 230, 262, 282, 283
in approach to panics and crises, 61–65, 108–9
confidence and, xvii–xviii, 50–51, 93, 95
distance preferences and, 100
effects of, 84–85
extreme, 54–55
invulnerability, 65, 134–39, 272, 273
shareholder and lender, 82

Wachovia, 163
Wall Street Journal, 259
Walmart, 91, 194, 198
Waste Management, 159
Weill, Sandy, 127
Weinstein, Harvey, 208, 209
Welch, Jack, 127–28
Wells Fargo, 163, 165
West, Richard, 142
Wirecard, 138, 208
work-related stress, 28–29
WorldCom, 208
World Health Organization, 51, 75, 98
World Is Flat, The (Friedman), 94

Xerox, 126

Yellow Vest, 198

Zelenskyy, Volodymyr, 115–16
zero-sum thinking, 120
Zillow, 45